MY GREATEST GAME

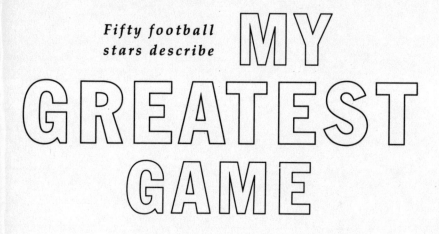

Fifty football stars describe MY GREATEST GAME

Edited by Bob Holmes

MAINSTREAM PUBLISHING

EDINBURGH AND LONDON

First published in Great Britain in 1993 by
MAINSTREAM PUBLISHING COMPANY
(EDINBURGH) LTD
7 Albany Street
Edinburgh EH1 3UG

ISBN 1 85158 579 6

A catalogue record for this book is available from the British Library

Phototypeset in Linotype Bembo by Intype, London
Printed in Great Britain by The Cromwell Press, Melksham, Wiltshire

Contents

Preface

Memory Lane is the favourite ground of all football romantics and one where season ticket prices can never be too high. It offers even better value when accompanied by legends and equipped with the 20/20 hindsight of newspaper reports and videos. Even so, asking players to recall the game of their lives is not as straightforward as it seems: there are those who will go for the obvious, but one or two will inevitably opt for the obscure. And some will go for games that a team-mate has already chosen so, in a couple of cases, we are talking about second choices. With all this as well as the occasional misty-eyed recollection, it is impossible to divorce the actors from the play – which is why the format attempts both a glimpse into careers as well as a look back on performances.

For the reader, whose romanticism may have been cured by the weight of memorabilia on the market, it is hoped that the choice of games offers some variety. For patriotic Trevor Francis it is simply his England debut and he – along with Jimmy Hill, Stuart Pearce and Sir Alf Ramsey – chooses the bitter taste of defeat! For most it is a major triumph, while for Ron Atkinson, Jimmy Johnstone and Norman Hunter it is a joyous celebration of pure football. Yes, Norman Hunter!

Fifty games and fifty heroes from the immediate post-War period to the present day is a daunting task . . . If it succeeds at all, it does so because of the legends themselves and through the sharpened focus of one unforgettable game of their choice. Whether it is Gazza gunning down Arsenal, Coisty finally convincing the reluctant Rangers faithful, Lineker's 'life-changing' hat-trick against Poland or Jock 'Jungle fighter' Wallace bellowing Berwick to immortality . . . *My Greatest Game* recalls many of football's finest hours and moments. But it is not just about epics, although Manchester United's unforgettable European Cup triumph is seen through the contact lenses of Nobby Stiles and Spurs' European Cup-winners' Cup victory comes courtesy of Jimmy Greaves. In an effort to broaden the spectrum, there are apocalyptic FA Cup upsets, personal struggles and poignancy, the latter from Davie Cooper, whose appearance as substitute for Scotland against Wales was the late, great Jock Stein's last tactical act.

This volume was conceived as soon as its precursor (*Match of My Life*) was started and there was the realisation that there is a surfeit of players worthy of inclusion. I thank Malcolm Allison, Ron Atkinson, Terry Butcher, Jimmy Hill, Jimmy Johnstone, Wilf Mannion, Frank McLintock, Steve Perryman and Martin Peters for their patience and hope their long-delayed appearances are worth the wait. To the others, I thank you for your time and trouble and hope you feel that our exchanges have been turned into pieces of which you approve. There is a necessary change of title and publisher but the format and the cause (for sufferers of multiple sclerosis) are the same. In attempting to celebrate football, I hope we will be a small step nearer to winning that greater game.

Acknowledgments

Ask any scribe and he'll tell you that getting hold of certain players can be a more daunting task than doing their biographies. That elusive nature does not desert them even when their boots have been hung up and their whereabouts range from nursing homes to dog tracks, blissful retirement to current hot seat, television studio to quiet backroom. I'm happy – and extremely grateful – to be able to say the great fund of good will that still exists within the game was frequently tapped in getting hold of the 50 players who have contributed to this book.

As before, the leading source of inspiration and direction was the indefatigable Jim Hossack whose contacts in the Scottish game, particularly, were a marvellous guarantee against withdrawal from the squad. Stewart Weir went further, tracking the untrackable in Ally McCoist, as well as Davie Cooper – the only catch being that he insisted on writing them himself! There must also be another special mention of John Maddocks, who is massively reassuring when you're unsure of the spelling of the Bilbao left-back who played against his beloved Manchester City a couple of decades ago.

Thanks are also due to fellow scribes Steve Acteson, Dave Armitage, Trevor Baxter, Duncan Hamilton, 'Tex' Hennessey, Dave Instone, Bill Marshall, Tony Stenson and Phil Yates, historians-cum-editors Mike Deavin, Andy Porter and Pat Woods, the persuasive bias of Geoff Bennett and John Casswell, and newspapers *The Bradford Telegraph and Argus*, *The Evening Standard*, *The Observer* and *Rangers News* without whom this would probably have still been on the drawing board.

A special word is also due to John Simkins at the Multiple Sclerosis Research Centre for his encouragement throughout.

Malcolm Allison

MANCHESTER CITY 5 SCHALKE 04 1
European Cup-winners' Cup semi-final: Maine
Road, 15 April 1970.

Born in Dartford on 5 September 1927, Malcolm Allison's displays for Kent Schoolboys earned him a trial with Charlton Reserves at 15 – and he scored a hat-trick. He was signed by the Valiants but had to do his national service before making his debut – as a pivot against Manchester City. Allison played in both defence and attack in his early days but in 1951 was sold to West Ham for £10,000 as a central defender. He wore the number six shirt until 1958 when he lost a lung, after suffering from tuberculosis, and was replaced by Bobby Moore. 'I couldn't understand how it could happen to me,' he said. 'And I remember the surgeon saying: "What else can you do apart from football?"'

Among those larger-than-life characters for whom even the ageing process may have once hinted at a special exemption, Malcolm Allison would rank highly. Entitled to a bus pass now, he is acting as a locum for ailing clubs, still dispensing tactical wizardry, still bawling out duffers on and off the field and still extracting blood from stones as easily as he does claret from old bottles. He is wiser and more mellow but the eyes are still capable of a sparkle and, in spite of enough dowsings to quell Vesuvius, his enthusiasm for the game seems fired by an eternal flame. Even now, getting him to fix a team is like asking Thomas Edison to change a light bulb.

In his prime, there was a cigar, a fedora and a trenchcoat

loosely fastened around the waist; jaunty London vowels and a genuine smile always breaking out on a craggily handsome face. There was expensive champagne and women of a much younger vintage; celebrated triumphs and sackings, suspensions, touch-line bans, divorces from wives and from clubs, relegation and exile. England and Juventus were spurned but Fisher Athletic and Bath City were eagerly embraced. There was also Plymouth and Portugal, Middlesbrough and Memphis, Turkey and Kuwait. But, above all, there was Manchester City.

Big Mal just sort of happened: he never had to work at it but B-movie looks and a cocktail cabinet the size of the Savoy lounge bar undoubtedly helped. So did Playboy Club companions and a lack of coyness with the press. Missing both a lung and international recognition, the former West Ham defender became managerial manna for the tabloids. But his teams had to keep winning. Or losing. Manchester City seldom do either in moderation but, under Big Mal and the benign gaze of Joe Mercer, they suddenly started winning on a regular basis. Winning the Second Division, the League Championship, the FA Cup, the League Cup. Nothing seemed beyond them until they bombed badly in Europe.

'It was my fault,' admitted Allison. 'We didn't prepare adequately,' which, for a coach, was a cardinal sin. But the season after that humiliating first round defeat by Fener-bahce, of Turkey, City found themselves back in Europe – this time in the Cup-winners' Cup. Having survived a severe test of character against Bilbao, the Blues came through 8–0 on aggregate against Lierse and 1–0 (on aggregate) against Academica Coimbra – not exactly the continent's aristocrats, and not everyone in Europe was impressed. Least of all Schalke 04, the crack West German Cup-holders who barred City's path to a first European final. 'I remember the things their coaching staff were saying about us – and about me, in particular,' says Alli-son. 'We couldn't do anything right in their eyes and then we lost the first leg 1–0 at their place. So the return at

Maine Road assumed terrific importance.' As he had said when City won the League, Allison believed in his men: 'I never doubted this team of vastly underestimated talents.' The side possessed as much character as class and with Big Mal's high-profile coaching, lesser players grew in confidence while stars like Lee, Summerbee and Bell grew into Maine Road legends. Schalke should have known better than to vastly underestimate the City mentor.

To be fair to the Germans, they were on a bit of a roll, having just avenged an 8–0 defeat by Cologne in the League. Not surprisingly, they had concentrated on shoring up their defence, which drew praise from Allison: 'They play it typically German – making it very tight at the back.' Mercer said: 'There is no hypocrisy about German football. It's hard but we prefer that to those teams who pretend innocence and then kick you all over the park.' But on the eve of the first leg, Allison declared: 'We have come here for a result. We want to win but a score draw would be satisfactory. However, to lose by an odd goal would worry me to death. I'd be scared giving a goal start to anyone.' The *Manchester Evening News* claimed that City were 'magnificent' in the first game and 'deserved to draw', but struck a note of warning on star winger Libuda with a headline: 'German Finney has City in a spin.' Allison's men had lost by the odd goal.

City, whose League performances did not inspire confidence, had a major scare when Corrigan broke his nose in training on the afternoon of the return leg but the 46,361 who filled Maine Road on that spring evening soon had their nerves settled. The giant 'keeper took his place and, having signalled their serious intent from the outset, the Blues were level on aggregate after just nine minutes. Lee made one of his characteristic surges before releasing Oakes whose low drive was deflected by Slomiany into the path of Doyle. Nigbur got his hands to the midfielder's shot but could not prevent it from crossing the line. Five minutes later City were ahead when Young, who had not found the net since 3 January, combined sweetly with Bell and Oakes before bringing the ball under control in the Schalke penalty area. He then rediscovered his homing instinct with a precise shot that went in off the far post. Driven on by Doyle and Oakes, City maintained the tempo and Young's second, after 27 minutes, had the crowd in ecstasy. Again it was the Bell/Oakes combination, followed by a Lee dummy, which allowed Young the space to run through the heart of the German defence. The searing, cannonball finish brought the house down.

The City faithful could not have asked for more as Schalke crumbled in the face of the Blues' onslaught. Switching the attacks with bewildering speed, the men from Manchester were simply unstoppable as they overwhelmed a skilful German team who had never been subjected to such a sustained onslaught. City were majestic, gloriously splicing techniques honed on the training ground with an abundant natural flair – the perfect riposte to unjustified criticism and what every coach worth his salt aspires to.

In the 52nd minute, the contest was over and City had booked their place in the final, Lee fiercely driving home a Doyle pass after Summerbee and Bell had begun the move. It was typical of that night – four or five players involved and a devastating finish. Nine minutes from the end there was another, with Bell rounding off a centre by Young, who, along with Doyle, was perhaps the outstanding figure of the night. 'That first goal was what I needed,' confided the winger. 'After that I couldn't do a thing wrong.' Libuda nicked a goal from close range a minute from time but it could not dull the lustre of City's performance.

Joe Mercer said: 'Despite our indifferent displays recently in the League, this proved that on our day we are capable of beating anyone.'

For Allison it was the sweetest victory. 'It's the game I recall giving me the most pleasure,' he says, 'particularly the way we played and remembering the comments of the German coach. We were brilliant that day and I remember our national coach, Alan Wade, telling me it was the finest example he had ever seen of countering a sweeper system.'

Vernon Addison wrote in the *Manchester Evening News*: 'Had it been cricket they would have called on the poets and Sir Neville Cardus would have written a book. No record, however, is really needed for the game was indelibly written in the minds of the 46,361 who saw it.'

It ensured City a final berth against Gornik, whom they beat to win the European Cup-winners' Cup but for Big Mal, ever the perfectionist, it was against Schalke that City provided him with his finest hour and a half.

Manchester City: Corrigan; Book, Pardoe, Doyle (Heslop), Booth, Oakes, Towers, Bell, Lee, Young, Summerbee (Carrodus).

Schalke 04: Nigbur; Slomiany, Becher, Russman, Fichtel, Wittkamp, Libuda, Neuser, Pohischmidt, Ermon, Van Haaren.

Ron Atkinson

MANCHESTER UNITED 3
WEST BROMWICH ALBION 5
League: Old Trafford, 30 December 1978.

Born in Liverpool on 18 March 1939, Ron Atkinson began his career with Lea Village School, then BSA Tools before moving on to Wolves, Aston Villa and Headington/Oxford United, whom he helped into the Football League and then into the Second Division. A commanding, inspirational half-back whose career was largely played out among the lower leagues, Atkinson was player-manager at Kettering Town, winning the Southern League Championship, before taking over at Cambridge United, whom he guided to the Fourth Division title in 1976/77. Typically, he referred to his honours at the Varsity towns as 'The Three Degrees'. He was well-qualified for the big time.

'We've got a real multi-racial side,' Atkinson loved to quip. 'Three blacks and two Browns.' But the vibrant Albion team he fashioned in the late Seventies was more than multi-racial – it possessed many diverse talents and was a potent mix of exciting individuals and hardy pros. Besides Tony and Ally Brown, Brendon Batson, Laurie Cunningham and Cyrille Regis, there were fresh new faces and more familiar ones who were at last giving vent to their skills, among them a young Bryan Robson. Under Atkinson's extrovert tutelage, they were playing thrilling football that was, at times, irresistible.

'West Brom are different,' wrote David Miller in *The Times*. 'They are probably more exciting than Vic Buckingham's side of the mid-Fifties.' That was some tribute as the Cup winners of 1954 were also runners-up in the League and undoubtedly one of the finest teams to grace the Hawthorns. But in 1978, the Throstles were in full cry again, and threatening to win the League for only the second time in the club's history – the perfect send-off for its centenary year.

The *Birmingham Post* certainly thought so as it headlined Albion as 'Artists with The Aura of Champions' after they had stunned 40,000 London fans by beating Arsenal at Highbury on Boxing Day. Gunners' boss Terry Neil called them 'The most positive side we have seen.'

After that victory, Atkinson acknowledged that his men were very much in contention: 'If you say that 18 points out of 20 is Championship form, then you would be right. But there is a lot of work to be done and a long way to go. If we can continue in our present form then we'll probably finish with 63 points but we have a tremendous battle to keep up with Liverpool and we've still not caught them. Our biggest strength is the ability of almost all of our players to score goals when they are demanded,' he added. 'We are rightly described as an attacking side but most of our play is based on sound defence. When we need to, we can do it. But I also like to think that we can break and catch opposing defences out – if we are given half a chance. We have some outstanding players that don't get the credit they deserve.'

Well before he took the Manchester United hot seat, Atkinson knew that there was nowhere better to announce your Championship credentials than Old Trafford. Predictably, he could hardly wait for the League fixture there on 30 December 1978, but what he didn't know was that he would become far more impatient after it was played – the game being scheduled in the middle of a busy, almost manic, holiday programme and just before a blizzard. Indeed, when non-Merseyside historians view the 1978–79 season they will conclude that the Siberian winter, which effectively shut down Britain for much of

17

the early part of 1979, did as much to halt West Brom's march to the title as a certain club which plays at Anfield. The shut-down occurred just as Albion were taking all before them, playing superlative football and catching Liverpool. 'When the programme resumed,' the Big Man reflected, 'we had played one game in 25 days. It stopped us in our tracks. But not before we'd played some of the best football – and the best game – I've ever seen.'

Albion were unbeaten in ten games but United had lost three of their last six, including two consecutive 3–0 defeats, one against lowly Bolton Wanderers. Still, some 45,000 turned up to see the Midlanders who were currently the talk of the game. The win over Arsenal had underlined their ability to handle awkward away fixtures and, with visits to Old Trafford no longer a matter of fear and trembling, Atkinson was quietly confident. Well, as quiet as a loquacious, bejewelled loud-dresser can be. 'The way we are playing, nothing is beyond us,' he said.

United fans were suitably wary and more than a touch jealous of the Midlanders who were playing the sort of football of which the Red Devils would have been proud. Those fans just did not know what to expect – even when they read their football *Pinks* that night. The headline roared: 'Red Magic in Goal Storm'. There was 'red magic', all right, but there had been even more 'blue heaven'. It was the sort of game that is a nightmare for early edition football specials – but a dream for the fans.

Albion could have been two-nil up before United took the lead when Brian Greenhoff volleyed powerfully past Godden in the 20th minute. Tony Brown had a fierce shot turned over by Bailey and then Batson had headed into the side-netting. But Brown brought the visitors level in the 26th minute after a lovely move involving Statham, Robson and Cantello. A minute later Cantello put Albion ahead after a deft back-heel by Regis. It was fabulous, uninhibited stuff but the game – and the goals – had hardly started.

The snow had – and no one noticed. In the 28th minute,

McQueen rose to head home Houston's free-kick and, amazingly, four minutes later United were back in front through McIlroy. Five goals in 12 minutes had the crowd in turmoil but Albion showed their mettle, Brown nipping in to level on the stroke of half-time. 'It's supposed to be a psychologically important time to score,' quips Atkinson. 'And it is – but it was so close to the half-time whistle that we weren't sure whether it had come before or after the ref had blown!'

The goal counted and Albion were boosted by it, taking complete charge of the second half. 'Bailey was their best player,' recalls Atkinson, 'and made some super saves. A proper score would have been ten for us.'

With Bailey proving consistently defiant and Greenhoff clearing off the line, it took the irrepressible Baggies until the 76th minute to regain the lead. A clearance by Godden was headed on by Regis for Cunningham, with a burst worthy of Best, to slot home. But the goal of the day was the fifth and clincher with five minutes to go. The rampant Regis, with all the flair you would expect from a man with a French Guyanan birthplace, gathered Ally Brown's pass and raced on to ram an unstoppable drive past Bailey. 'It was the perfect finish,' says Atkinson. 'A red-hot performance in Arctic conditions. Even the United fans gave us a standing ovation.'

Albion's players had the accolades showered upon them – and so did their manager. If ever a team reflected its gaffer's personality, this was it – a choice blend of grit and flamboyance. But after the weather abated, Albion did not quite recover their swagger, having to settle for 60 points and third place – behind Liverpool and Forest. However, their spell at the end of 1978 warmed the hearts of everyone who saw them – right through the chilly depths of 1979.

Manchester United: Bailey; B. Greenhoff, Houston, McIlroy, McQueen, Buchan, Coppell, J. Greenhoff (Sloan), Ritchie, McCreery, Thomas.

West Bromwich Albion: Godden; Batson, Statham, T. Brown, Wile, Robertson, Robson, A. Brown, Regis, Cantello, Cunningham. Sub: Johnston.

Bertie Auld

CELTIC 3 LEEDS UNITED 1 (ON AGGREGATE)
European Cup semi-final: Elland Road and Hampden, 1 and 15 April 1970

Born in Maryhill, Glasgow, on 23 March 1938, Bertie Auld joined Celtic in March 1955 after an apprenticeship that took him from Glasgow Schools to Partick Thistle Boys Club, Panmure Thistle and Maryhill Harp. Ferocious in the tackle, Bertie had been a full-back until Harp gave full vent to his attacking instincts, converting him to the left wing. He had a spell on loan at Dumbarton but returned to Parkhead to win his three Scottish caps before being sold to Birmingham City for £15,000 in May 1961. With Birmingham he was a finalist in the Fairs Cup but that was a dry run for the honours that flowed after his return to Celts in 1965. At a give-away £12,000, he was one of Jock Stein's most astute purchases and became a stalwart in the 'immortal' team of the Sixties, collecting medals from four League Championships, three Cups and four League Cups, besides the European Cup in 1967. A dynamic, inspirational player who made the Celts buzz, he was sold in 1971 to Hibernian where he became coach. He has managed Partick Thistle (twice), Hamilton and Hibs.

'Britain came to a standstill both nights,' was how Bertie Auld describes the interest in the titanic, two-legged confrontation between Celtic and Leeds in the 1970 European Cup semi-final. 'If anything could follow being the first British club to capture the trophy in 1967, it was beating the English champions in style. They fancied themselves, all right,' Auld remembers, 'and had every right to – they hadn't conceded a goal in the tournament and were near their best. Not only that, some people were saying we were over the hill: Lisbon was three years ago and we hadn't won it since. But we were ready for them.'

For all Don Revie's meticulous attention to detail, Leeds were clearly not ready for Celtic. The Yorkshire fans arrogantly assumed that the Scots would be a push-over and though Revie did not fall for that, he was not prepared for a side as motivated as the Celts were on the great European occasions. Winning the trophy had become an obsession with Revie after first Celtic and then Manchester United had lifted it on those glorious nights in 1967 and 1968. Acutely aware that his hard, machine-like team were not going to be compared with either the Lisbon Lions or the Red Devils unless they did likewise – and probably not even then – Revie set his stall out to land the coveted crown after finally securing the League Championship in 1969. And when Leeds reached the penultimate stage with a clean sheet and the Scots barring their path to the final, he acknowledged: 'It will be our toughest test yet.' But still, they could not have known what was about to hit them.

Anglo-Scottish clashes have traditionally assumed greater importance north of Hadrian's Wall, but this match fully justified the billing 'Battle of Britain'. Leeds were desperate to win, all right, but so were Celtic, who were imbued with the fervour privy only to Scots about to repel Sassenachs. 'The Scots seem to want to beat us more than we want to beat them,' is a familiar cry from English players, for whom Bannockburn and Culloden might hold no more significance than, say, membership of the Highland League or a place to park the caravan in summer. After a century of having the eardrums pierced by the Hampden Roar and the anatomy rearranged by dervish-like commitment on the park, they have got the message but, it seems, are still incapable of responding in kind.

Except on this occasion. As far as the huge trophy was concerned, Leeds were the *hungrier* side and there were no lengths to which Revie would not go – even to seeking a psychological advantage from the colour of the socks. As both clubs wore white, Revie riled Celtic by offering a choice of two colours – 'Ulster' orange or 'Rangers' blue. It was a mistake and backfired badly – with less than two minutes of the first leg gone, the Greens were a goal up.

The Celts tore into the attack and, with the Yorkshire-men floundering, a raid down the left ended with Connelly shooting past Sprake, the ball going in off a Leeds defender. There was joy unconfined among the Celtic ranks and a stunned disbelief on the Leeds players' faces, now as pale as their Persil strips. A goal down and without the injured Hunter, the English champions looked worried – and wobbled every time Celtic poured forward. However, motivated by Bremner, affectionately known by the Elland Road faithful as 'ten stones of barbed wire', and, of course, a Scot to boot, the home side belatedly counter-attacked. But in their desperation, their passing lost its normal accuracy: they resorted to power-plays – and got nowhere. Even when the giraffe-like Jack Charlton threatened, he foundered on the granite outcrop known as McNeill, while Leeds were always vulnerable to the genius of Johnstone on the right – teasing and tormenting one of his favourite 'bunnies' in the otherwise brilliant Terry Cooper. Auld remembers: 'We really turned it on on both nights and Jinky was tremendous.' But it was the fiery left-footer, himself, who thought he had set up the clincher just 50 seconds into the second half – only for Connelly's effort to be controversially ruled offside. Auld, however, was now in command and immediately shrugged off the disappointment. He fed Johnstone as often as he could and maintained the pressure on Leeds, who were denied the chance to even get on terms, let alone build a lead for the second leg. It ended 1–0 to Celtic.

Of course, Parkhead was far too small to accommodate the hoardes who wanted to witness what they were sure would be a ritual slaughter of the Sassenachs in the return. Hampden had to do but Perthshire might have been better. 'I can remember it vividly to this day,' says Auld. 'Walking on to the Hampden turf that night was something else. I've never known an atmosphere like it – not even at Old Firm games or internationals. It was like being in a dome – looking up at the crowd, I never seen the sky. It was as if there was a roof of breath and smoke . . .'

Hunter was back for Leeds but their jinx had struck again when Reaney broke his leg against West Ham, Madeley moving to number two. However, Revie's men showed their mettle after just 14 minutes when Bremner burst through to level the match with a powerful drive from 20 yards. 'It was greeted with a deathly silence,' says Auld, 'and you could hear the Leeds players congratulating each other. There were 134,000 there and not many of them were for Leeds.' The goal lifted the visitors, who sensed they could yet snatch the tie, but Auld ensured that they didn't get carried away. Taking charge of midfield, he engineered many of the more penetrating Celtic raids and, for a while, Sprake's goal had a charmed life. Two minutes after half-time, Auld crossed for 'Yogi Bear' Hughes to head home. Then Sprake was injured and replaced by Harvey whose second touch was fetching it out of the net. It was the Celts' second on the night and third in all, coming after Murdoch and Johnstone essayed a lovely one-two. According to the *Daily Record*, Murdoch's lethal *coup de grâce* 'brought the greatest Hampden roar of all time'.

For Auld, it capped a night of nights. 'I had read that I wasn't the most popular player amongst the Leeds lads so I set out to make my presence felt,' he said. 'Bremner spent 45 minutes trying to get me after I'd done something he thought was a wee bit naughty [a tackle on Jones] but he never caught me. We had all the satisfaction, especially as we were bringing one or two younger players on. Yes, it lived up to the hype.'

So the Celts became the first British club to reach two

European Cup finals and proved beyond doubt that they were the best team in Britain. Auld avoided the 'barbed wire' and the country resumed normal life.

First leg – Leeds United: Sprake; Reaney, Cooper, Bremner (Bates), Charlton, Madeley, Lorimer, Clarke, Jones, Giles, Gray.

Celtic: Williams; Hay, Gemmell, Murdoch, McNeill, Brogan, Johnstone, Connelly (Hughes), Wallace, Lennox, Auld.

Second leg – Celtic: Williams; Hay, Gemmell, Murdoch, McNeill, Brogan, Johnstone, Connelly, Hughes, Auld, Lennox.

Leeds United: Sprake (Harvey); Madeley, Cooper, Bremner, Charlton, Hunter, Lorimer, Clarke, Jones, Giles, Gray.

Joe Baker

ENGLAND 2 NORTHERN IRELAND 1
Home International: Wembley, 18 November 1959.

Born in Liverpool on 17 July 1940, Joe Baker was the second son of a Scottish mother and English merchant seaman father. Elder brother Gerry was born in the United States. Both boys were raised in Scotland and became international footballers, albeit for different countries. Gerry was capped by the USA, while Joe caused a sensation by becoming the first Scottish League player to turn out for . . . England! Apart from a brief spell on the Chelsea groundstaff, the pair never played together, Joe graduating from Scottish Schoolboy honours to the England Under-23 team, having made his name with Hibernian. At 5'9" and 11st 7lb, he was not a heavyweight number nine but was good in the air, with electric acceleration and the ball-playing skills of an inside-forward. Torino paid a massive £73,000 for his talents in 1960 but Joe returned to Britain after an unhappy year in Italy. He restored his appetite for goals at Arsenal before becoming a folk hero at Forest. Joe was capped just eight times before eventually making it back to Hibs via Sunderland. He hung up his boots at Raith Rovers in 1974.

London cab drivers are a cynical lot and know a weirdo when they see one. But they will still manage to keep one eye on the road and the other on the fare. Very occasionally, they will waive the fare in the interests of safety or sanity. The driver who collected a wide-eyed, callow youth at Heathrow on a chilly November morning in 1959 felt that this was one of those occasions. The kid looked harmless enough but soon convinced the cabbie that he was well short of the full set. Clearly, this passenger should not be out in public and, doing his citizen's bit for the capital's well-being, the cabbie slid his partition window shut and radioed for the cops. After all, he reasoned, who in their right mind would claim to be a member of the England football team while speaking in a barely decipherable Scottish accent?

'He really thought I was a nutter,' chuckles Joe Baker at the memory of his welcome to old London town. 'And the police soon appeared on the scene. I had a job convincing them, too, because they couldn't understand me either. My mistake was asking for the England team's hotel – the Windsor – but, luckily, one of the officers had read about me in the papers and they let me go. The driver apologised and drove me straight there.' After that, and all the stick he'd endured before he came down, it was a wonder Baker still wanted to represent the country of his birth. Because England was not his country in any other respect.

Apart from his Merseyside birthplace, the teenager was as Scottish as haggis 'n' neeps. He not only talked 'Scottish', he led the Hibernian line with such a dash that he might have been played on to the field by bagpipes. Lacking the height of a Lawton or a Lofthouse, Baker was an essentially Scottish centre-forward possessing both the passion and persistence to make up for his modest build. And his saucy scissor-kicks, searing pace and bullet-like headers made him the talk of Edinburgh and beyond. 'He has the heart of a lion and moves like greased lightning,' said Tommy Docherty. 'Which is no' bad.' With goals by the trawler-load, he was rated by many as a genuine successor to Lawrie Reilly and potentially the finest Scottish centre-forward since Hughie Gallagher. The only trouble was . . . he was English.

Once the auld enemy realised that the hottest property north of the border was eligible to play *for* and not against them, they did not waste a second. Billy Wright, who had been given a run-around by Baker when Wolves met Hibs in a friendly, alerted England boss Walter Winterbottom and, although Baker had been capped as a boy by the Scots, the Sassenachs were swift to award him Under-23 honours. The following season he was chosen to play for the senior team against Northern Ireland at Wembley. 'Walter was a brave man,' remembers Baker. 'There was a lot of uproar in the papers while I had to take a fair bit of ribbin' myself in Scotland.' To accommodate this tartan teenager, fellow new boy Ray Parry and the return of Johnny Haynes, England left out Brian Clough, Jimmy Greaves and Bobby Charlton. As if the raw, braw 'McBaker' did not have enough on those inexperienced shoulders . . . 'I am very proud to be picked for England,' he would say when interrogated about an honour that Scots regarded as blasphemous at best – and that was in diplomatic circles. 'I shall do my best – just as I always do back home for Hibs,' he would tell them. 'I was in a no-win situation and wondered if I was being fully accepted on either side of the border. But it was not my fault – I didn't make the rules.'

England had been experiencing a dismal run since the Munich disaster had ripped the heart and soul out of an emerging side. Only three matches out of 16 had been won and none of the last seven. Baker, however, appeared blissfully unaware of the past as he covered the Wembley grass with the verve and sprightliness of a Newmarket colt. Betraying few signs of nerves, he created openings for both Haynes and Parry, whose shots were blocked on the line, before silencing the sceptics by scoring in the 16th minute. Anticipating Allen's quick free-kick, Baker moved toward the penalty spot, allowed the ball to drop on his right side and unleashed a rising drive into the top corner of the net. 'It was a brilliant way to start,' says Baker, 'and the crowd really warmed to me.' Bobby Charlton later told him: 'I thought there was only me who could hit 'em like that.' But England fell away after this, apparently content with a one-goal lead. *The Times*, whose correspondent deigned not to mention Baker's name until more than 300 words into his report, claimed the teams reminded him of 'two chess players brooding over their moves, quietly trying to search out the weak spot for checkmate'.

With Haynes experiencing a quiet return, Parry only threatening spasmodically and neither Clayton nor Flowers quite themselves, there was a lack of creativity about the home performance that was alleviated only by the eagerness and obvious class of the new centre-forward. Indeed, Northern Ireland should have levelled before half-time when McIlroy's penalty was saved by Springett. Heartened by the scare they had given the English, the green shirts laid siege as soon as the second half started. Four shots rained in on the English goal but the wall would not be breached. Not yet.

With just three minutes of the mostly dreary encounter remaining, McParland fastened on to a Blanchflower clearance and embarked upon one of his lethal sorties. Howe could not stop him but as Springett came out, the 'keeper managed to block the shot. The danger appeared to have been averted but the livewire Bingham latched on to the ball and levelled. England looked for inspiration and found it in Baker, who had almost added to his tally with a diving header early in the second half. With seconds to go, Baker worked the ball down the left before sending over a beautiful diagonal ball for Parry to ram home. Even *The Times* thought the finish 'tingling', while the *Daily Express*'s Desmond Hackett roared: 'Bravo McBaker, the new darling of Wembley.'

To save his new sensation the inevitable media inquisition, Winterbottom arranged for Baker to slip out of the stadium by a side door and catch his plane. 'I don't know about the "darling",' he laughs, 'I was more like the ghost of Wembley.'

The manager may have ensured that his centre-forward caught his flight but as Baker sat on the plane he may have wished he had stayed to savour his finest hour. As far as the Scots were concerned, he was now playing football with an English accent. But at least he had no trouble getting a cab.

England: Springett; Howe, Allen, Clayton, Brown, Flowers, Connelly, Haynes, Baker, Parry, Holliday.

Northern Ireland: Gregg; Keith, McMichael, Blanchflower, Cunningham, Peacock, Bingham, Crossan, Cush, McIlroy, McParland.

Tony Barton

ASTON VILLA 1 BAYERN MUNICH 0
European Cup final: Rotterdam, 26 May 1982

Born in Sutton, Surrey, on 8 April 1937, Tony Barton won England Schoolboy and Youth caps before playing on the right wing of the entertaining Fulham side that included Johnny Haynes and Bobby Robson. He had two-and-a-half years at Forest before a cruciate injury ended his career at Portsmouth. He became chief scout and then joined Ron Saunders as assistant manager at Villa, where he was made caretaker after Saunders's abrupt departure to Birmingham City, and then given the job of trying to haul the club to safety while maintaining England's hold on the European Cup.

Top European coaching appointments can be accompanied by fanfares of trumpets, a lakeside villa, a Merc and a contract that can double the national debt. When Tony Barton took over England's European Cup representatives in 1982, all he got was the Villa. Barton was suddenly landed with the daunting double task of not only keeping the English champions in Europe but of keeping them in the First Division – on a caretaker basis. They were fifth from the foot of the table when Ron Saunders walked out to join rivals Birmingham City and were simply not the same team that had thrillingly captured the title the previous season. But that was not all: far from being fêted as a new Messiah, Barton, seven years a loyal assistant, was said by Saunders to be 'a dogsbody', while even the fans referred to him as 'Tony Who?'

With no managerial experience behind him and references like that, the quietly-spoken Barton could have been forgiven for agreeing with his former boss that the job was, indeed, 'too much for him'. The kindest comment Saunders made was: 'The way I left that club, any idiot could run it,' but Barton had too much dignity to be dragged into a war of words and, characteristically, let his team do the talking. They could not have spoken more eloquently, recapturing the verve and style of the previous season in rising to safety in the League and reaching the latter stages of the European Cup. 'To be honest,' reflects Barton, 'dogsbody is not an entirely unfair description. Under Ron, I worked in the shadows, organised the scouting and assessing opponents; but I used to fetch the mail for him, too.'

Perhaps that is why it took the Villa board almost two months to give the 45-year-old Barton a contract. And when they did so, it was for a lot less than Saunders had been earning. Nor did it include a new Merc every two years. But from the way the players reacted, you would have thought they'd chip in with the difference. Barton relied entirely on the same squad, merely loosening the straitjacket that Sergeant-Major Saunders had stuck them in and, the dread of failure removed, the team began to play. With the joy back in their game, Gordon Cowans, Tony Morley and Gary Shaw, in particular, were scarcely able to believe their luck at the change.

Apart from being male and Caucasian, there were no obvious similarities between the affable Barton and the forbidding Saunders, one being the chalk to the other's cheese. 'Discipline is vital,' says Barton, 'but you've got to allow individuals a bit of licence. People think I've worked a miracle but all I've done is add little things to the set-pieces and make the young players believe in themselves again,' a view confirmed by skipper Dennis Mortimer. 'He lets players go out and express themselves and treats people with a bit more respect than Ron did.' But was it the stuff that brings Europe's most coveted prize?

After being reluctant to enter the competition when it began and then taking another 12 years to win it, English clubs had finally got the hang of the European Cup. Liverpool had won it twice in a row, then Forest took over for two years before handing it back to Liverpool. In 1982, Aston Villa were drawn against Dynamo Kiev in the quarter-final and played the away leg first under their new caretaker boss. It was his first crisis. The game was switched to the warmer Crimea due to the Soviet winter but Barton recalls: 'The training ground was diabolical and the hotel was crummy. We had a meeting with UEFA but were banging our heads against a brick wall. I just told the lads to make light of it and we amazed the Russians by laughing and joking all the time. We did well to get a 0–0 draw and won 2–0 at home.' The second crisis came in the semi-final when an intrusion by fans had threatened Villa's place in the final. Barton's defence had done marvellously in holding Anderlecht to a 0–0 draw but their efforts could have been in vain. 'I told the lads they had done their bit and not to worry about it, but it was an anxious time waiting to hear if we might get kicked out.'

Villa survived, albeit with a fine and a subsequent game behind closed doors, but their attention was now firmly focused on Bayern Munich, the West German hot favourites who bristled with experienced internationals. 'I was still having to pinch myself that I was in charge,' recalls Barton, 'and they had people like Hoeness, Breitner, Rummenigge and Augenthaler. Everyone was telling me that we'd done well to get to the final but I watched several tapes of theirs and spotted a few things that suited us. We were quietly confident and just tried to make the whole thing as lighthearted as possible. Our main worry was the 'keeper, Jimmy Rimmer, who had a neck injury that needed a painkilling injection just before the kick-off. But after only a few minutes, he had to come off. Nigel Spink was our sub, a big lad whose ability I never doubted. He was promising, all right, but he'd played only one League game.' Spink, who had been considering becoming an apprentice plasterer due to limited first-team opportunities, told Barton: 'Don't worry, boss, I won't let you down.' If the beleaguered manager found these words less than reassuring, worse was to come. 'I'll never forget him running on the field,' recalls Barton, 'and saying: "Cor, my Mum won't half be pleased."'

Mrs Spink was more than pleased. As the Bayern machine eased into gear with the smoothness of a BMW automatic, the shots rained in on the Villa goal. The mighty Rummenigge, twice European Footballer of the Year and built like the *Bismarck*, gave her boy . . . well, a bit of a plastering, but Nige was equal to it. In fact, the young 'keeper was equal to anything the Germans could throw at him and the Villa defence held firm. 'I had a few butterflies early on,' he said, 'but they soon went – I am not surprised at how well I played because I'd been playing well in the Reserves . . .'

With service to Villa's front-runners at best sporadic, the game followed the pattern of the 1980 Final, when the German champions had taken charge but could not break through against a brave English defence and its brilliant 'keeper. Then it had been Brian Clough's Forest with Peter Shilton defying Kevin Keegan's Hamburg after John Robertson snatched a breakaway goal. Could Villa manage a repeat? 'We had played well in the first half,' claims Barton, 'but they took over in the second. Even so, I still felt we could score on the break – we had the players to do it.' Morley was one of those players and, after one of his more ineffectual nights, the winger produced a moment of magic in the 66th minute. Barton remembers it as if it were yesterday: 'He latched on to a super ball from Gary Shaw, went inside and outside the full-back with a sway of the hips and crossed to Peter Withe. The ball bobbled and I think it hit his shin. But in it went.

'They threw everything at us after that and the last half hour was the longest of my life. Spink made more courageous saves, Swain kicked off the line and Hoeness missed completely. But we did a magnificent job and held on to make a lot of people eat their words. After the cele-brations, I remember going to my room and tying the Cup to my bed. The European Cup! The brothers Grimm could not have written a better fairy tale. If, in January of that year, someone had told me that I would be made Villa manager on April Fools Day and go on to manage the European Champions, I'd have told him he was a bloody idiot.'

Aston Villa: Rimmer (Spink); Swain, Williams, Evans, McNaught, Mortimer, Bremner, Shaw, Withe, Cowans, Morley.

Bayern Munich: Muller; Dremmler, Horsmann, Weiner, Augenthaler, Kraus (Niedermayer), Durnberger, Breitner, Hoeness, Mathy (Guttler), Rummenigge.

Liam Brady

ARSENAL 3 MANCHESTER UNITED 2
FA Cup Final: Wembley, 12 May 1979

Born in Dublin on 13 February, 1956, as a teenager Liam Brady captained Ireland's Schoolboys, won 11 Youth caps and became a homesick Arsenal junior. He once went home for Christmas and vowed not to return, but was valued so highly the club's backroom staff spent weeks changing his mind. Elder brothers Ray and Pat had already paved the way in League football but little 'Chippy' – for his love of chips – was something special. Brady made his first team debut in 1973 and gradually became a midfield maestro for both club and country. He was capped 73 times, 14 as captain, scoring nine goals. Probably the best player the Republic has produced, Brady's legendary left foot carried his country for a decade. He raised the standards at Arsenal, too, where he made 294 appearances before gracing the Italian League. There, he bucked the trend of English League failures by helping Juventus, whom he joined in 1980, to two consecutive titles. He went to Sampdoria, Inter and Ascoli before ending his career at West Ham in 1990.

There was sufficient of the leprechaun in Liam Brady for a host of players, mostly lunging defenders, to suspect the little Irishman of sometimes having the ball laced to his left boot. As he trapped it, an impish look would appear on his face and he would shimmy around a couple of tackles. But just as they would swear that it was 'fastened', Brady would release one of those defence-splitting passes or that surprisingly fierce shot. So the foot became known simply as 'The Claw'.

As the hard-running journeymen began to darken the landscape of the late Seventies, Brady remained a defiantly creative genius. His control, perception and poise illuminated a long tunnel of negativity and it is a tribute to his skill that he did so in a side whose other components epitomised the functional at the expense of the fun. For all their rigid endeavours, Arsenal had still won nothing since the Double and Brady's desperation to halt the drought ended in misery in the 1978 final. Having insisted on playing when not fully fit, the Irishman had been substituted and then apologised to his team-mates after a 1–0 defeat by Ipswich. This year's road to Wembley had not been easy, a five-match epic being required to see off Sheffield Wednesday in the third round and a slice or two of 'Arsenal luck' to remove Forest in the fifth. Manchester United stood in the way and the bookies made the Red Devils narrow favourites. 'I was just glad to get another opportunity,' said Brady.

Neither side had enjoyed a particularly successful League campaign but United's two inspiring performances to dispose of Liverpool in the semi-final had earned the tighter odds. As far as a spectacle was concerned, Arsenal fans were always less fastidious: whereas United's followers *demanded* a win in style, the Gunners would have settled for a win. And often had to. To Dave Sexton, who had taken over at Old Trafford after the sudden departure of Tommy Docherty, much would depend on Arsenal's approach. 'They tend to play an off-side game so if we avoid that trap we should be able to put pressure on their defence and it will be a full-blooded match,' he declared. 'It will be even better if either side scores an early goal.' He was being diplomatic – most neutrals were hoping for an early *United* goal to make Arsenal play. What they didn't want was an early Arsenal goal. Two Arsenal goals would kill the game.

It was not a little ironic that the most entertaining player on the park had set his stall out to do just that. 'We were all very keen to make up for last year,' remembers Brady, 'and came out to make an early impact. To win the Cup is still every kid's dream.' With Brian Talbot, an Ipswich hero in last year's final, already playing for the Londoners as if his life depended on it, and Rix and Price also affording energetic support, Brady was able to take charge. Eluding the terrier-like attentions of Macari, the 'Clawman' made the most of Wembley's broad acreage and released Stapleton out wide. The ball went to Price before being turned in by the hurtling Talbot, who reached it just ahead of team-mate Sunderland. Barely 12 minutes had been played. United's response was immediate, McIlroy, Thomas and Macari taking the game into the Arsenal half and big Joe Jordan getting the better of Young in a niggling clash of giants. But Arsenal were not wholly reliant on soaking up the pressure, Brady looking capable of engineering a second goal with his every touch. He struck at the cruellest moment – a minute before the interval.

Breaking from midfield, the Irishman embarked on a run that took him into the United penalty area and, with Albiston and Buchan left floundering in his wake, he crossed. United may have been expecting him to switch the ball to his favoured left foot but he hit it with his right, Bailey could not get to it and Stapleton's head did the rest. It looked all over but there were some lionhearts in the United ranks: McQueen, Macari, the ubiquitous Thomas and Jordan refusing to accept the inevitable. However their sweat-soaked efforts were easily absorbed by the retreating Arsenal defence. And to anything that pierced the yellow shirts, Jennings was its equal. Arsenal concentrated on protecting their lead and in a Wembley final they could not be blamed for that. Even so, neutrals began to shuffle towards the exits.

With their fatigue as visible as their mounting desperation and their fans fearing the worst, United raised themselves for one final surge. But the Londoners were already celebrating, their supporters singing themselves hoarse while substitute Steve Walford was allowed a run on the hallowed turf, replacing Price with just five minutes remaining. Watching in the studio, Jack Charlton told ITV viewers: 'Wrong. Five minutes to go and the whole balance is upset. Arsenal might even be in trouble now!'

It was as if United had heard him. Redoubling their efforts, they roused their faithful and with just four minutes remaining, a Coppell free-kick found Jordan. 'Jaws' sent the ball back into the middle for McQueen to thrust out a long left leg and surprise Jennings. Perhaps it was being ahead for so long or maybe it was their desperate desire to make up for last year's disappointment? Brady admits: 'With no disrespect to United, up to that point they were dead. But when they scored their first goal out of the blue I thought we might panic and we did.' Gone was the defensive drill and 'military' organisation as United pounded the Arsenal rearguard. And found it cracking. Two minutes later, it collapsed. McIlroy, who had played throughout as if building to this climax, twinkled his way through tottering defenders and stroked the ball past a horrified Jennings. Delirium broke out in the stands, on the bench, but, most significantly, on the field. United were entitled to their celebrations and their relief was overwhelming. But for Brady, it was a terrible moment. 'When they equalised I thought we'd blown it because now we were dead – dead tired – and they were lifted by the goals.'

At that point, United would have been favourites with every bookmaker in the land, probably after extra time. Indeed, Brady, himself, had settled for another half-hour. 'I thought there was going to be extra time so all I really wanted to do was keep the ball in their half,' he explained. But as United's relief washed over their aching limbs like Radox, their concentration wavered. Brady's didn't. With the icy composure that only the maestros can conjure on such occasions, he crossed the half-way line, the ball held tightly in the 'claw'. United were caught in exhausted retreat, their defence hopelessly square. Brady coolly weighed the options. 'Graham Rix must have made 40 or 50 yards to get alongside me,' he recalls. Brady pushed the ball to him and when the centre arrived, Sunderland was there to joyously thump it past a disbelieving Bailey. Ecstasy and incredulity broke out at the other end. And later, much, much later, one half of north London was still singing 'There's only one Liam Brady.'

Defeated Manchester boss Sexton admitted: 'It was a cruel result.'

Former legend Bobby Charlton said: 'It shouldn't happen to a dog,' while Matt Busby had tears in his eyes.

But Brady's eyes were smiling. Socks down to his ankles, arms held aloft, his dream of FA Cup glory had at last been realised. 'I can now live with the memory of the previous final when I had a nightmare,' he said. 'I doubt if there'll ever be a finish to match it.'

For United, claimed Lawrie McMenemy in the BBC studio: 'It was like being sentenced to death, being reprieved at the last minute – then walking from the courtroom and being run over by a bus.' Driven by a man with a ball stuck in his 'claw'.

Arsenal: Jennings; Rice, Nelson, Talbot, O'Leary, Young, Brady, Sunderland, Stapleton, Price (Walford), Rix.

Manchester United: Bailey; Nicholl, Albiston, McIlroy, McQueen, Buchan, Coppell, Jimmy Greenhoff, Jordan, Macari, Thomas.

Peter Broadbent

WOLVERHAMPTON WANDERERS 4
MOSCOW SPARTAK 0
Friendly: Molineux, 16 November 1954.

Born in Elvington, Kent, on 15 May 1933, Peter Broadbent played for Kent County Schools and Dover before signing as a pro for Brentford in 1950. In just 16 games, this stylish inside-forward made a big enough impression for Wolves to pay £10,000 for him – a lot of money for a 17-year-old in those ration-book days. His educated right foot and excellent control soon became vital components in Stan Cullis's irresistible Molineux machine during its 'old golden' age of the mid-Fifties. A team man, Broadbent's vision and passing accuracy ensured that all forwards got in on the act – and the scoresheet. He earned seven England caps but was competing for the schemer's role with the incomparable Johnny Haynes. No mug in front of goal himself, Broadbent notched 138 goals in 629 League appearances in a 20-year career. After Wolves he played for Shrewsbury, Aston Villa and Stockport.

'All England will be looking tonight,' thundered 'Commentator' in the *Express & Star*. 'Today is the most eagerly-awaited in Wolverhampton's history.' If the local football correspondent appeared to be a terminal case, the rest of the country also seemed to be suffering from a severe dose of what he called 'Spartakitis'. The famous old Molineux ground could have been filled twice over for the visit of the formidable Russians, while for every other citizen a vigil in front of a grainy, black and white tele-

41

vision picture was as obligatory as it had been for the Coronation. Modern students may point out that this clash between the runners-up in the Soviet League and the leaders of the English First Division was a mere 'friendly', but no subsequent encounter in 'proper' European competition ever contained more of a Cup-tie spirit – or Cold War overtones. 'We sensed the whole country was with us,' remembers Broadbent.

Indeed, you might have thought that World War III was looming from the pre-match hype. 'The hammer and sickle has been hoisted over Molineux,' announced the *Express & Star* solemnly. The Spartak players were subjected to a 'welcome' by anti-communist protestors who showered them with pamphlets, while both the BBC and Radio Moscow pronounced on the significance of the game. Yet the match appeared in serious jeopardy on the Monday as thick fog blanketed the West Midlands. The weather men said: 'It is likely to get worse.' Reports of the 'molestation' of the visitors added to the intrigue but may have owed much to 'visibility being reduced to a few feet'. To take their minds off the forthcoming confrontation, the Soviets went to the cinema where they saw *The Yellow Mountain*, a Western, heartened perhaps by mischievous thoughts of what the fog might do to the Wolves' long-ball game.

When the blanket lifted sufficiently to permit a work-out, Spartak terrified 'Commentator'. 'Every player is a gymnast,' he observed through the retreating mist. 'They high-kicked, writhed and skipped their way through training.' The Wolves of Stan Cullis were undaunted, however. Typically, their only contribution to the build up was to announce that Ron Flowers had passed a late fitness test, while Peter Broadbent can remember, 'just doing our normal preparation'. Cullis kept his men well-cossetted but even Broadbent admits: 'I had never known an atmosphere like it.'

Spartak had beaten Arsenal 2–1 a week earlier. England had twice been humiliated by the Hungarians and the awesome burden of restoring national pride fell on the men in the old gold shirts. Mercifully, the fog cleared and there were 55,184 crammed into the ground when the Russians ran to each side of the field and bowed. Even 'Commentator' admitted: 'There was just the slightest touch of jitters – understandable enough since Wolves were carrying all Britain's prestige on their golden clad shoulders.' Indeed with this kind of load, it was hardly surprising that the lords of the long ball began in uncharacteristically tentative mood. Not until the quarter hour did they reveal the aggression that had devoured all-comers in the domestic game, but then they found the Russian 'keeper, Piraev, equal to the task as he saved twice from the head of Slater. After that Wright had to make one of his trademark tackles to halt the dangerous Simonyan, and Williams saved well from Paramonov. With the crowd finding its voice and Broadbent finding his men, Wolves at last began to pound the Iron Curtain – but had to be wary of the Soviet counters. It was classic European fare and balanced on a knife-edge.

Broadbent's authority grew after the resumption, his prompting and probing, measured passing and close control helping to steer the more frenzied home attacks toward their target. He ensured that Johnny 'Mighty Atom' Hancocks became a major influence and gradually ushered the fraught Midlanders towards a breakthrough. 'We were beginning to wonder when it was coming,' he recalls, 'as we had been on top for a while. And they were very dangerous in breakaways.' Hancocks twice went close, bringing a marvellous save from Piraev and then rattling the bar before the mounting pressure eventually took its toll. As the evening wore on it was clear that even the composed Spartak defenders did not have to withstand this kind of battering on a regular basis. Their supremely drilled and disciplined ranks had resisted stoutly but at last began to waver. 'We thought we had 'em after an hour,' says Broadbent, 'as we had begun to play a bit.' Shot after shot rained in on the Iron Curtain and, with the crowd

43

sensing a breakthrough, it finally parted. There was another sustained bombardment before Denis Wilshaw got the crucial touch in the 63rd minute. Molineux erupted and witnesses claim that the Midlands had heard nothing like it since the Luftwaffe dropped its load on Coventry. The Russians responded by making a substitution – unheard of in Britain but accepted in this 'friendly' – once the referee had been told. Isayev replaced Paramonov and, as the old gold shirts retreated in numbers, Spartak mounted their customary 15-minute finale. Now it was Wolves' turn to hang on and somehow they survived the onslaught, Slater and Stuart both heroically blocking 'certain goals'.

However, with nine minutes remaining, the diminutive Hancocks (5'4", size two feet but heart of a lion) decided the match. Darting, jinking, dazzling his way around three dazed Russian defenders, he finally put the game beyond the visitors with a killer strike. Pandemonium broke out – and that was just in the press box. 'My shoulders ache from the pounding they received,' complained 'Commentator', 'from one of the most dignified and well travelled of national soccer writers.' Before the uproar had subsided, Hancocks was at it again, sending Swinbourne through for the third. With Spartak well and truly spent, the ball was in the net again but it was disallowed. And then Hancocks slotted home a fourth.

'Unbelievable,' is how Broadbent remembers it. 'We would have been happy just to win. Scoring four was almost too much for the crowd.' Others compared it to VE Day. Perhaps some had really swallowed the propaganda?

Among the fascinating footnotes is that Cullis explained his failure to substitute the injured Stuart, by saying: 'It is against British tradition.'

In the Russian tradition, Radio Moscow refused to mention the defeat in their all-night broadcasts to domestic listeners but, on their North American service, admitted: 'It was a bitter pill to swallow.'

Cullis claimed: 'It was the club's greatest achievement – better even than winning the FA Cup.'

But the last word must go to 'Commentator'. 'Even St George in his shining armour,' he began, 'could not have fought more gallantly for England than did Wolves in their shining golden•shirts on the battle-scarred Molineux turf last night.' And no one had done more than Peter Broadbent.

Wolverhampton Wanderers: Williams; Stuart, Shorthouse, Slater, Wright, Flowers, Hancocks, Broadbent, Swinbourne, Wilshaw, Smith.

Moscow Spartak: Piraev; Orgonkov, Sedov, Parachin, Bachachkine, Netto, Tataschin, Paramanov (Isayev), Vorochilov, Ilyin.

Terry Butcher

ABERDEEN 1 RANGERS 1
League: Pittodrie, 2 May 1987

Born in Singapore on 28 December 1958, son of a serviceman, Terry Butcher played for Lowestoft Schools and joined Ipswich Town in 1976, making his debut the following year. At 6' 3" and 14st 5lb, he was a giant of a defender and soon earned England Under-21 and 'B' honours before being capped against Australia in 1980. He won a UEFA Cup-winners' medal in 1981 and went on to become the central bulwark of the Ipswich and England defences. He was transferred to Rangers for an Ipswich record of £720,000 in 1986 and captured both the League and League Cup at Ibrox in 1987. It was to prove an eventful year as he was involved in a notorious Old Firm incident, which led to a court appearance, and then broke his leg. The injury cost Rangers and England dearly but Butcher confirmed his mental and physical toughness by coming back to produce many more courageous performances for club and country. He became player-manager at Coventry and then switched to Sunderland, and is recognised as one of the most dominant defenders of the modern era.

'Sleepy' and 'backwater' are two of the more frequent descriptions of the Suffolk football outpost of Ipswich. In spite of the celebrated feats of Sir Alf Ramsey and Bobby Robson, who both went on to manage England, the words just about sum up the football stature of the town that is tucked away from the game's mainstream near the East Anglian coast. But it can be said with absolute certainty that 'sleepy' and 'backwater' will never be used to describe Glasgow Rangers. Terry Butcher, giant of a man, giant of a defender, had waged an ultimately losing battle to sustain the élite status of Ipswich for a decade before yielding to the blandishments of Britain's most fervid football hotbed. An established international, he sought wider acclaim at club level and a chance to win something. So when English giants Manchester United and Spurs dithered over signing him in 1986, it took one whiff of a rarefied Ibrox for him to lead the English exodus over the border. He relished his reception in the simmering cauldron and made an immediate impact. Rangers had the foundation stone for their late-Eighties revival and Graeme Souness may never make a better signing.

The Rangers fans took to Butcher as swiftly as he took to them. A teeming, throbbing theatre was what he had longed for and, although he had an affectionate fan club in Suffolk, Portman Road could never produce the fervour generated in the best stadium in Britain. And, as if that were not enough, Gers fans were even more stoked up than usual as, after an intolerably long fallow period [for them], they sensed a new era of greatness dawning. Butcher could hardly believe what he had let himself in for. 'Forget about the pressure of playing for England,' he said soon after his move. 'It's much tougher playing for Rangers. It's the toughest job in world football.'

Butcher was particularly taken aback by the Old Firm games and declared: 'You hear people talking about Arsenal v Spurs, Everton v Liverpool and they speak of it as something red-hot. They are nothing, absolutely nothing, compared to what goes on in Glasgow. You can't name anywhere else in the world where the pressures on the players are so great.' The big man has been made more graphically aware of the vehement intensity of those encounters with Celtic than perhaps any other Englishman – erstwhile team-mate Chris Woods apart – and when Rangers travelled north to play Aberdeen in the Granite City on 2 May 1987, Butcher was embroiled in both a personal crusade and an 'Old Firm' struggle on a bigger scale. Celtic were the Blues' only challengers for the title which Rangers and Butcher craved, and the 'other half' of Glasgow were at home to lowly Falkirk for whom relegation loomed large. Moreover, the Gers had won only once at Pittodrie in 23 outings since the Premier League was instituted in 1975. They had not won there for five years and it was the last place they would want to go to clinch their first title in nine long seasons.

Even so, some fans thought it was all over and Rangers, holding a four-point lead and a vastly superior goals difference with just two games to go, were undoubtedly in the box seats. Still, Butcher tried not to think about it. 'The only time to talk about celebrating the title is once we've won it,' he said. Davie Cooper added: 'The fans think we've already won it but until we've done it, I won't believe it. Going to Aberdeen has never been easy for us. No way is it going to be any different this time.'

Aberdeen boss, Ian Porterfield, confirmed Rangers' worst fears: 'The match is vital to both clubs for different reasons. Our two remaining games are crucial to our chances of playing in Europe next season. We have the players capable of beating Rangers and we've already proved that this season.' In the light of all this, it was of little comfort to Rangers to know that Falkirk would be fighting for their Premier League lives at Parkhead. If Celts won and Rangers lost, there would only be two point in it . . . This then was the background to that furious decider on the east coast – a few hundred miles north of Suffolk but a few light years away in sheer, unbridled fanaticism.

The opening was predictably fierce and Woods had to produce a superb diving save to stop Irvine's powerful header in the third minute. Moments later Irvine was involved again, being badly fouled by Souness who was booked. The tone had been set and when Robertson hit the deck following an off-the-ball incident with McCoist, McLeish was given a yellow card for arguing. Robertson was booked on 27 minutes, either side of which Rangers had the ball in the net but both times it was ruled offside. The game might have been played on a tinder box and, sure enough, the explosion occurred in the 31st minute, Souness giving referee Duncan no option with a late challenge on the unfortunate Irvine. As the manager trooped off, Butcher led the Rangers protests only to be given a yellow card himself. It was the second time Souness had received a red card in his first season in charge and was hardly the start he or his men would have wished for against a formidably charged-up Aberdeen. But the Gers need not have worried – their saviour from Suffolk was in control.

One of the most persuasive lines Souness used to gain Butcher's signature was his intention 'to make Rangers the best club in Europe, maybe the world'. 'The potential is here,' he was fond of saying. 'You can feel it.' Butcher certainly felt it but he was also aware of the potential for disaster when Souness left them with just ten men. It could have been a catastrophic turning point but Butcher himself led the way. When McKimmie fouled Cooper, the winger took the kick and there was Butcher to power in a header past Leighton – and send the Blues fans into raptures. But the first half was not over yet and when Munro fouled McKimmie, there was time for the ubiquitous Irvine to turn in the equaliser.

With Philips on for Fleck at the start of the second half, Rangers had settled for a cautious approach although that didn't apply to their tackling, the tally of yellow cards reaching nine in a tempestuous encounter. Aberdeen, a man to the good, held the upper hand and Rangers, heroically marshalled by Butcher and urged on by their fanatical followers, funnelled back but held firm. Joe Miller hit the woodwork and then brought a great save from Woods but Aberdeen could not break through. A minute from time, Bett, who had appeared to have been booked earlier, was given another yellow card!

Perhaps the referee had forgotten but one player on whose mind every event of the day is indelibly etched is

Butcher. 'I'll never forget it,' he says. 'It had been nine years since the club had won the League and I could never have imagined how badly the fans wanted it until I came up here. And we were nine points behind Celtic at Christmas! It just shows the sort of team we are building at Ibrox.'

Butcher thought the signing of Roberts was the turning point in the season and certainly the former Tottenham defender's toughness and resolution were crucial as Aberdeen had thrown everything but its granite foundations at the Rangers defence as they sought a winner. 'It was one of the hardest battles I've been in,' admitted Butcher, 'but it was a terrific feeling to have that following behind us. And then we heard that Falkirk were winning . . .' A painful irony for Celts was that Jimmy Gilmour, who scored the winner, is a nephew of the great Jimmy Johnstone but of much, much greater import was that the brash new regime on the other side of Glasgow had finally succeeded. And their big money signings were the heroes. None more so than Butcher whose resolution in the face of an all-out Dons onslaught was magnificent. It was a mean and nasty match but the sort you have to win if Championships are to be taken.

'This is only the beginning,' said Butcher. 'You ain't seen nothin' yet. It has been an unbelievable year.' Butcher was all but deified by the Rangers faithful, while in Suffolk they did not begrudge him his moment of triumph. But hero-worship was the music Butcher wanted to hear – it is always preferable to a quiet round of applause.

Aberdeen: Leighton; McKimmie, Robertson (Grant), Irvine, McLeish, W. Miller, Gray, Bett, J. Miller, Simpson, Hewitt.

Rangers: Woods; Roberts, Munro, Souness, McPherson, Butcher, Nicholl, Fleck (Philips), McCoist, Durrant, Cooper.

Tim Buzaglo

WEST BROMWICH ALBION 2 WOKING 4
FA Cup third round: The Hawthorns, 5 January 1991.

Born in Surbiton on 20 June 1961, Tim Buzaglo played for Waysiders in the Surrey Intermediate League and joined Woking in 1986. He has found the net regularly throughout his career but was better known as a scorer of runs with the Gibraltar cricket team for whom he qualified through parentage and whom he represented in three World Cups – until a certain Saturday in the winter of 1991.

When you operate computers for a living and your greatest claim to sporting fame is scoring 41 not out against East Africa in cricket's World Cup you do not expect to become the stuff of FA Cup folklore. But Tim Buzaglo not only became famous for causing one of the great Cup upsets of all time, he did so in just 15 minutes. The striker's second half hat-trick in Woking's 4–2 demolition of West Brom lifted the humble Vauxhall Premier League side into the fourth round and turned the unlikely name of Buzaglo into one with which the nation's households were suddenly familiar. The scene – a wintry West Midlands landscape – might have been painted by Lowry yet the script on that January day was pure *Boy's Own*: watched by 4,000 of their own fans, the 5,000–1 outsiders came from behind to inflict the greatest humiliation on Albion in the Throstles' 112-year history.

Albion fans stayed behind to demand the head of their

unfortunate manager, Brian Talbot, but had the heart to cheer the non-Leaguers in their hour of triumph – and chair Buzaglo off the field. For the sometime international cricketer, it was the climax of a week which he had begun by punching keys in deepest Surrey but ended by punching holes in a Second Division defence – and telling the tale as a guest of *Match of the Day*. Inevitably, the Monday after was a different story. 'I got no work done at all,' he confesses. 'I spent about £20 on Sunday papers but it still didn't sink in. Only when I went to work and got no peace at all from colleagues or the phone did I realise what I'd done.'

The Woking faithful might have been forgiven for thinking that their giant-killing in the 1990–91 season had begun and ended with a 2–1 win over Bath City in the fourth qualifying round. After all, Bath were members of the non-League élite in the Vauxhall Conference and a considerable scalp. Indeed, Dereck Brown described scoring the winner as 'a dream come true'. Little did he know what he'd started. The Cards' reward was another home tie against Conference opposition and this time they required two replays to dispose of Kidderminster, a healthy 3,249 watching the first match at Woking. The interest was beginning to build.

Goals, however, were a problem and a below-par Buzaglo was in and out of the side. For him the coming glories were not even a twinkle on his keyboard and he was not alone. After being held 0–0 at home in the league by Redbridge Forest, the *Woking News & Mail* screamed: 'Dozy Woking suffered a severe bout of "before the Lord Mayor's Show!"' The big occasion was the replay with Kidderminster. It took them 191 minutes to find the net against the Worcestershire side and manager Geoff Chapple admitted: 'We are working hard but just don't look like scoring.' Buzaglo returned for the third encounter and his shot, which the Kidderminster 'keeper could not hold, led to the equaliser before Andy Russell grabbed a late winner. Merthyr Tydfil were next and the biggest crowd at Kingfield for 11 years witnessed a 5–1 walloping of the Welshmen, 'Tiger' Tim getting the scent with his first goal for six weeks. So Woking were in the FA Cup third round for the first time in their history and not even an away draw at West Brom could temper their euphoria. 'We proved that not all non-League teams play ale-house football,' said hat-trick hero Mark Biggins. Albion should have listened.

The Midlanders were having a poor season and the Surrey side travelled with hope in their hearts. 'We thought we had a glimmer,' said Buzaglo. 'Geoff [Chapple] had done his homework and felt we could do it.' 'Old Buz', as he's also affectionately known, had regained his scoring touch with eight in six games. Against him was renowned hard man Graham Roberts, who had not so long ago been collecting silverware with Rangers and Spurs, and, alongside him was £500,000-rated Gary Strodder.

Perhaps sensing that they were on a hiding to nothing, the Baggies opened in determined mood. Sparing neither the offside trap nor their opponents' limbs, they seemed bent on intimidating the upstarts from the whistle. But the Cards, who included a bank clerk, a fireman, an engineer, a salesman, a Ministry of Defence employee and a painter and decorator, refused to bow – and played the better football. Woking should have gone in front but Mitchell's shot was headed off the line before Albion took the lead against the run of play, West heading in from a corner in the 34th minute. Unabashed, the visitors continued to battle and Buzaglo recalls: 'Although we went in 1–0 down at half-time, we said to ourselves: "We can win this or at least take 'em back to our place."'

Continuing to play to feet, the Cards equalised just before the hour, a triangular passing movement being capped by Buzaglo's curler from 15 yards. 'I always knew it was going in,' he smiles. With Woking fans now at fever pitch and the Baggies fearing the worst, the Cards went for the jugular. Read's long clearance was headed on by Brown and Old Buz gleefully headed home the rebound after his first shot was blocked. 'It was a nice, little bounce,' he acknowledges. At 2–1 with 25 minutes remaining, the fans could hardly believe it – but there was more. Woking's and Buzaglo's places in the FA Cup pantheon were guaranteed in the 74th minute when he rifled home a left-foot shot from a Biggins' cross from the right. Delirium among the Woking fans, despair for Albion. For Talbot it was the final nail – the sack came 48 hours later – while for Buzaglo it meant celebrity status. 'All I had thought about during the week,' he said, 'was scoring one goal . . . as long as we won. I can't believe this.'

But Woking had not finished. Two minutes from time, substitute Worsfield made it four with a diving header and Bradley's goal for Albion in the dying seconds was irrelevant – and flattering. 'We knew we had won when the third went in,' says Buzaglo. 'We tore them apart and by the end were skinning them.' Chapple, who described the occasion as 'the greatest day of my life', and did not mind a ducking in the bath when fully clothed, said of his hat-trick hero: 'He's a tremendous player but he's had an indifferent season. I've been pulling my hair out with him the last six or seven months. But we always pick him because we know what he can do and today we saw his class.' Talbot, close to tears, observed: 'We couldn't cope with Buzaglo and the result is a humiliating one for myself and the club. Everyone has to hold up their hands and say that Woking deserved it. They did their little town proud.'

The Cards' reward was a home draw with Everton which they switched to Goodison and, after an heroic battle, lost 1–0. To add to their memories, the players did a lap of honour of the famous ground, received a civic reception back in Woking and went on to win two Cups – the Surrey Senior and the AC Delco. But the last word must be on Old Buz. As they lifted him to their shoulders, the Albion fans had chanted in one voice: 'Sign him on!' It was a pity they didn't – after Goodison, the Cards came back to earth on the Tuesday by playing Walton and Hersham in the Surrey Demolition and Excavation Senior Cup. The following Saturday – just a week after 34,274 had saluted them in the Merseyside shrine – Buzaglo was stretchered off after the third vicious foul in the first four minutes of a league match with St Albans. 'I didn't even have the ball when the guy clouted me,' he said. 'But being injured gave me more time to watch the video [of the West Brom game]. Without that I'd think I had dreamt it.'

West Bromwich Albion: Rees; Shakespeare, Harbey (Palmer), Roberts, Bradley, Strodder, Ford, West, Bannister, McNally, Robson.

Woking: Read; Mitchell, Cowler, Pratt, Baron, S. Wye, Brown, Biggins, Franks (Worsford), Buzaglo, L. Wye.

Eric Caldow

SCOTLAND 4 SPAIN 2
World Cup qualifier: Hampden, 8 May 1957.

Born in Cumnock, Ayrshire, on 14 May 1934, Eric Caldow played with Cumnock Academy and Glenpark Juveniles before joining Rangers in 1952. At 5'8" and 10st 5lb, Caldow was slight in stature but more than made up with his class and speed. He won two Under-23 caps before making the full Scotland team in 1957. He stayed first choice until his leg was badly broken in a tackle with Bobby Smith at Wembley in 1963. A finalist in the European Cup-winner's Cup in 1961, he collected five League Championship medals with Rangers, two Scottish Cups and three League Cups. Once in the national side, he was an automatic choice for six years, oozing quality and calm assurance. A sure shot with penalties and excellent in his distribution, Caldow was the complete full-back and a natural choice to succeed Bobby Evans as his country's captain. Crisp in the tackle and exceptional on the turn, he was a challenge for the great wingers of his day. Not many got past him. Caldow left Rangers for Stirling Albion in 1966 and took over as player-manager of Corby Town in 1968. He managed Hurlford United and Stranraer before becoming scout for Queen's Park Rangers in 1975.

According to one critic at the World Cup finals in 1954, 'Scotland's defenders stood around like grazing Highland cattle.' He was referring to the 7–0 defeat by Uruguay, a result which condemned the dark blues to an early exit and one of the biggest humiliations in their history. Long before Ally McLeod, there was failure and near-farce, except that on this occasion, there was no manager – Andy Beattie having resigned on the eve of the match. Scotland came bottom of a four-nation group but there were other embarrassments: the ridiculously small squad of 13 – one goalkeeper – was overworked, under-prepared and contained no Rangers players – they could not be spared from a club trip to the USA. The Scots had slipped up badly in almost every respect, possessing no obvious leader in the absence of George Young, no pennant to swap with their opponents and not enough strips for training. Practising in their club shirts, Willie Fernie famously remarked: 'We look like Liquorice Allsorts.'

Eric Caldow was spared the confusion. Although he had only just broken into the side for the qualifying campaign for the 1958 World Cup finals, it was immediately obvious that he was exactly what had been needed in Switzerland. More like a greyhound than a grazer, Caldow brought pace and authority to the defence. And when Spain arrived in Glasgow for the first group game in 1957, his presence in the side suggested that the painful lessons of three years ago had been learned. The only trouble was . . . on Spain's left wing lurked a fellah called Gento, a Real Madrid superstar who happened to be the most explosive winger in the world. 'They said he'd roast me alive,' remembers Caldow, 'and I was aware of his reputation.'

Real were, of course, the wonder team of Europe and, besides Gento, provided Zarraga and the great Di Stefano. With the team made up from just three clubs, Real, Barcelona and Bilbao, there should have been no shortage of understanding to go with their undoubted skills. Indeed, England team boss Walter Winterbottom had fancied Spain for the World Cup in 1954. Their failure had less to do with ability than temperament, and it was still a formidable line-up facing young Caldow as he made only his second appearance in the dark blue jersey. 'We were real underdogs,' he recalls, 'and even the Scottish press said we were not in their class.' Indeed, the *Daily Record*'s 'Waverley' thought Scotland's best hope was an early goal and . . . the Latin temperament. His final word to the players was: 'Don't be shy about using the shoulder though the continentals don't like it.'

Before a crowd of 87,000, it was the Spaniards who went for the physical stuff, turning a howling Hampden into a huge bull ring as one Scot after another was tossed unceremoniously on to the slippery turf. But keeping admirable composure, the Scots responded in the best way possible – by scoring. It came from a corner after Baird's shot had hit the woodwork. Blackpool's Mudie turned Smith's kick on to the bar but made no mistake with the rebound. Five minutes later, Spain were level: a fortuitous mis-kick by Kubala struck Younger's leg and eluded the 'keeper's grasp. With Mudie coming in for some especially rough treatment, Scotland almost scored again following a thrice-taken free-kick. All that was missing from the majority of the challenges was a pair of horns but the rattled visitors were punished when the Scots regained the lead from the spot. Hewie's kick carried too much pace for Ramallets after Olivella had tripped Ring. With Caldow in charge of Gento and Di Stefano having to drop deeper to set up attacks, Spain were on the receiving end from the rejuvenated Scottish forwards. The Liquorice Allsorts were sorted and two minutes into the second half, the magnificent Mudie rounded Ramallets but again the woodwork intervened. Profiting from the escape, the Spaniards drew level again when Younger could only palm away a Di Stefano pile-driver, Suarez doing the rest. With 20 minutes of the second half gone, Mudie restored Scotland's lead with a 20-yard drive into the roof of the net but the best was still to come. A three-man move begun by McColl ended when Mudie swept home Collins's pass for a richly-deserved hat-trick. With Young setting a captain's example, McColl and Docherty tackling like demons and Caldow and Hewie keeping Gento and Gonzalez at bay, there was no way back.

It had been Caldow's first encounter with Gento, whom he had not allowed a kick all night. The winger told him:

'You're the best and fastest full-back in the world.' The press agreed. Caldow adds: 'I met him a few times after that and always matched him for pace. He was certainly the best winger I ever played against. To beat Spain was great but to be acclaimed the fastest full-back in the world really made my night.' On a night when the Spaniards' behaviour had been far too bullish, it was pleasing to report that there was absolutely no grazing on the part of the Scots.

Scotland: Younger; Caldow, Hewie, McColl, Young, Docherty, Smith, Collins, Mudie, Baird, Ring.

Spain: Ramallets; Olivella, Garay, Verges, Campanai, Zarraga, Gonzalez, Kubala, Di Stefano, Suarez, Gento.

Jack Charlton

LIVERPOOL 0 LEEDS UNITED 0
League: Anfield, 28 April 1969

Born in Ashington, Northumberland, on 8 May 1935, Jack Charlton is related to the famed Milburn family and is the elder brother of Bobby. Jack played for East Northumberland Schools and Ashington YMCA prior to signing amateur forms for Leeds in 1950. He was recommended to Elland Road by his uncle Jim Milburn, a brother of the legendary 'Wor' Jackie, but his career was put on hold due to national service in the Royal Horse Guards. He returned to become a fixture as Leeds' pivot, making his first team debut in 1953 in a 1–1 draw with Doncaster Rovers. From this undistinguished beginning, Big Jack gradually developed into the best centre-half in the country. Known as 'The Giraffe', he was a stalwart of both Don Revie's Leeds and Alf Ramsey's England, winning 35 caps including a World Cup winners' medal in 1966. He followed Bobby as Footballer of the Year in 1967 and made a record 629 League appearances for Leeds, scoring 70 goals. An outspoken television pundit, he is among a rare breed to have matched his success as a player in management. As a manager he led Middlesbrough back into Division One, revived Sheffield Wednesday and, after a brief, unproductive stay at Newcastle, has enjoyed an astonishing reign in charge of the Republic of Ireland.

Success came late to Jack Charlton: after his apprenticeship at Elland Road had been interrupted by the army, he learned his craft almost unnoticed in the lower reaches of the Second Division. Leeds were languishing while younger brother Bobby was making headlines with Manchester United and England. Unsung Jack was in his late twenties before he played in the First Division and only a month away from his 30th birthday when he won his first cap. Almost every honour in the game followed but, even with Leeds, he had to wait. Agonizingly. After finishing runners-up twice in a row upon their return to Division One and losing to Liverpool in the 1965 Cup Final, the Yorkshiremen had to go to Anfield, of all places, to clinch the elusive League title.

'This,' he insists, 'was the most memorable occasion of my Leeds career – no doubt. We had had a terrific season but Liverpool were still in contention. So going to their place was a real test. It couldn't have been tougher but we were confident as we had hardly lost a game all season.' Even so, the 'lion's den' nature of the contest called for the stoutest of hearts as well as great skill, but Leeds knew they could not have had anyone better equipped to deal with the inevitable onslaught. Not only had Charlton been undaunted by taking the number five shirt from the great John Charles as a youngster, he was still towering over Europe's top centre-forwards at an age when his contemporaries were seeking the softer options of the lower leagues. Big Jack would handle anything Liverpool, Shanks, the Saint or the Kop could hurl at him.

Leeds still had another home game to come but it was of little comfort to a club already imbued with superstition and a sense of failure after their near-misses of recent seasons. They wanted no mistake at Liverpool and, as Revie said, 'Apart from Elland Road, there is no place in the country I'd rather clinch it than Anfield.' Charlton, a one-club man whose loyalty was as fierce as his tackle, agreed and felt that his mission in the game would not be complete until he could add the League Championship to the Jules Rimet trophy. But the Leeds luck, the Elland Road curse or whatever it was that denied them their full quota of silverware in the Revie era, was already beginning to manifest itself – the pessimists suspecting that the fixture planners had dealt them a poor hand. Charlton was not among them.

'If people didn't say we were worthy champions after this, when would they?' he reasoned. As indomitable in the dressing-room as he was in the penalty area, Big Jack lifted his team-mates as easily as he alarmed opponents and, on this memorable spring evening, Leeds were ready for their titantic decider. The Kop gathered in anticipation of one of Anfield's greatest nights and 53,750 squeezed into the famous ground. The atmosphere was of a high voltage even by Liverpool's standards and, sure enough, the Reds hurled themselves at Leeds as if their lives depended on it. With Smith, Strong and Hughes augmenting a livewire attack ably led by St John, and Callaghan and Thompson darting dangerously down the flanks, it called for defending of the highest class. Gary Sprake in the Leeds goal had prepared for a night of nights and, sure enough, wave after red wave kept coming at the white-shirted defenders. But Sprake did not have a shot to save until the 35th minute – and that was a speculative long range effort from Callaghan. There was a simple explanation – the indestructibility of Charlton and Hunter.

The pair gave one of their finest performances in tandem at the heart of the Leeds defence, tackling, covering, controlling the box and generally appearing impassable to even the most imaginative of attacks. Charlton had had to fight for recognition as a player, which he gradually achieved as the Leeds revival took shape. He was often described as an 'old-fashioned' centre-half because of his command of the stratosphere and the ruggedness of his tackling. And while it was rumoured that he could inflict bruising through eye contact alone, the timing of his challenges, his menace in the opposing penalty area and his knack of scoring vital goals were the attributes of an extraordinary player. As cussed as he was consistent, the sight of The Giraffe loping into the opponents' box was one of the most menacing of the age. All of this, however, meant nothing to Liverpool who maintained the siege at an intensity that was special even by their standards. Eventually, their persistence looked to have paid off as Leeds hesitated but Evans wasted the chance and the white shirts closed ranks again. At the other end, Bremner had a shot deflected and almost beat Lawrence but, well before the break, it was looking as if one goal would decide it.

It was hard, it was unflinching, it was frenetic and there was no let-up in the second half. But still Sprake was relatively untroubled – apart from holding a curler from Callaghan on the hour. Although a watertight defence was a priority, Leeds were not idle in attack and Lawrence had to be alert to the probing counter. The pace quickened and the football, desperate at times, was accompanied by an unrelenting din from the terraces. But as the Kop grew more impassioned, Revie's men remained steadfast. The understandable anxieties of the Leeds faithful were eased by one look at the magnificent Charlton and Hunter and, as their shrill whistles pleaded for the end, the Kop raised one final crescendo. Liverpool came again but Leeds held firm and, finally, it was all over.

'I've never known such relief,' says Charlton. 'We were stunned and it didn't sink in for a minute.' The Liverpool players left the field but Leeds walked towards the Kop, uncertain of the reception awaiting them. At first there was sullen silence but, tentatively, a Leeds player raised his hand. Others followed. And then, like rolling waves of thunder, the Kop gave its salute. 'To stand there as a Leeds player and be cheered by the Kop . . . that was something. I'll never forget it,' says Charlton.

'It was simply fantastic,' observed Revie. 'What a great gesture!'

Reaney added: 'You would have thought *their* team had won the League.'

But there was more. Shankly declared: 'The League Championship is the greatest prize in the game and I'm glad they've won it at last.'

Leeds beat Forest two nights later to end the season with nine club records, a total of 67 points, only two defeats, 27 wins (18 at home) and just 26 goals conceded. The Giraffe had been sticking his neck out for his club for 16 years and now his ears were flapping with deserved acclaim.

Liverpool: Lawrence; Lawler, Strong, Smith, Yeats, Hughes, Callaghan, Graham, Evans, St John, Thompson.

Leeds United: Sprake; Reaney, Cooper, Bremner, Charlton, Hunter, O'Grady, Madeley, Jones, Giles, Gray.

Chin and chest – a close shave for Jimmy Hill. Seen here at Craven Cottage, Hill was an entertainer long before he became a TV pundit – as a talented member of Tommy Trinder's famous Fulham 'showbiz' side of the Fifties

A centime for his thoughts? Michel Platini listens to the Marseillaise *in Mexico, one of three World Cups he graced without lifting the Jules Rimet trophy*

Steve Perryman, the baby-faced assassin, releases the ball in front of caged admirers. A terrier in the tackle, Perryman shows his determination for Spurs even when unchallenged

George Graham strolling into history. Graham levels against Liverpool in the 1971 FA Cup final to help Arsenal to the Double – with one of the 'softest' goals of his career

Million-pound overheads! Britain's first £1m player blasts a bicycle kick against the Bulgarian wall at Wembley

Tottenham's 'Colossus of Wales', Mike England, towers above Palace forward Jim Scott at Selhurst Park

Familiar pointers from Kenny Dalglish as he celebrates scoring the goal that clinched the League championship for Liverpool at Stamford Bridge in 1986

Ray Clemence shows why it took Bob Paisley only ten minutes to decide he was right for Liverpool. Here he clutches a high ball, watched by Ian Gillard of Queen's Park Rangers

Terry Butcher relaxing in his 'secondary' role for England – on this occasion against Uruguay. The giant of a defender claimed playing for Rangers was 'the toughest job in world football'

Ray Clemence

LIVERPOOL 3 NEWCASTLE UNITED 0
Wembley: FA Cup Final, 4 May 1974

Born in Skegness on 5 August 1948, Ray Clemence played in local schools and youth football – at left-half! He never wanted to be a goalkeeper but fate took a hand when his first game between the posts was seen by a Scunthorpe scout. He joined 'The Irons' in 1965 and made 48 appearances before taking the momentous step to Anfield – for just £18,000 in 1967. After a two-year apprenticeship as understudy to Tommy Lawrence he established himself in the first team in 1969.

A whisker under six feet and weighing 12st 9lb, Clemence was not huge for a 'keeper but possessed the reflexes of a cat. Add sound positioning, command of the area and adhesive handling, and you have one of the finest 'keepers ever to don the gloves. He won four Under-23 caps before making his full England debut in 1974. In all he earned 61 caps and was generally preferred to Peter Shilton during the Seventies. One of five Liverpool players to appear in the club's first three European Cup finals, he gained an FA Cup-winners' medal in 1974. After 470 games for the Reds, Clemence went to Spurs for £300,000 in 1981 where he won yet more honours, including a second Cup-winners' medal in 1982, and took his total number of first-class games to over 1,000 before successfully turning to coaching.

Maybe it was because he had Shanks as a boss and Shilts as a rival; or that he played behind the meanest defence in the land. Some suggested it could have been down to his working as a deckchair attendant on Skegness beach . . .

and seeing enough flapping to last a lifetime. Whatever the reason for Ray Clemence's surety of touch with high crosses, his mastery of this most difficult aspect of his art earmarked him as one of the finest goalkeepers of all time. Yet he might so easily have been lost to the game: rejected by Notts County and on the wrong end of some heavy beatings in the Scunny 'A' team, he was thinking of becoming an accountant. But he seized his chance in the first team as if fielding a well-flighted centre – and kept the goals against column well within budget. Bob Paisley saw enough in ten minutes to take him to Anfield.

Besides having the reactions of a Formula 1 driver, the elasticity of a gymnast and the concentration of a chess champion, Clemence had gloves lined with Evostick – precisely the qualities Liverpool were looking for as insurance for their almost impervious back four. A Reds 'keeper might have just one shot to deal with per game but it could be enough. Clemence kept so many clean sheets (227) in his 14 years at Anfield that he could have opened a laundry business. And one of his fondest memories is of keeping one at Wembley, one of the easiest afternoons of his career which came after the mouth of Malcolm Mac-Donald had been threatening to do much more than soil the linen.

'I played many times at Wembley, of course,' says Clemence, 'with England and in various finals. But winning the FA Cup for the first time is still a special occasion – especially when you've been on the losing side a few years before.' Clemence had been in goal when Arsenal had pipped Liverpool 2–1 to land the double in 1971 and still felt the scars of that grave disappointment. Three years later they were back with Newcastle as the opposition. 'A tricky one for us,' he recalls, 'as they had all the publicity, although we were favourites. The papers were just full of what Malcolm MacDonald was going to do to us.'

Supermac had scored in every round and was the hero of Tyneside. He was a dangerous, left-footed centre-forward whose goals output was only exceeded by his confidence. The precise number he was going to put past Clemence depended on which paper you read. Failure? The Geordies would not countenance the idea and, to be entirely fair, they had never known it, winning all five of their previous finals. Under the managership of Joe Harvey, who led them to their last triumph in 1955, they had an excellent side with good players in key positions, most notably Kenny Hibbitt, who laid them on for MacDonald, Supermac's co-striker John Tudor, and defensive marshal and current captain Bobby Moncur. For once, the Merseysiders would not have it all their own way in the choral department, either. But perhaps the greatest factor in the Magpies' confidence was luck. Harvey declared: 'It's our year.'

Newcastle had needed replays to subdue both non-League Hendon and lowly Scunthorpe after being embarrassingly held to home draws in the third and fourth rounds. But the greatest chunk of fortune came in the quarter-final when the Tynesiders somehow survived the misdemeanours of their own fans. An infamous pitch invasion, when the Magpies trailed Nottingham Forest 3–1, caused a re-start and two replays, Newcastle eventually winning through when many felt they should have been kicked out. With the fates seemingly on their side, it was no wonder several pundits opted for an upset.

Shankly, however, was not among them. 'We'll beat Newcastle,' he said, and prepared as if it was just another away match in London. 'Keep it simple,' he told his players, 'and stick to the normal routine as much as possible.'

Having prepared in a quiet country hotel, Liverpool looked much more relaxed than their hyped-up opponents, although they only just edged a disappointing first half. 'I had a few shots to save,' insists Clemence, 'but not as many as I'd been expecting, Phil Thompson doing a marvellous job on MacDonald.' After a competitive opening quarter-of-an-hour, Liverpool had gradually taken charge but it was not until 13 minutes into the second half

67

that they went in front. With nothing either seen or heard from MacDonald, Hibbitt labouring after twisting a knee and Moncur being increasingly tormented by Keegan, Geordie apprehension grew: and it was fitting that it was Keegan who lashed a Smith centre past McFaul after Hall had ducked to allow the cross to reach him.

'It was all Liverpool now,' says Clemence, 'and I was really enjoying it.' Indeed, the 'keeper created the second goal with a huge kick which Toshack headed on for Heighway. The Republic of Ireland star, who had scored against Arsenal three years earlier, anticipated it beautifully, ran into space and cracked it past McFaul. Fifteen minutes remained and Shankly motioned from the bench for his players to knock it around. They did. With the Mersey sound now drowning Tyneside's plaintive cries, Liverpool played exhibition stuff as if to underline their superiority. Smith and Callaghan, the only two survivors of the 1965 triumph, felt 1974 was a superior performance and the team turned on a high-class show in the second half. Hughes was rampant, Hall busy, Lindsay oozed class, Keegan simply covered every blade of grass with increasing menace and Thompson was as parsimonious as a jailer. They confirmed Shankly's claim that 'Liverpool have been the best team in the country for three months.' For the Geordies, it was sheer misery but through it all McDermott played magnificently.

There was, however, no stopping the relentless Mersey tide. Clemence remembers: 'The third goal was from a really great passing movement between several players before Kevin Keegan slid it home.' It was actually 12 passes, seven players and the 'keeper himself had started the move. MacDonald managed two late, despairing lashes which inevitably prompted the Mersey taunts: 'Supermac . . . Superstar . . . How many goals have you scored so far?' It was a fitting finale for Shanks who stunned the football world by retiring in the close season. As for Clemence, it was music to his ears – his afternoon had been so easy he could have spent it in a deckchair.

Liverpool: Clemence; Smith, Lindsay, Thompson, Cormack, Hughes, Keegan, Hall, Heighway, Toshack, Callaghan.

Newcastle United: McFaul; Clark, Kennedy, McDermott, Howard, Moncur, Cassidy, Smith (Gibb), MacDonald, Tudor, Hibbitt.

Bobby Collins

CELTIC 3 RANGERS 2
League: Parkhead, 13 August 1949.

---

*Born in Govanhill, Glasgow, on 16 February 1931, Bobby
Collins played for Polmadie Hawthorn Juveniles and Glasgow
Pollok before becoming a Celt in April 1948. At 5'4", he was
the 'standard size' for an old-style Scottish winger but possessed
the ball skills and vision which would eventually make him a
great inside-forward. With Celtic he won Scottish Cup-winners'
(1951) and League Championship (1954) medals, and landed
two Scottish League Cup wins (1957 and 1958). He made 15
appearances for the Scottish League and won the first of his 31
caps against Wales in 1951. Having added a few pounds, he
moved to inside-forward, where he proved a ferocious tackler and
a dynamic midfield general, and for a few years in the late 1950s
and early 1960s, he was among the most complete inside-forwards in Britain, knocking in the goals as well as orchestrating
almost every attack from his central role.*

*Collins was a big money signing by Everton at £23,500 in
1958 but when he was sold to Leeds for £1,000 less three-and-a-
half years later, it was generally assumed his career was on the
slide. But inside the wee stocky frame there beat a massive heart
and at Elland Road he achieved even greater things. In 1964 he
inspired the Yorkshiremen to the Second Division title and a year
later became the first Scot to be voted Footballer of the Year in
England as he earned a recall to the Scotland side at 34 – after a
six-year absence. Only Denis Law and Jimmy McMenemy have
worn the dark blue jersey for a longer period but, sadly, his
international career did come to an end when he broke his thigh in
the same year. Still, he was not finished at club level and he*

staged a magnificent comeback for the emerging Leeds in the First Division. He joined Bury (1967) and Morton (1969) before going to Australia for a spell. He was Down Under but still not out, coming back to play League football for Oldham in 1973 – at the age of 42. He also played for Shamrock Rovers before returning to begin a managerial/coaching career which took him from Oldham to Huddersfield, Leeds, Hull, Blackpool and Barnsley.

If it was possible to be a commanding figure at 5′4″, Robert Young Collins was that man. Tigerish in the tackle, terrier-like on the ball, he became a player of immense influence in the Fifties and Sixties. In the Forties he was just a wee young winger who could turn a full-back inside-out on an old tanner, belt to the byline and place his cross on the centre-forward's forelock. Such players were ten a penny in pre- and post-war Glasgow, but few had Collins's unique bag of tricks and tenacity. Celtic, proudly parading the subtle genius of Charlie Tully, sought desperately to wrestle free from the post-hostilities dominance of Rangers. Sensing perhaps that the 'Gers were beginning to show their age, Celtic tossed in two juniors for the first Old Firm encounter of the 1949–50 campaign. It was a massive gamble but Collins and Haughney would not let them down.

'We were really thrown in at the deep end,' recalls Collins. 'It was my first-team debut and though I played until my forties, nothing since has made such an impression. Rangers . . . Old Firm . . . 70,000 people at Parkhead . . . and I was up against the great Tiger Shaw . . . it had everything.'

The tribal fanaticism which had characterised Glasgow clashes before Hitler's intervention had resumed undiminished once hostilities on the larger stage had ceased. Indeed, the ravenous appetite for the game which saw the war-weary, ration-hungry hordes descend on football grounds in the late Forties and early Fifties like worker ants on a left-over feast, appeared, if anything, sharper, so fuelling the already considerable hatred that existed between the two halves of the football city. Mercifully, it did not extend to the players. 'Religion?' asks Collins. 'Nobody gave it a thought. We were just concerned about winning the game.'

Concerned? Such a massive understatement of the craving to topple the ancient foe was tantamount to heresy but says much for the commendable perspective from which Collins has always viewed such encounters and goes a long way to explaining his amazingly uncluttered approach to the baptism of a lifetime. 'I played outside-right and Mike Haughney was outside-left,' he remembers. 'We were two youngsters up against two of the most experienced backs in the game – I faced Shaw while Mike was up against George Young.' The gulf in stature between the two old Rangers lions and the pair of weans that Celtic threw at them just about reflected the Blues' post-War domination: of the 12 games played between 1946 and 1949, Rangers had won nine, Celtic two with one drawn. But the Celts had no intention of making any further sacrifices – it took courage to send out a couple of kids and it was courage which Celtic played with on that August afternoon.

Marshalled magnificently by Bobby Evans, Celtic overcame the inconvenience of an early goal to take the game to Rangers. And with McAuley and Boden completing a superb half-back line, the dangerous Blues forwards rarely got a look in. The portents had suggested otherwise when Waddell put Rangers ahead after McGuire had brought down Duncanson in the 12th minute, but ten minutes later Celts were level – also from the spot. 'I was whipped down for our penalty,' recalls Collins whose trickery and control had already begun to trouble the Rangers defence. McPhail rammed home the kick and with it Rangers' sense of superiority vanished.

With unexpected parity came a confidence that saw the wing pair of Collins and Haughney torment their stalwart markers while Tully, worshipped by the green and whites since his £8,000 switch from Belfast the previous year, was beginning to turn it on. On the half-hour, Tully headed toward goal and when it rebounded off the bar, the statuesque Rangers defenders allowed McPhail to leap and nod home.

There was tumult now on the Parkhead terraces as a famous victory could be sensed and it was the green half of the city that enjoyed the half-time taunts. With the Blues attack effectively neutralised, Collins and Haughney had more of the ball and they used it to great effect. For a pair of juniors, their response to the occasion was tremendous and Collins, more than his left-wing colleague, turned the game. Modestly ignoring the rave reviews 40-plus years on, he can just about be forced into acknowledging: 'It was a marvellous game.'

But Rangers were not the mighty 'Gers for nothing and under Bill Struth they weren't to surrender until the last blast of the whistle. In the 62nd minute they were level. It was an opportunist strike by Willie Thornton who used his lightning reactions to capitalise on an unlucky rebound off McAuley.

With the tension now weighing heavily on gnarled veterans, Celtic were splendidly served by the youth of Collins and Haughney who were able to shrug off the tension as easily as their stalwart markers. And with 20 minutes remaining, it was Haughney who crowned a marvellous debut with the winning goal. A McPhail shot was turned on to the bar by Rangers 'keeper Brown and there was Haughney to tap home. 'It was a great way to finish,' says Collins. For both wingers, it was a great way to start.

Celtic: Miller; McGuire, Baillie, Evans, Boden, McAuley, Collins, McPhail, Johnstone, Tully, Haughney.

Rangers: Brown; Young, Shaw, McColl, Woodburn, Cox, Waddell, Finlay, Thornton, Duncanson, Rutherford.

Davie Cooper

WALES 1 SCOTLAND 1
World Cup qualifier: Ninian Park, Cardiff, 10
September 1985

David Cooper was born in Hamilton on 25 February 1956. A trainee printer, Cooper was content to play amateur football with Hamilton Avondale and then Clydebank before being persuaded to turn pro by Bankies' owner Jack Steedman. Plying his new trade with increasing effect, it did not take long for Cooper, a natural left-footer, to become noticed by bigger clubs and Rangers paid £100,000 to take him to Ibrox in 1977. A genuine wing wizard with beautiful balance and touch, he made six Scottish Under-21 appearances before winning the first of 22 full caps in 1979. He made the 1986 World Cup finals in Mexico and only missed Italia 90 because of a foot injury. At Ibrox, he collected three Championship medals, three Scottish Cups and no less than seven League Cups before moving to Motherwell for a give-away £50,000 in 1989. The honours did not end there as he helped the Steelmen to a famous Scottish Cup triumph over Dundee United in 1991.

Still delighting crowds and driving full-backs to distraction in the 1992–93 season, Cooper has gained many admirers, among them Ruud Gullit, who thought the Scot was one of the best players he had ever seen. A dead-ball expert, Cooper's accuracy from set-pieces caused problems for many defences, whether providing for others or delivering free-kicks that Brazilians would be proud of. With respect to his former trade, Super Cooper has left an indelible imprint on Scottish football.

'You always think you know your favourite game,' admits Davie Cooper, 'until you start talking about others. There was the 1981 Scottish Cup Final when I was dropped for the first game and came back for the replay. Or there was the Skol Cup Final when I scored *that* free-kick [a shot driven• from over 20 yards and with such ferocity that Aberdeen 'keeper Jim Leighton only touched it, so the story goes, on the way back out]. And there was the Scottish Cup Final win with Motherwell, and the thrill of travelling on an open-top bus for the first time – despite all the trophy wins at Ibrox. But,' he insists, 'football is all about emotions, highs and lows, winning and losing. The game that best sums everything up is against Wales, the World Cup qualifier at Cardiff in 1985.'

Scotland, having lost to Wales at Hampden, had to get at least a point and were without skipper Graeme Souness (suspended), Alan Hansen, Kenny Dalglish and Mo Johnston (all injured). A win would ensure qualification; a draw would guarantee a play-off with Australia, defeat would almost certainly be the end of the road. Cash-strapped Wales sacrificed their 'lucky' ground at Wrexham for the financial security the bigger Cardiff gate would bring, but remained confident – up front they had Rush and Hughes, whereas the Scots had Sharp and Speedie. Cooper was on the bench.

The Scots in the end succeeded but at a terrible cost as Cooper recalls. 'We lost a goal in the first half when Mark Hughes scored. After that it's fair to say that Scotland struggled a wee bit against a very passionate Welsh side. At half-time we had to change 'keepers, Alan Rough coming on for Jim Leighton [who had lost a contact lens]. So when it came to changing things, there were not many options open to Jock Stein.'

Indeed, the Scots, who had never looked like scoring, seemed on their way out at half-time but, urged on by about half the 40,000 crowd, were battling for their lives in the second half. Tragically, they were not the only ones. Stein, who had had a prostate operation in the summer, was still trying to shake off a virus and was now being harassed by a photographer. But still he remained capable of one last piece of tactical wizardry in the 54th minute. 'Basically,' recalls Cooper, 'he briefed me to have a real go down the Welsh right. I didn't feel any pressure knowing that I was the last throw of the dice. In fact, I was looking forward to getting on. There are some matches that you really fancy yourself to do well in and this was one of those occasions.' Cooper replaced Gordon Strachan and within minutes was making an impression. 'To start with they only put one marker on me so I decided to take him on and had a fair bit of success. I remember one run in particular when I went right to the by-line, cut back inside and squared the ball across the goal – but there were no takers.'

But with just nine minutes remaining, it was left to Cooper to take an unexpected offering. 'We were pushing Wales back and having a go at them,' he remembers. 'In those situations sometimes you earn a break more through hard work than skill. I think the penalty award comes into that category. All I recall is Graeme Sharp getting a knockdown which David Speedie hooked on to the arms of Dave Phillips. If you are Welsh, it was a soft award. For us, it was a stonewall penalty. I was in the habit of taking penalties for Rangers, but I hadn't planned on taking this one. I didn't have much option when Roy Aitken – a Celtic player entrusting a Rangers player with the most important spot kick in years – handed me the ball and walked away. By the time I turned around, there were ten Scotland players facing the other way so I sort of got the message. I just placed the ball on the spot and walked back to my mark. I was always planning on hitting it low and left – generally a goalkeeper's weakest spot. I didn't think about missing.

'It was not the best penalty I ever struck,' Cooper admits, 'and Neville Southall got quite a bit of glove on it but only succeeded in pushing the ball inside the post. If I had missed, it would have been a terrible effort but it went in and the rest is history.'

Sadly, Cooper's penalty kick was quickly forgotten. 'As soon as we came off the park, we were told that the Big Man had taken ill,' he says. 'That sort of cooled things a bit.' Stein, increasingly agitated by the photographer midway through the second half, collapsed. Thirty minutes later, the price of Scotland's World Cup survival would be known. 'Then we were told that Big Jock had died,' says Cooper. 'I have never felt as cold or as lonely. Everyone was numbed. What could anyone say? One minute the man was giving me instructions, the next he was away.'

On the way back, myself and one or two of the boys were asked to keep an eye on Jimmy Steel, one of the backroom staff with Scotland who had been with Jock all through the great times at Celtic. Obviously, Steely felt it more than most but there was nothing said and nothing really to say.' Even the previously raucous Tartan Army was reduced to stunned silence as they roamed the Welsh capital scarcely believing what they had heard. Stein, the former miner who had belatedly turned to football at the age of 27 and gone on to become a giant in management, had died before they could even get him to hospital. The sense of loss was profound. As *The Observer*'s Hugh McIlvanney put it in his marvellous tribute, 'the essence of his gifts as a manager was seen to reside in . . . his capacity to make men do for him more than they would have been able to do for themselves.' McIlvanney adds mournfully, ' . . . there were many others in many places who felt last week that they did not have to go down a pit to know what real darkness was'.

The father figure of Scottish football was dead but Scotland's World Cup dream of reaching a fourth successive finals tournament lived on. And Cooper, the man whose accuracy from the set play maintained the Scots' interest, was again to feature when Scotland took the next step on the road to Mexico. 'The draw in Wales earned us a point to take us to a play-off with Australia,' he continued. 'It was always going to be tough. The Australians were never going to play much football, content with packing the defence and not conceding goals. But we were always going to get chances and happily I took one of them. After about an hour, we got a free-kick. Their 'keeper, Terry Greedy, placed his wall but left a gap. I could see the inside of his right hand post. So I just hit it low, hard and with a bit of curl on it and in it went, scraping the paint off the post. Frank McAvennie got another and we were as good as in Mexico.'

So Cooper, more than anyone, had kept that dream alive – which is what Stein would have insisted upon. A true genius of the genre, the winger was at last able to display his talents on the world stage. Perhaps he was still doing it for the Big Man . . .

Wales: Southall; Jones, Van den Hauwe, Ratcliffe, Jackett, James (Lovell), Phillips, Nicholas, Thomas (Blackmore), Rush, Hughes.

Scotland: Leighton (Rough); Gough, Malpas, Aitken, McLeish, Miller, Nicol, Strachan (Cooper), Sharp, Bett, Speedie.

Ray Crawford

COLCHESTER UNITED 3 LEEDS UNITED 2
FA Cup fifth round: Layer Road, 13 February 1971.

Born in Portsmouth on 13 July 1936, Ray Crawford rose from a £2–10–0 office boy with Portsmouth Council to become one of the most prolific scorers of his age. Notching 290 goals in 476 League games with six clubs, he was unlucky to earn just two England caps, scoring against Austria. He led the Ipswich line in tandem with Ted Phillips in Alf Ramsey's Championship-winning side of 1962 and retained his knack in front of goal throughout his career.

Jack Charlton minces words as often as he missed tackles. As self-effacing as he was uncompromising, he is once alleged to have claimed: 'I can't play – but I can stop those buggers that can.' The best centre-half in Britain of his day had indeed 'stopped' such celebrated leaders of the line as Uwe Seeler and Jose Torres, Bobby Smith, Joe Baker and Ian St John. But there was one unsung compatriot whom he had seldom been able to subdue – which was why, during a fourth round FA Cup replay in Essex, Big Jack may have been secretly siding with Rochdale. *Rochdale?* 'Dale were at Colchester United, having surrendered a 3–1 lead at Spotland on the Saturday. The Lancashire side were already rueing what was dubbed 'The Great Escape' by the visitors when the winners of the tie were 'rewarded' with a home draw against the mighty Leeds. Relishing the prospect was the scorer of Colchester's first goal, an ageing centre-forward who had cost a princely £3,000 from Kettering. The fellah, as they said in countless transfer negotiations, had 'been around a bit and always knew where the net was'. Especially when marked by Charlton. 'I can score against Leeds as easily as a farmer knocks off rabbits,' said Ray Crawford, matter-of-factly.

Of the has-beens and never-will be's in the United dressing-room, Crawford was undoubtedly the star. Nicknamed 'Jungle Boy' after doing his national service in Malaya, he had emerged unscathed from two very different fields of conflict. Indeed, the Hampshire man's heart was never in doubt but his mild manners and modesty belied a military precision in front of goal. And now with his sixth club in his 34th year, he had retained sufficient sharpness to remind his colleagues that he had found the target almost 300 times in the League, been the main hitman for Ipswich's title-winning side in 1962, and been capped by his country. So when he spoke, Colchester listened. Crawford's words were music to the ears of manager Dick Graham who was trying to convince himself, let alone his motley squad, that Leeds were beatable – assuming Rochdale were.

In contrast, Don Revie's problem was – with one notable exception – complacency. 'If we lose, we should all be sacked,' was Terry Cooper's reaction to the draw. 'Where's Colchester?' chimed Billy Bremner.

But Graham, himself, did not exactly ooze confidence: 'If we beat them, I'll eat my hat – and climb the castle wall,' he promised.

Once Rochdale had been disposed of in the replay, Graham discovered that his Grandad's Army, as they were affectionately dubbed, had been lifted off such a lofty scrap-heap that they were not about to look up to anyone – not even Leeds. The Yorkshiremen were at their all-threatening-but-not-quite-conquering peak while their opponents languished – as ever – in the lower reaches. Revie's men had been runners-up in both the League and FA Cup the season before, they were insured for over £1

million and boasted ten internationals. Colchester were in
the Fourth Division and the team had cost . . . £15,000.
No matter, Graham, of sergeant-major demeanour,
bellowed: 'We can win this. It's the match of the round
and everybody's going to be there – television, radio, all
the papers . . . We must enjoy every minute of it. It's
going to be something you remember for the rest of your
lives.'

Crawford sensed it, too, and recalls: 'I told myself
before the tie that this would be my last time in the fifth
round – my last chance of glory. The other veterans felt
the same and it was a case of now or never. I knew things
were going well for us when the Cup week began. Everything fell into a pattern, the training was right, spirits high
and confidence soared. We knew we were going to have a
good result.'

Maybe it was the club's epic win over Huddersfield in
1948, maybe because the match was on the 13th but, more
likely, it was because he did not leave anything to chance
that Revie visited Layer Road on one of his renowned,
collar-turned up spying missions. And after seeing the U's
beat Cambridge 2–1, he declared: 'Colchester are a very fit
side and never stop running. I think it's going to be a very
fine match.' He had also seen Crawford score a couple of
goals.

The atmosphere built steadily and neither the inevitable
presence of *Match of the Day* cameras nor a near trebling of
ticket prices could prevent a sell-out in two hours. And
with Graham now convinced that his side would win –
'beyond all shadow of doubt' – the scene was set. Leeds
had prepared in their meticulous manner, flying down the
day before, and it only remained for Colchester to limber
up on the beach, the stands to fill and for Graham to have
'a sudden attack of butterflies' on his way to the ground.
But one look at his players' faces and he calmed down. He
knew they were up to it.

Before a capacity 16,000 crowd, Leeds were mindful of
their manager's warning. 'The pitch is small and my play-

ers could feel hemmed in. The early stages could be vital,' Revie had said, perhaps unwisely. Relying on physique instead of finesse, Leeds committed several crude fouls early on and looked uncomfortable.

Crawford was among the first to spot it. 'I had no idea they would be so vulnerable. After all, Jack is four inches taller than me. I thought I would have a chance if the ball was driven chest high or along the ground, but I was winning high ones as well. My plan had been to release the ball quickly – *before* the tackle came in,' he chuckles. 'We had also been practising free-kicks all week and sure enough it was from one of those that we scored. Jack fouled Dave Simmons and when the free-kick came over, Gary Sprake came out, hesitated and I nodded it in.'

One–nil after 18 minutes. Ecstasy among the U's fans but Leeds did not panic. Not yet. Six minutes later it was beginning. 'Bobby Cram sent Brian Gibbs away down the right,' recalls Crawford, 'and I headed his cross against the back of Paul Reaney. There was a scramble, I was on the ground and just before Sprake could get to it, I somehow hooked it past him.'

The half-time score was the talking point on every ground in Britain and by many it was dismissed as 'the wrong way round'. Until it became 3–0 soon afterwards. 'We thought we could do it if we picked it up again early in the second half,' says the hero of the hour. 'We decided we weren't going to sit and wait for them to come at us.' Ten minutes into that half, as the local paper roared, 'the fantasy was true'. Crawford began the move with a pass to Lewis and his cross was again too good for Sprake whose hesitation allowed Simmons to head home.

'It was unbelievable,' says Crawford. 'A bunch of has-beens 3–0 up against Don Revie's Leeds. And the fans chanting "Easy". But we could – and should – have had more. I had a great chance for a hat-trick but was too knackered to hit it. And then they pulled one back and we thought, "Oh, no . . ."'

Leeds suddenly began spraying the ball about and Revie

finally rumbled Graham's man-for-man tactics. Hunter notched a rare headed goal from a Lorimer corner and Giles made it two with 17 minutes left. Both Crawford and Graham admit they were the longest 17 minutes of their lives. 'They played some super stuff,' says Crawford, 'and came at us from everywhere.'

The crowd could hardly bear it and with six minutes to go, Giles headed narrowly over from a corner. Colchester's Grandads looked spent but still found enough spirit to frustrate the Leeds machine as it rolled inexorably forward. Four minutes from time and Jones had a shot saved. Two minutes left and Hunter went wide. A minute to go. The fans couldn't take it any longer. Neither could the players. With exhausted defenders at last forgetting their drill, Jones only had to head home from 'unmissable' range and the fantasy would be over. But Smith somehow saved it, Jones hung his head and Leeds knew it was not their day. 'It was pure instinct,' said Smith. 'I was too close to think. I just grabbed the ball and hung on.'

The ref blew and Layer Road exploded. The fans raced to Crawford, the players to Graham who confessed: 'It's the greatest day of my life.'

The papers heralded it in suitable fashion: 'Probably the greatest Cup upset of all time,' roared the *Sunday Mirror*. 'The most incredible result in soccer history,' screamed the *Colchester Express*. It all but shoved news off the front page on the day Britain went decimal.

Revie admitted: 'We were well beaten,' while Charlton said: 'We came home with a feeling of shame.'

For Crawford, 'The day stands out even above playing for England and winning the Championship. You've got to remember that only weeks before I had been in the Southern League and before that on the dole.'

Colchester United: Smith; Cram, Hall, Gilchrist, Garvey, Kurila, Lewis, Simmons, Crawford, Gibbs, Mahon.

Leeds United: Sprake; Reaney, Cooper, Bates, Charlton, Hunter, Lorimer, Clarke, Jones, Giles, Madeley.

Kenny Dalglish

LIVERPOOL 2 NEWCASTLE UNITED 0
League: Anfield, 23 August 1977

Born in Dalmarnock, Glasgow, on 4 March 1951, Kenny Dal-glish first came to light with Glasgow Schools, Drumchapel Amateurs and Glasgow United. He played for Scotland at Schoolboy and Youth level, becoming a Celt in August 1967. But, as he once memorably related, life was not easy for an apprentice joiner on the fringes of the European Champions' first team: 'I spent my time shovelling shavings and hitting nails, mostly my own.' His description of himself? 'A wee fat number four.' Pretty soon, however, he started hitting the net and cast his shovel aside for a trophy cabinet. Rapidly developing into a modern great, Dalglish won titles as often as he was capped, with Hampden a second home. Much more than a prolific goalscorer, his vision, close control and ability to turn on an old sixpence were his most noteworthy trademarks. But he was also dispos-sessed as easily as a polar bear is separated from its cubs. Unselfish, yet single-minded, he opened doors for his colleagues and was a constant threat to the most accomplished defenders in Europe.

At the age of 26, a peak for many strikers, he left Celtic for Liverpool – and went on to scale even greater heights. He took his international caps to a record 102 and won the European Cup three times, the English Championship five times, the FA Cup once and the League Cup four times. He also did the double – as player-manager. He scored 168 goals in 481 games. As manager, he won the League three times, the FA Cup once and was 'Manager of the Year' three times before his sudden resignation in

1991. After a spell away from the game, he became boss of Blackburn Rovers whom he took to the Premier League in 1992.

There are times when 20–20 hindsight can be a hindrance; and even the sharp focus provided by a perpetually high profile only serves to blur the vision. Yes, it is difficult to assess the importance of Dalglish's Anfield debut when it is glimpsed through such a dense thicket of subsequent achievement. But suffice to say, though he has won enough honours to demand a personal wing in the British Museum, he opted for his first appearance before the Kop as the most memorable of his life.

It stunned football when Liverpool smashed the transfer record by paying Celtic £440,000 for his services in August 1977. The inspirational, irreplaceable Kevin Keegan had gone and Dalglish was landed with the 'impossible' task of filling his shoes. There was, of course, no doubting Dalglish's pedigree – 47 international caps and umpteen titles with Celtic – but Scottish skills did not always make it over Hadrian's Wall unscathed, the Borders being littered with as many spectacular failures as there had been Gallachers, Jameses and Laws. And Keegan, with the stamina of Red Rum and the persistence of the Red Brigade, was a particularly hard act to follow. Not least because he was idolised by the Kop.

Liverpool boss Bob Paisley knew that he would have to sign 'somebody special' to take over from Keegan. And slapping a huge price tag on that somebody's shoulders was hardly going to lessen the expectations – or, should it be, demands – of the Anfield faithful. As Tommy Smith wrote in his column in the Liverpool *Football Echo*, 'You can't take a world-class player out of your side and not suffer for it.' He added thoughtfully: 'It is essential that Liverpool win something this year to take the pressure off Dalglish, and off Liverpool for selling Keegan.' Smith, as ever, had his finger on the pulse but, like Paisley, pointed to the newcomer's virtues: 'There's no question about his ability . . . and he has proved he can score goals in Europe because, like Liverpool, Celtic are in Europe every year.'

The manager was even more confident. 'I never had any doubts that Kenny would make up for Kevin's departure as he was already a well-established Scottish international,' said Paisley.

Dalglish had actually been to Anfield as a schoolboy trialist but went home determined to launch his career in Glasgow. Now, on his return a decade later, he would need the same single-minded approach and much, much more. There was even a suggestion that he might lack a bit of pace! Tommy Docherty, who gave him his first Scottish cap, provided the answer to that one: 'Aye, but he's ten yards faster upstairs.' And anyone who saw Dalglish shield a ball, turn, send the defender sprawling like a jack-knifed rig which had shed its load, and blast a fierce shot from an acute angle was made instantly aware that here was somebody *very* special. Not simply for his sublime skills on and off the ball but for his character which oozed through his every game. Whether it was a grin or a grimace, Dalglish wore the look of a man who was not interested in coming second – even on the training ground. Immediately people sensed that he was a fellah who could cope with the daunting burden being placed on his broad shoulders, and the fans began to sense it, too, even before they had had a proper look at him. He had scored on his League debut – in a 1–1 draw at Middlesbrough – and had impressed at Wembley in the Charity Shield game a week earlier. So there was a feeling that that Tuesday night in August was going to be one of those special Anfield occasions – even though it was the first of the season.

'Nothing since has ever come up to that night for me,' says Dalglish. 'My home debut for Liverpool . . . there's nothing like the first time you play there. I was under pressure but I'll never forget the reception I had from the fans. It was the start of a long relationship I had with them.'

There had been a chance that not all of that night's attention would be focused on the new acquisition but when Bell's Whisky postponed the award of the Manager of the Year trophy to Paisley, all eyes were inevitably trained on the Scot. The portents were good: he had not only looked the business against Boro', he had also fitted into the Liverpool style. So there were over 48,000 packed into the ground for the visit of injury-hit Newcastle, who seemed to accept that their role was merely subordinate. Anfield was always prepared to welcome another great to the fold and the name of the latest candidate was on everyone's lips. For those Scousers who were unsure of the exact pronunciation, the Kop was already offering elocution lessons: 'Dalgleesh,' they roared. It was the welcome Kenny had wanted.

Against a side defending in numbers and with the pre-season rust not entirely removed, Liverpool took until the second half to get into their stride. But the new boy had made some promising touches, his class was obvious and, most important of all at Anfield, he looked to be a team player. The veteran Ian Callaghan probably stole the honours from Emlyn Hughes in the first half but the second period belonged to only one man. It was just 75 seconds old when Callaghan began the move that will long be remembered with affection by the Kop. He passed to Kennedy whose lofted ball was picked up by Dalglish. Beating his marker Bird for pace, the Scot allowed 'keeper Hardwick to come out before he lifted the ball over him and into the net. Neatly. Precisely. And in front of the Kop. Dalglish raised both arms to salute his new admirers. They reciprocated. Deafeningly. Their new king had arrived.

The fuse finally lit, Liverpool exploded into action, ripping apart their outclassed opponents. Dalglish almost had another but, aiming for the far corner, placed his shot inches wide. McDermott, Kennedy, Hughes and Neal all went close after swift, searing moves that had the Magpies' defence reeling. At the other end, Clemence had to be alert to save from Cassidy and Hughes blocked a close-range shot from Burns, but Liverpool always looked the more likely scorers. And with Dalglish already unveiling his stylish repertoire, a second seemed inevitable. It came after Dalglish found Heighway with a telling cross-field ball. The winger slipped it inside to McDermott who coolly picked his spot. There were just three minutes remaining but Anfield would have another decade in which to savour the reign of its new king. Pretty soon the banners were claiming: 'Kenny's from Heaven'. Among the countless honours he would come to receive were the MBE and the Freedom of Glasgow in 1985. He had been given the freedom of the Kop much, much earlier.

Liverpool: Clemence; Neal, Smith, Hughes, Jones, Case, Callaghan, McDermott, R. Kennedy, Heighway, Dalglish.

Newcastle United: Hardwick; Nattrass, Bird, McCaffery, A. Kennedy, Barrowclough, Cassidy, Craig, Blackhall (Oates), Burns, Gowling.

Roy Dwight

**NOTTINGHAM FOREST 2
LUTON TOWN 1**
FA Cup final: Wembley, 2 May 1959.

*Born in Belvedere on 9 January 1933, Roy Dwight played for
Kent and London Schools before joining the Fulham groundstaff
as a boy. A powerful and direct winger, he earned representative
honours with England Youth and joined Forest for £15,000 in
1958. His goal-scoring ability made him a formidable attacker
who was on the fringe of England selection at his peak. He was
the hero of the Nottingham side that lifted the Cup, achieving
immortality by scoring and breaking his leg in the '59 final. He
recovered full fitness but was allowed to leave by new boss Andy
Beattie and wound down his career at Coventry and Millwall
where he eventually became a coach.*

The sternest 'defender' that Roy Dwight came up against
on that memorable May afternoon was a staff nurse at
Wembley General Hospital. He remembers her standing
on the steps, straight of back and resolute, as he was lifted
from the ambulance. 'You are not going anywhere until
you've been X-rayed, Mr Dwight,' she said firmly. 'Oh,
yes I am,' insisted the Forest winger. 'I am going straight
to a TV set and I'm not moving till it's over.' The game
was already over for Dwight but his hard-pressed team-
mates still had more than half an hour to hold out. In the
days before substitutes, their tired limbs needed all the
help they could get on a hot afternoon – and Dwight was

not going to desert them. Well, not a second time, anyway.

The scorer of the opening goal in the 1959 Cup Final was wheeled around the nurse as if she had been a statuesque Luton full-back and his right leg had still been in one piece. Dwight and the ten men of Nottingham were in defiant mood, and the nurse finally relented. Forest's survivors were still cursing their colleague for not coming out for the second half when he found himself in a ward, surrounded by patients whose sympathies lay with Luton. Undaunted, he persuaded the ambulanceman to park him in front of the set and inquired politely of his fellow patients: 'Do you mind if I have a look?' He goes on: 'I remember the bloke next to me, a Luton fan, turning round and saying, "Cor, stone me." You see, I still had my red Forest shirt on.'

But no sooner had the Luton supporters recovered from the shock of seeing the opposition hero in their midst than it was Dwight's turn to suffer. 'Pacey pulled a goal back and I suddenly felt the pain in my leg. It had been numb until then. But the Luton fans, who couldn't have been nicer, helped me put it on a board and rest it until the final whistle.' When asked if he had feared the worst at that point, Dwight admits: 'I did – for a minute. But then I thought of what we'd been through to get to Wembley. And knew we'd had worse moments than that. Far worse. And survived.'

One of them was the freezing January afternoon when the Reds trailed Tooting and Mitcham 2–0 at half time. Tooting and Mitcham? The tiny Isthmian League amateurs led the First Division side on merit to stand on the verge of one of the great Cup upsets. Dwight remembers it well: 'The match should never have been played as the pitch, which had been ploughed up to help drain it, froze solid with ruts four inches deep. But somehow we got out of a real hole – thanks to a very fortunate penalty – it hit the bloke's shoulder! – and an own goal.' After winning 'fair and square at our place', Forest comfortably accounted for Grimsby in the fourth round but then met old Midland rivals Birmingham at St Andrews. A crowd of 55,300 saw City go in front and it looked curtains for the Reds until Tommy Wilson levelled – in the last minute. The replay was another tense affair with Dwight, himself, equalising – in extra time. And so to neutral Leicester where the right-winger rifled in a glorious hat-trick in a 5–0 romp. 'We played 'em stupid that day and people began to take us seriously,' he says. Lofthouse's Bolton were dealt with next before Aston Villa were edged 1–0 in a nail-biting semi at Hillsborough. 'That win meant so much to me,' says Dwight, 'as only the previous season I'd been in the Fulham side that had lost at the same stage to Manchester United. Losing a semi-final is the worst experience of the lot.' But now, sitting helplessly in a hospital ward with his right leg fractured, he began to question that. Losing now would be far worse, he realised. He looked anxiously at the clock. There were still 20 minutes of the match remaining.

Luton's anticipated second-half onslaught did not materialise and Forest stood firm. As the minutes ticked away, Dwight wondered if the club's name might just have been on the old trophy. As he and his unsung colleagues were making their tortuous way to Wembley, he was well aware that the glamour sides were knocking each other out. And it had left only modest Luton standing in the way of Nottingham's first Cup victory since 1898. Forest were made favourites but it was a final in which the London press were at their most disparaging. 'We were made to feel like nonentities,' remembers skipper Jack Burkitt. 'But we knew we could play and we were determined to put on a show.'

Forest may have lacked the household names of Manchester United, Wolves and Newcastle but not even Fleet Street could deny that they could turn it on with the best of them. But for 67 agonising minutes, it was not their quality that was being examined but their character. As Luton skipper Syd Owen acknowledged, 'Forest began like greyhounds.' Playing superlative attacking football, they swept forward in relentless red waves. One observer wrote: 'Forest flitted like fireflies in their scarlet shirts.' After the ruts of Tooting, Wembley's lush lawn must have felt like Axminster carpet and they stroked the ball about with suitable aplomb. Dwight recalls: 'We didn't have too many tactics. It was just a case of passing to a red shirt whenever you could and that way we had become recognised as one of the best footballing sides in the country.'

They underlined their status with one of the most superlative openings to a final Wembley had seen. Disdainful of the fumbling attempts to halt them, Forest went 2–0 up in a quarter of an hour. Dwight takes up the story. 'If we had a rule, it was to get out of Stuart Imlach's way once he was in full flow. After ten minutes, Stuart was away, taking a pass from Burkitt and flying down the wing. I came inside and I vividly remember the cross coming right past Syd Owen and on to me. It was probably the best left-foot shot I ever hit.'

If that was a classic strike for its simplicity, there was more to come, Billy Gray wandering out to the left flank and Wilson meeting his long centre with a Lawtonesque flourish. 2–0 after a quarter of an hour. Finals were not meant to be like this but while there may have been a lack of glamour, there was no shortage of class and Forest threatened a hatful. Owen somehow managed to keep them at bay for another 18 minutes but it seemed only a matter of time before they would add to their tally. Then the Wembley hoodoo struck.

Dwight recalls: 'Jeff Whitefoot hit one of his typical passes into a gaping hole in the Luton defence. The only defender in sight was Brendan McNally but I reached it first. He arrived a split second later and as I tried to nudge the ball forward, he caught my right shin. It was a pure accident and at first I didn't feel any pain. I didn't think it was serious and neither did referee Jack Clough, who just wanted to get on with the game. Our trainer, Tommy Graham, ran on and treated my leg as if it was a piece of washing waiting for the mangle. He wriggled it back and forth, said "OK?" and ran off. I got to my feet but as soon as I put my weight on it, I felt it go. I didn't tell the lads and at half-time Billy Walker still kept it from them as they were going to have to play the whole second half with ten men. He wanted them to think I was coming back at any moment and just told them I had trapped a nerve. He even waited for them to get back on the field before letting the ambulance take me away. By the time the lads realised they were on their own, I was watching them on TV.'

As Luton mounted a last desperate assault, tightening muscles and taut nerves took their toll on Forest's defenders and Brown was only inches wide with a header from Bingham's cross. But it proved the last throw and Burkitt held the Cup aloft to tumultuous applause. For Dwight it meant his X-ray was due but his weekend was far from over. 'Billy Walker and the lads brought my medal and the boss said he'd arranged a car to take me to St Pancras for the journey back to Nottingham. I wasn't going to miss that for the world but when the car didn't come, I offered the driver of a limousine £20 to get me to the station on time. That was a lot in those days and he drove through red lights, up pavements and straight on to the platform, but we made it. I have never been so glad to part with £20 as the reception in Nottingham was unbelievable.' Indeed, the city has seen nothing like it before or since. There were 70,000 people in the Market Square alone and over 300,000 lining the streets. They were welcoming 11 heroes but Dwight, in a wheelchair, was the name on everyone's lips.

Nottingham Forest: Thomson; Whare, McDonald, Whitefoot, McKinlay, Burkitt, Dwight, Quigley, Wilson, Gray, Imlach.

Luton Town: Baynham; McNally, Hawkes, Groves,

Owen, Pacey, Bingham, Brown, Morton, Cummins, Gregory.

Mike England

BRAZIL 3 WALES 1
Friendly International: Sao Paulo, 16 May 1962.

Born in Holywell, Flintshire, on 2 December 1941, Mike England first impressed with Flint Schoolboys and joined Blackburn Rovers in 1959. He made his League debut against Preston at just 17 and earned his first cap against Northern Ireland in 1962, gaining selection for Wales's summer tour of South America – although still not a regular in the Rovers side. At 6′2″ and 12st 11lb, he was good in the air and ferocious in the tackle, but also a threat in the opposing penalty area – especially from set pieces. He became a commanding figure in the Blackburn defence but grew frustrated when Rovers refused to allow him to join a bigger club. He threatened to quit the game before Rovers finally relented, selling him to Spurs for £95,000 in 1966 – a record for a defender. A worthy successor to Maurice Norman, he made 300 League appearances for the Londoners, winning the FA Cup in 1967, the League Cup in 1971 and 1973, and the UEFA Cup in 1972. He left White Hart Lane in 1974 and played for Seattle Sounders and Cardiff City, whom he helped to promotion from Division Three in 1975–76. He made 44 appearances for his country before becoming Wales manager in 1980, a role he carried out well with limited resources until he was sacked in 1988. He was awarded an MBE for his services to Welsh soccer.

'You've been nowhere and seen nothing until you have been to Maracana,' wrote Geoffrey Green in his autobiography, *Pardon Me for Living*. Mike England agrees. As a wide-eyed youth of 20 and still unsure of his place at

Blackburn Rovers, England experienced 'the mind-boggling thrill' of coming in to land at Rio, seeing the city below nestling among the hills, the great bay and Green's beloved Maracana Stadium – as the writer put it, 'a circular colossus pinned like some giant flying saucer come to rest on earth'.

England recalls: 'That was pretty good for starters. But even better was the reception that greeted the Brazilian team, in particular Pele, whom they worshipped like a god. There was a tremendous roar and then rockets and firecrackers – I'd never seen anything like it in my life. There were 154,000 there. I'd only played one international – against Northern Ireland – and remember that, in some ways, it was a relief not to be in the team for this one. But the lads did well to hold them to 3–1, with Pele scoring a blinder. And then I was told I was in for the next match – four days later in Sao Paulo. My job? Marking Pele.

'It could have been worse,' insisted the big lad from Blackburn. 'At least I had John Charles playing alongside and Terry Hennessey, who, like me, was just making his way in international football. So I had one great and one fellow-beginner for company. Not bad, really. It was just the bloke I was supposed to be marking . . .'

England was right: it could have been worse. But not much. For all their gallantry, Wales had been outplayed in the first match and now Len Allchurch had an ankle injury and Vic Crowe was unwell. The party had included only two wingers so Phil Woosnam switched to the right wing to partner Roy Vernon. Woosnam had played on the wing before, he said – 'for my village team'. But throughout the tour there was the massively reassuring figure of John Charles towering over everyone. The Gentle Giant was the only man in the Welsh side who would have walked into a composite team, a man whom the Brazilians respected and rated perhaps the best centre-half in the world. Yes, it could have been worse – Charles might have missed the plane.

Surprisingly released by Juventus at the last minute, Charles caught his flight with only minutes to spare but came up against a Brazil which manager Jimmy Murphy rated 'better than the team which won the World Cup in '58'. Charles agreed. 'They seem to have improved on the side that played us in Sweden,' he said. And they still had Gilmar in goal, both Santos brothers, Garrincha on the wing, Vava and Didi, whom many now felt was no longer a 90-minute player. And they had Pele. Harder and more mature than the coltish 17-year-old who exploded on to the scene four years earlier, Pele was beginning his long reign as the undisputed king of the game.

'Stick to him like glue,' Murphy told England. He said: 'Follow him everywhere – if he goes to the toilet, follow him there, too.'

With Charles his usual magnificent self, Murphy had been proud of the Welsh performance in the first game. 'I was very pleased with the lads,' he said. 'We played well as a team but hope to do better in the second game.'

Cliff Jones, on the left wing, also came in for generous praise, especially from the hosts. 'He's one of the best wingers in the world,' they claimed. But the undisputed Number One was still the 'Little Bird' Garrincha whose early goal had set the home side on their way. It was hardly comforting for Wales when they saw Garrincha and Vava among the substitutes for the Sao Paulo match. They would have recalled that Garrincha had a knock and left the field in Rio. With Pele also off and the subs used up, Brazil were down to nine men. But still Wales could hardly get a kick.

The second game began more promisingly for the visitors, who kept a tight rein on their opponents – and a clean sheet – until the 35th minute. 'We were doing very well,' says England. 'I followed Pele everywhere, as instructed, and with Terry Hennessey doing a good job on the other side of John Charles, we were holding 'em. Charles was just Charles, totally commanding.' But, in spite of this spirited display, Wales couldn't stop Vava, who came on for Coutinho, from opening the scoring. Didi had earlier rattled the woodwork and Wales also had chances, but hesitation cost Ivor Allchurch and Woosnam dear either side of half-time. 'Still, to go in just one-nil down was not bad,' says England.

Indeed, with a population less than that of Sao Paulo's, Wales were doing wonderfully well to live with the world champions, but it may have looked as if they had had enough when they did not reappear for the second half! Brazil took the field and had to wait for their opponents who were eventually called out by a linesman. 'We were waiting for the usual bell,' explained Welsh Secretary, Herbert Powell. 'But it did not ring. We meant no discourtesy.'

The delay was soon forgotten as both sides missed chances, even Vava blazing over in the 50th minute. Seven minutes later Wales suffered a blow when 'keeper Jack Kelsey was injured in a collision and had to be replaced by Newcastle's Dave Hollins. But midway through the second half, with England 'growing in confidence with every minute that passed' and the crowd becoming restive, Wales were not only avoiding a thrashing, they were back in the match. Allchurch sent Woosnam away down the left and the makeshift winger's cross was perfect – substitute Ken Leek throwing himself full-length to head it home. It was a goal worthy of the champions and the crowd began barracking their men as a draw looked likely.

Brazil responded with an all-out assault on Wales but the thin red line held. England takes up the story: 'It was looking good. There were only ten minutes to go and we were still holding them. Then I did an unforgivable thing – I got complacent. I told myself: "You've done a great job here," and as soon as I'd said it, I lost concentration – and Pele scored. In fact, he got two in the last ten minutes and we lost 3–1! One, I'll never forget – the ball was driven hard towards his chest and I was right up his backside. I thought, "He can't go anywhere," but he let it hit his chest, dipped a shoulder, swivelled and hit it – in one movement. And it was in the net. Sheer genius. He is without doubt the greatest player I've ever seen. He got another to wrap it up but we hadn't done badly and nearly got a second at the end.'

Murphy said: 'I think we did very well and played much better than we did in Rio.'

For England: 'It was a privilege to play against Pele and he taught me a valuable lesson.' In an illustrious career for club and country, England says: 'This match stands out above all the rest.' Indeed, in terms of going somewhere and doing something, marking Pele in Brazil takes some beating. For after that it was back to Ewood Park . . . and Blackburn Reserves.

Brazil: Gilmar; Djalma Santos, Jurandir, Nilton Santos, Mauro, Zequinha, Jair, Didi, Coutinho, Pele, Zagalo. Subs: Vava, Garrincha.

Wales: Kelsey; S. Williams, Hopkins, England, Charles, Hennessey, Woosnam, Vernon, Moore, I. Allchurch, Jones. Subs: Hollins, Leek.

Trevor Francis

Born in Plymouth on 19 April 1954, Trevor Francis first 'starred' as a seven-year-old winger with Pennycross Junior School and then Plymouth Schools. He was just 16 when he burst on to the back pages with 12 goals in his first eight games for Birmingham City. He also played for England Youth and was immediately labelled a wonder boy.

Francis had electrifying pace, a sure first touch and a knack for goals which soon earned him the idolatry of the St Andrews faithful. A quiet, intelligent sort, Francis was able to absorb the lessons of playing alongside experienced quality strikers such as Bob Hatton and Bob Latchford and seemed destined for greatness. After five Under-23 caps, he made his full England debut in 1977 and the only question mark about him was his possible fragility – but that did not stop Brian Clough making him Britain's first £1 million player when he took him to Forest in 1979. Not renowned for his heading ability, Francis repaid his gaffer by nodding the winner in the European Cup Final in 1979 and his all-round brilliance went a long way to helping Forest retain the trophy the following year. Francis missed the final through injury – the start of a miserable sequence of absences that was to plague his career.

Forest recouped their million from Manchester City in 1981 but 18 months later he was sold to Sampdoria. He went on to Atalanta before Graeme Souness took him to Ibrox in 1987. Later he became player-manager at QPR and then Sheffield Wednesday. Francis won 52 caps for England but may have doubled that number had it not been for injuries.

When Trevor Francis made his England debut against Johan Cruyff's Holland, manager Don Revie did not put a man on the Dutch master; the *Daily Mail*, however, put a couple of men on Francis. A photographer snapped the prodigy, wife Helen and parents Phyl and Roy with a special 'Wembley' cake to mark the occasion, and a reporter sat with Mum and Dad to record their observations on their son's eagerly awaited first game for his country. An England shirt meant a lot to the Francises which is why Trevor, after a distinguished career in England and Italy as a million-pound striker, a half-century of caps and a European Cup triumph, chose a humiliating 2–0 defeat as the game of his life.

For the 90,000 faithful who filed up Wembley Way that night, two players provided the main talking points: the untried Francis and the maestro Cruyff. Since Holland's marvellous performances in the 1974 World Cup, the Dutchmen had spread their talents among foreign clubs and the kind of vibrant football that entranced the world in West Germany three years earlier had since proved elusive. In the 1976 European Championship semi-final they were a disgrace, losing 3–1 to Czechoslovakia and two men to referee Clive Thomas. Cruyff was booked for his patter and the question remained whether his genius could reunite his capricious countrymen. For Francis, the task in this friendly international was more straightforward but even more difficult: at 22, he was expected to use all of his precocious talent to give a lift to a lumbering England, still in the international wilderness. Winning the match? That was never really on, and so it proved.

Revie, who had not seen the Dutch since 1974, declared: 'If we start worrying about Cruyff, Neeskens, Rensenbrink and the rest we will forget what we are out there for.' But without key defenders Roy McFarland and Emlyn Hughes, England were always going to be up against it and, on Wembley's stage, it was a near certainty that the Dutch would rediscover at least some of their former mastery. With Cruyff orchestrating their every move, Holland simply outclassed a hapless England, who were reduced to chasing shadows in their own half. Up front, the talented but disparate trio of Francis, Keegan and Bowles hardly had a kick as the midfield was out-fought, out-paced and over-run. Playing what their care-taker manager, Jan Zwartkruis, called 'circulation football' against England's 'kick and rush', Holland assumed a haughty control from the kick-off, the swagger very much back in their suave, one-touch approach. Revie's patched up defence somehow held out until the 30th minute when Cruyff, from his favoured left-side, sent Neeskens through a statuesque defence. The midfielder found Peters who easily beat Clemence. Eight minutes later, and after Brian Greenhoff had gone off with a damaged elbow, the Dutch scythed through once more, Peters again being the executioner after turning Beattie inside-out.

Characteristically, the visitors did not choose to rub it in, strolling through a second half but giving England only a fleeting glimpse of their own goal. The best chance fell to Francis whose shot was blocked by Schrivers's feet but no one was deluded into thinking that the Dutch wouldn't have found another gear if they had had to. Not even Revie. 'They taught us a lesson,' he was honest enough to admit. 'We've got to go out into the world and find out what it's all about. They were absolutely magnificent. They have such wonderful control and feel for the ball. We never got to grips with it in the first half but battled away in the second. Our players are very despondent and bat-tling is not enough. You have got to have craft, guile and control.'

Zwartkruis added: 'Cruyff was brilliant tonight. He was like the Scarlet Pimpernel. You saw him here, you saw him there, you saw him everywhere.' According to the match statistics, Cruyff had a remarkable 61 touches of the ball and, of his 50 passes, 30 were forward. In contrast, Francis enjoyed just 21 touches yet still managed to pro-vide about the only crumb of comfort for England.

It was not a great debut and his most memorable contributions were being the victim of a foul by Rijsbergen that brought a yellow card and having England's best effort blocked by the 'keeper. For much of the time he looked a forlorn figure up front as England chased the orange shadows in their own half. But when he did get the ball, his touch was confident and his acceleration suggested he could become a threat at the highest level.

Even his Mum and Dad admitted that Holland were a 'different class' but they joined the Birmingham contingent who cheered him off at the end. Biased? Indeed, but the rest of the crowd were indulging in that familiar refrain, 'What a load of rubbish!' Not since Hungary destroyed the myth of invincibility in 1953 had England looked so demoralised but Francis could at least hold his head high. The night had belonged to a Dutch master but in the youngster with the West Country burr, the home side possessed a genuine class act for the future. And so it proved: injuries prevented Trevor Francis from fully realising his 'wonder boy' potential but he possessed enough craft, guile and control to help lift his country back to international respectability and his next club to undreamed-of glory.

England: Clemence; Clement, Doyle, Watson, Beattie, B. Greenhoff (Todd), Madeley (Pearson), Brooking, Francis, Bowles, Keegan.

Holland: Schrivers; Suurbier, Rijsbergen, Krol, Hovenkamp, Van Der Kerkhof, Peters, Neeskens, Rep (Kist), Cruyff, Rensenbrink.

Paul Gascoigne

ARSENAL 1 TOTTENHAM HOTSPUR 3
FA Cup semi-final: Wembley, 16 April 1991.

Born in Gateshead on 27 May 1967, Paul Gascoigne was kicking a ball as soon as he could stand. He even annoyed his parents by juggling it under the dinner table at meal times. At six he wanted to play for England and at eight he was bamboozling kids two years his senior at Redheugh Boys Club. At ten he won his first trophy and at 14 joined Newcastle as an apprentice where he cleaned the boots of Kevin Keegan. Opinions differed: Ipswich's Bobby Robson was among a clutch of managers who turned him down while youth development officer Peter Kirkley noted, 'He was small and chubby and a bit of a plodder – but he had exceptional skill.' Heathfield High School's Geoff Wilson said: 'He had a round face, round body and round legs but I've never seen such skill in a player.'

No sooner had he unveiled his dazzling repertoire to the Newcastle faithful than his departure in the footsteps of Waddle and Beardsley seemed inevitable. Spurs broke the British record by paying £2 million for him in 1988 and two months later he made his England debut as a sub against Denmark at Wembley. With his precocious talent and practical jokes, he was always destined to become a target for the tabloids but never has a player received quite the treatment Gazza has endured since leaving his native north-east. He came of age in the 1990 World Cup in Italy, where he helped England to the semi-finals before his tears captured the hearts of millions. Gazza had surprised many with his vision, virtuosity and defensive covering to emerge as a far more complete and mature player than the headline writers suggested.

Even Robson had said he was 'as daft as a brush', but now he seemed set to sweep all before him.

It was George Best who said: 'He is accused of being arrogant, unable to cope with the press, and a boozer. Sounds like he's got a chance to me.' And it is with Best whom Gascoigne has most frequently been compared – even though the similarities are more obvious off the field than on it. Where Best was a wraith-like winger of bewitching genius, Gascoigne is a stocky midfielder still to break out from the foothills of greatness, let alone approach Best's heights or longevity. As personalities, both have epitomised the lovably wayward working-class hero, struggling to adjust to the gaze of the spotlight. And even though Best pulled more birds than Gazza has pints, both have met distractions with a mix of quietly chaperoned success and spectacular, splash-headline failure. So far Gazza has yet to achieve either Best's eminence on the field or his notoriety off it but perhaps his greatest accomplishment is that his talent has illuminated an otherwise bleak landscape. His genius flourished when all those about him were being strangled at birth; he has also had to overcome serious injuries and the culture shocks of shifting from Newcastle to London to Rome. His best – subject to fitness – is surely still to come.

If Italia 90 was where he surprised many good judges by the sheer breadth of his game, it was in the 1991 FA Cup semi-final against Arsenal that his genius was most memorably glimpsed. Just a month after a much-publicised groin operation and one tie before his notorious '15 minutes' in the final against Forest, Gazza earned his club a famous victory over their deadly north London rivals in an exuberant and breathtaking hour. In fact, he demoralised the Gunners in just 11 minutes. The first semi-final to be held beneath the twin towers had all the hallmarks of an epic. Arsenal v Spurs would be a full-blooded affair if held on Hackney Marshes but there had never been as much to play for – and that's not forgetting the famous clash in 1971 when Arsenal secured the first half of their double triumph. The Gunners were homing in on a repeat performance but Spurs had even more at stake – they were fighting for their very existence!

Following their financial misadventures, the erstwhile stockmarket high-flyers were resigned to selling their two biggest playing assets, Gascoigne and Lineker. Not only would their departure keep the liquidator from the White Hart Lane door, but the inestimable bonus of a Cup final appearance and a possible place in Europe could pacify the creditors. The match hardly needed Gascoigne! Barely 50 per cent fit but 200 per cent motivated, the game's most talked about player was back after his op. Even more than usual, he was the joker in the pack.

Unable to sleep before the match, Gazza channelled his hyperactive energy into a blistering assault on Arsenal, scoring one and making another in the first 11 minutes. Inevitably he tired and was substituted and, just as inevitably, Arsenal threatened a comeback, but Gascoigne had put the game beyond them in that unforgettable opening. The Londoners went for each other's jugular from the kick-off and when Limpar was fouled by Samways in the first minute, and then kicked on the ground by Van den Hauwe, the seething Swede seemed hellbent on revenge. By the fifth minute, Paul Stewart had become his victim but the offence occurred so far out that Arsenal, normally so well drilled in these matters, barely mustered a protective wall in front of Seaman. Even so, only Gascoigne would have had the cheek to think of beating the England 'keeper from 35 yards. But up he ran, to a roar from the Spurs faithful, and drove an absolute pearler into the top corner. Seaman got his fingertips to it but it brought the house down and, very nearly, the stanchion.

There was no stopping Gazza now and, with the hapless Michael Thomas, who had drawn the short straw of marking him, reduced to chasing his shadow, Spurs added a second. Buzzing like he has never buzzed before, Gazza produced another piece of magic – a double one–two with first-time flicks – to send Allen away and, from the result-ant cross, there was Lineker to do the rest.

'We lost it then,' admitted Arsenal boss, George Graham, who was shaking his head in disgust at his men's initial ineptitude. But the players disagreed, battling back with some spirit once they'd recovered from that opening blitz. Cautions were given to Samways, Stewart and Dixon, while Gascoigne and Thomas became embroiled. But the Gunners, desperate to preserve their double dream, knew they had to reduce the deficit before the break and kept going as Spurs relaxed. Smith lashed wildly over from Winterburn's cross but made amends on the stroke of half-time, nodding in Dixon's corner to give his side a lifeline. Graham's pep talk was hardly needed and Spurs seemed to buckle under the sustained bombard-ment. But the chances went begging and the impetus was lost. Gazza, who was now showing visible signs of his lay-off, was called off – to receive a standing ovation.

His replacement, Nayim, gave Spurs a new dimension and Arsenal tried to do likewise with Groves coming on for Limpar. With Gascoigne an anxious and animated spectator on the bench, it looked as if his day could yet be spoiled as Arsenal pressed but Spurs still had a man on the field who knew how to kill a game stone dead with one lethal strike. Leaving the lumbering Adams in his wake and using Samways as a decoy, Lineker ended the agony of the Tottenham fans by rifling past Seaman, who might have done better, in the 79th minute. Gazza leapt for joy, knowing that, unlike the World Cup, his team had made the final and he would be playing. Terry Venables, like the good boss he is, tried to say it was 'a great team effort. To be honest,' he added, 'apart from the free-kick, I don't want to overdo it talking about him. But to get that much power as well as bend and dip was phenomenal.'

He was right and he was wrong – it was a great team effort but only one man could have blasted Arsenal out of it in the first 11 minutes. 'That's why,' said Gazza at the time of writing, 'it has to be this match.' The football world sincerely hopes that there will be many more.

Arsenal: Seaman; Dixon, Winterburn, Thomas, Bould, Adams, Campbell, Davis, Smith, Merson, Limpar (Groves).

Tottenham Hotspur: Thorsvedt; Edinburgh, Van den Hauwe, Sedgeley, Howells, Mabbutt, Stewart, Gascoigne (Nayim), Samways (Walsh), Lineker, Allen.

George Graham

LIVERPOOL 1 ARSENAL 2 (AET)
FA Cup final: Wembley, 8 May 1971

Born in Bargeddie, Lanarkshire, on 30 November 1944, George Graham was capped at every level after learning his craft with Coatbridge Schools. His Scottish schoolboy international performances attracted Aston Villa who signed him as a pro in 1961. He earned Youth and Under-23 honours at Villa Park and was a finalist in the 1963 League Cup. He landed a winners' medal two years later after being sold to Chelsea for a bargain £6,000. Graham, though, eventually became a six-figure player, going to Manchester United for £100,000 in 1972, but his best years were with Arsenal, whom he joined in part-exchange in 1966.

A cultured, multi-purpose forward, the cool-headed Graham brought class and consistency wherever he played. Composed on the ball and good in the air, he was one of the principal cogs in a Gunners' machine known more for its efficiency than its finesse. The Double was thought beyond them but Graham's intelligence and opportunism were crucial in clinching the League and Cup inside a week. He was a member of the side that won the Fairs Cup the previous year but could never match this success at Old Trafford. He wound down his playing career with Portsmouth and Crystal Palace before embarking upon an equally distinguished career in management, first with Millwall and, since 1986, with Arsenal, winning the League in 1988–89 and 1990–1, and the unique double of FA and League (Coca-Cola) Cup in 1992–93.

It was the ideal occasion for 'The Stroller'. Five days after snatching the League title in the most dramatic fashion, the Double was on the line. It was the Cup final, Bill Shankly's Liverpool were the opponents and a place in football history was at stake. Just the sort of game George Graham took in his stride. When it came to keeping your head, there were few players in this otherwise frantic era who came near to the immaculate Scot. He looked as he played: calm, unruffled, slipping neat, measured passes to colleagues in space, making penetrating runs, decisive interventions. In what was sure to be a blood and thunder encounter, it was clear that he would be a key man. While others about him were falling in the trenches, Graham would simply stroll through. Never was that quality more desperately needed than during two tense hours on a May afternoon in 1971.

With only the second League and Cup Double this century – and the fourth in history – at stake, Arsenal were never in danger of submitting to the tiredness of their limbs. But the tension of such a monumental game so soon after the almost unbearable strain of a Monday night at White Hart Lane invited suggestions that even their celebrated composure and strength of character might just buckle under the Wembley sunshine. Facing a side managed by Shankly was sufficient, alone, to make the toughest troops tremble but, as if the likes of Lloyd, Hughes, Smith and Toshack were not formidable enough, the combined weight of doughty opponents and dicing with history would surely prove beyond them.

The daunting millstone was immediately apparent as the two giants locked horns on the lush Wembley turf freshened by recent rain and verdant under a bright sun. It was a perfect setting, the traditional north–south clash given added piquancy by Arsenal's joust with the record books. A nation waited but, as is often the case with such epoch-making events, the afternoon became heavy with anticlimax. Liverpool were perhaps the more culpable as Arsenal did at least have their strength-sapping victory over Spurs to offer as an excuse. As draining on the limbs

as it had been on the emotions, it was understandable that
they should play it canny. But Liverpool, blissfully free of
such burdens, were hardly more enterprising. The upshot
was 70 minutes of unremitting tedium. Even the Kop was
silent.

Storey, that poor man's Nobby Stiles, had betrayed the
Londoners' anxiety as early as the first minute when he
crudely chopped down Heighway, and Rice and McLintock soon followed with assaults on Toshack. When Simpson fouled Evans, the crowd were justified in demanding:
'We want football.' What little there was came in the fleet-
footedness of Heighway, the generalship of McLintock
and the perception of Graham, a quiet thinker on a day
for Philistines. But not even Graham could capitalise on
Radford's defence-splitting pass with just eight minutes of
the first half remaining. There had been other chances to
bring the dreariness to a swifter conclusion but Clemence
saved superbly from Armstrong just before half-time and
Kennedy twice badly miscued soon after the resumption.
Arsenal, doubtless, would not have minded clinching their
elusive Double in such a workaday manner but places in
history, thankfully, are not granted so easily. In the 70th
minute, the experienced Thompson was introduced and
immediately Liverpool found another gear.

Attacking with gusto down both flanks, the Merseysiders pounded the Gunners' goal and Wilson had to be at his
alert best. Kelly had replaced the injured Storey for
Arsenal and, in a rare foray, Graham's header came back
off the bar. But when the whistle sounded for the end of 90
minutes, it was Shankly's team who looked the more
likely winners. Thompson had aroused the Kop from its
slumbers and, in another two minutes, had them in full
voice. Pouncing on the ball in the middle of the park, the
veteran winger moved menacingly forward before releasing Heighway on the left. This flank had been Arsenal's
Achilles heel all afternoon and, as the Liverpool man
advanced, the Gunners' defence gathered in force to cover.
But Heighway's elusive dribble took him past Rice and

almost to the by-line; Wilson came out to shut him off but was surprised by a low drive which went in off a post from the narrowest of angles. Shankly was on his feet, the Kop in rapture and Arsenal looked to have kissed goodbye to a dream. 'I was expecting Heighway to cross it,' explained Wilson.

The great stadium was now deluged with the Mersey sound, the decibels dulling the senses if not Arsenal's despair. But just when Liverpool felt they had grabbed a killer goal, the Londoners again displayed their remarkable resilience. Wilson saved from Hall at point blank range, which inspired an Arsenal surge. Their canary-yellow shirts glistening with desperation, they went upfield in numbers. The Trojan Radford hoisted the ball into the Liverpool area and when neither Hughes nor the indefatigable Smith, Liverpool's skipper, could clear, the ball came off Kelly into the path of Graham. Cool amid the confusion, the Stroller got the touch and Arsenal were level. 'That was the goal that turned the game,' said Shankly. 'It was their first real break. For us it was a silly goal to concede.'

For Graham it was one of the softest of his illustrious career. Yet it was his most valuable. 'It was the most memorable goal I ever scored but I think I was standing on the line,' he chuckles. 'But I thought Eddie Kelly did very well to win the ball.'

Wembley was at full volume now, alive with a clamorous anticipation. The roars cascaded from the terraces as the rival legions sought to outdo the other with their passionate exhortations. The contest that the crowd and the country had been waiting for had finally materialised and it was still evens on who would triumph. With McLintock marshalling his men, Kelly probing and Graham orchestrating, Arsenal had the greater impetus, theirs being the greater prize. But Liverpool, too, had chances, the best being a Toshack header which was blocked on the line. Just as a replay looked the most likely bet, the hitherto anonymous Charlie George emerged the hero.

113

The creator was once again Radford who found the gifted 20-year-old in space outside the penalty area. With London voices rising, George controlled it and went past Smith with the ease of a master. Then he hit it. Sweetly. It seemed to gather pace, rising above a despairing Clemence and into the net. Lloyd later claimed it took a deflection but that hardly takes anything away from George's moment of glory. Not even the mighty Liverpool could come back from that – Arsenal had fired both barrels and the Double was theirs.

Graham said: 'I am honoured to be voted Man of the Match' and described it as 'the most memorable of my career'. It had been anything *but* a stroll.

Liverpool: Clemence; Lawler, Lindsay, Smith, Lloyd, Hughes, Callaghan, Evans (Thompson), Heighway, Toshack, Hall.

Arsenal: Wilson; Rice, McNab, Storey (Kelly), McLintock, Simpson, Armstrong, Graham, Radford, Kennedy, George.

Jimmy Greaves

TOTTENHAM HOTSPUR 5 ATLETICO MADRID 1
European Cup Winners' Cup Final: Rotterdam, 15 May 1963.

Born in Poplar, London, on 20 February 1940, Jimmy Greaves appeared innocuous in the air, lacking in physical presence and without an explosive shot, but Greavsie was the greatest goal-poacher of his era. Scoring at every level, from every angle, he was justly acclaimed the 'Fagin' of the penalty area. A chirpy, Cockney sparrow, he once said: 'I was born with a natural gift for sticking the ball into the net, and wasn't interested in doing much else.' With 357 goals in 514 League games, he didn't have to, slipping the ball home with an aplomb that one critic likened to 'closing the door on a Rolls Royce'.

Having made his name at Chelsea, Greavsie could cut a swathe through the tightest catenaccio and was snapped up by AC Milan in 1961. Brought 'home' to Spurs for £99,999 five months later, he added an even deadlier dimension to the fabulous Double-winning side. In Bill Nicholson's immortal words, 'he could pass to the stanchions', but was eventually part-exchanged for Martin Peters and ended his career playing in the midfield wilderness at West Ham. A period of personal crisis followed his retirement before he re-emerged as a household name in the role of television pundit. Complete with chirp.

When you are the greatest finisher your country has ever produced and you are 'dropped' for the biggest game in its history, you are entitled to hesitate over the match of *your* life. But only Greavsie could say: 'I can't think of one', with any conviction. Even when pressed, he would only mutter: 'Honest, I ain't got one.' As The Saint might have put it, 'Now come on, Jim. OK, you missed the 1966 World Cup final but you played in two FA Cup finals and won 57 caps for England, scoring 44 goals. And if none of those grab you, you starred in countless "Glory, Glory" nights for Spurs in Europe having got sackfuls for Chelsea. And you can't pick a match?' 'Oh, all right then,' mumbled Greavsie . . . 'Atletico!'

By his own extraordinary standards, he did not have a blinder in this European Cup Winners' Cup final. Nor were his obligatory brace of goals pulled from the very top drawer. But the significance of the victory is not lost on him: 'It was the first time a British club had won a major European trophy,' he reminds you. And neither the intervening three decades nor his self-deprecatory tone can disguise the pride he still feels. Besides setting the course for the Celtics, the Manchester Uniteds and the Liverpools, the win almost made up for missing out on the European Champions Cup the previous season. In a frenzied semifinal with Benfica, the gods had conspired against Spurs and only stone-hearted Arsenal fans did not feel for the North Londoners after a 4–3 aggregate defeat.

'Benfica was the first tie in which I had been eligible since coming from Italy,' Greaves explains, 'and we did fancy ourselves a bit then.' Indeed they did, but not without good reason. The Tottenham of Blanchflower and Mackay, of Jones, White and Greaves fancied they could rule Europe. Even without Greaves, they had waltzed to the first Double of the century and, with a now irresistible blend of power and panache, felt they could even out-Real Real. Undoubtedly one of the great club sides of all time, the swashbuckling Spurs of the early Sixties was built on a resolute defence, where the brilliant Bill Brown was in goal and that solid, if unsung pair, Peter Baker and Ron Henry, were at full-back. Mighty Maurice Norman was a centre-half colossus who had the fearsome Dave Mackay on one side and master tactician Danny Blanchflower on the other. Seldom have wing-halves dovetailed more splendidly: where Mackay thundered, Blanchflower simply thought . . . and had the class and authority to run any game. If the power was in the half-back line, the glory was up front: dashing wingers in Terry Dyson and Cliff Jones, the 'ghostly' creativity of John White, the blunderbuss of Bobby Smith and, latterly, the rapier of Greaves. In full flow, they were a thrilling and unstoppable sight, and there were many white hot nights at White Hart Lane. 'But it was in Rotterdam,' claimed Nicholson, 'where people told me we played like Real. For me that night made up for losing to Benfica.' But for Greaves? You sense the disappointment still rankles.

'What I remember most about the final was the prematch team talk,' he says. 'We weren't expected to win . . . probably because no British club had ever won a European trophy before and they were the holders. We'd also suffered a big blow when Davie Mackay got injured. Before the kick-off, we were all a bit nervous but we got a damned sight more so when Bill Nicholson began singing the praises of Atletico! He was saying what a super side they were, that the centre-half was a great player, the goalie was unbeatable, the centre-forward was 9'3" and so on until Danny Blanchflower stepped in. The skipper said: "Hang on a minute, boss. Can you imagine their team talk?"'

'Bill asked: "What do you mean Danny?" '

'And the skip went on in that Irish voice of his: "Their boss will be saying what a great side *we* are. There's big Maurice Norman – about 9'6", Cliffie Jones – the fastest winger in the world, John White – one of the great inside-forwards. They must be frightened out of their minds facing us." And he really lifted us. In fact, I think we had it won before we went on to the park.'

Inevitably, however, it was the irrepressible Greaves who sent them on their way. Too modest to relate that he was Blanchflower's trump card as 'the greatest finisher in the game', Greaves was swift to underline his status on the field. In perfect conditions, with Blanchflower in total command and tens of thousands of Tottenham fans roaring out the Spurs anthem, the skipper started the move and White carried it on. Smith sent Jones away down the right and when the cross arrived, Greaves was there with a lovely half-volley just inside the post. When Greaves scored, defences would often feel that their pockets had been picked, as they looked in vain for the culprit, who would be lost among his team-mates' congratulations. And just 15 minutes into this memorable night, it was already 'Halleluja Greavsie!'

But the Spaniards, with the subtlety of Mendoza and speed of Collar posing the greatest threats, were not the Cup holders for nothing and Spurs soon knew they were in a match. Greaves, relishing the big occasion, was having one of his more industrious nights and, ten minutes before the interval, wandered to the right wing from where his deep cross was dummied by Smith. The ball went to Dyson who hammered it against the bar for White to whip home. Now oozing confidence, Spurs turned on the champagne football but, within a minute of the restart, it suddenly went flat. Henry had handled Chuzo's shot and Collar made it 2–1 from the penalty. Perhaps they recalled Nicholson's words, perhaps they recalled Benfica and felt the prize would once again elude them. Or maybe they just missed Mackay? Whatever it was, Spurs, previously swashbuckling, were now buckling.

Twice shots went within a whisker of Brown's posts as Atletico forced four corners in five minutes. But the Tottenham line held, Marchi proving an admirable replacement for Mackay and Norman being at the heart of everything. Up front, too, Spurs did not want for spirit as Jones ran the legs off every defender, Dyson darted hither and thither and Greaves, in Nicholson's words, 'brought his Italian experience to bear – never getting flustered when the tackles were flying'. But, as the ex-Milan star graciously conceded, 'it was really Terry Dyson's night'.

The tiny winger began his rise to giant status midway through the second half. 'We needed something,' admitted Greaves. They got it from Madinabeytia who allowed Dyson's centre to slip under the bar. The 'keeper was never the same again and nor were his colleagues, Spurs restoring their grip with two more goals. Now playing the game of his life, Dyson, a mere 5'3", went into overdrive, centred and Greaves nonchalantly did what he does best.

But the greatest moment was still to come. With the Spaniards now broken, the aristocrats of N17 resumed their swagger. 'Nobody was going to stop us now,' says Greaves. How ironic then that perhaps the least gifted player of all should administer the *coup de grâce*! There were just three minutes remaining when Dyson, taking a pass from White, darted through the Madrid defence to lash home a 25-yarder. Greaves recalls walking off at the end when Bobby Smith 'ruffled little Terry's hair and said: "You should retire now – you'll never play as well as that again."'

As the accolades poured in and the team paraded the Cup around the ground, Greaves suddenly left the joyous throng to thank Mackay, who was on the sidelines – and reduced the Iron Man to tears. 'I just broke down when I knew that my part in this win had been remembered,' said the Scot.

Among the plaudits was a claim from a Spanish newspaper: 'What Spurs did is the start of a new age of football in the British Isles which could have its confirmation in the World Cup of 1966.' The poignancy is not lost on Greaves for whom this 'Glory, Glory Night' in Rotterdam will do very nicely, thank-you. Even if it did need a bit of prompting.

Tottenham Hotspur: Brown; Baker, Henry, Blanchflower, Norman, Marchi, Jones, White, Smith, Greaves, Dyson.

Atletico Madrid: Madinabeytia; Rivilla, Rodriguez,

Ramiro, Griffa, Glaria, Jones, Adelardo, Chuzo, Mendoza, Collar.

Kevin Hector

DERBY COUNTY 3 BENFICA 0
European Cup: Baseball Ground, 25 October 1972.

Born in Leeds on 2 November 1944, Kevin Hector played for South Leeds Schools before joining Bradford where he scored 113 League goals in just 176 appearances. Even in those more prolific times, it was a remarkable record and for a striker of unremarkable build (10st 9lb and 5'9"), but the Yorkshireman had those precious ingredients of pace, balance and a gift for goals. He even notched five in one game as the scouts descended on Park Avenue and it took the football world by surprise when he joined the cash-strapped Rams for £34,500 in September 1966. It was a big fee in those days – especially for Derby – but Tim Ward's massive gamble would not take long to pay off – even if Ward did not last long enough to see it.

From Second Division obscurity, Derby were to dice with the aristocrats of Europe under Brian Clough and Peter Taylor – and Hector, nicknamed 'the King' – was one of their stars. He earned belated and all-too-fleeting international recognition when Alf Ramsey sent him on for the last two minutes of England's heart-breaking World Cup qualifier with Poland in 1973 – and was a kneecap away from becoming a national hero. His predatory skills did not desert him even when the Clough-Taylor era ended but he was sold to Vancouver Whitecaps in 1978, playing the English seasons with Burton Albion and Boston United. He returned in 1980 and scored the goal that kept Derby in the Second Division in his last match. It brought his appearances to a club record 581 and his goals to 201 – a tally surpassed only by the legendary Steve Bloomer.

When you hear that your club's first ever League Championship has been 'clinched' while you are lying on a Majorcan beach, you are entitled to sweet dreams about European football – especially when denied a chance to play in the UEFA Cup through 'administrative irregularities' two seasons earlier. Having completed their programme with a 1–0 win over Liverpool and jetted off to the Med to await the outcome, Derby duly celebrated the subsequent failure of both Liverpool and Leeds to overtake them – and then wondered what they had let themselves in for. 'It was all new to us,' says Kevin Hector, 'and we did not know what to expect. All the big European clubs were there – Real Madrid, Bayern Munich, Celtic, Juventus, Benfica. And we had nobody with any real experience. We had played in Europe on pre-season tours but that was about it.'

Indeed, once the Majorcan holiday was over, that naivety might well have turned to nightmares as the enormity of the task sank in. Even though they were champions, Derby were still building their side, old hands were departing and new boys were arriving. And the one battle-hardened veteran who knew all about floodlit continental campaigns was gone. Dave Mackay was replaced by Colin Todd while Dave Nish also came to bolster the defence. Brian Clough and Peter Taylor were undaunted by Europe and were making sure their players weren't either.

When the draw was made Derby avoided the big guns and found themselves up against the Yugoslavian champion, Zeljeznicar. With just one win in six League games in August, Derby were grateful for unknown, unpronounceable and unthreatening opposition, sailing comfortably (2–0, 2–1) through to the second round. 'It did us a lot of good,' says Hector. 'The first game in a European competition is always a sticky one but this [tie] gave us a lot of confidence.' Derby never really recovered from their inauspicious start in the League but soon realised that the tight confines of the Baseball Ground were a considerable asset in Europe. Nothing if not committed, Derby fans tended to produce more decibels than performances often merited and although small, the double-decker ground could be an intimidating arena. Besides, the place became a mecca as Clough and Taylor were the talk of football. Nothing seemed beyond them and Hector, who had arrived before them, blossomed under their tutelage.

His knack of scoring vital goals had earned him the adulation of the Derby faithful as well as a place on the fringes of the England squad. One look at his poise in the penalty area had convinced Clough that he was a striker capable of piercing the tightest continental defence so when former Derby stalwart Jimmy Hagan brought his star-studded Benfica team to the Midlands for the first leg of the second round, neither Hector nor the Rams batted a collective eyelid. Hector recalls: 'We did nothing different in our preparation and treated it as if it was a normal game.' With an unimpressive run of performances in the First Division that included seven successive defeats away from home, Derby were not too dismayed that the first leg was in familiar surroundings. But when asked if they could lift themselves for the big one, Taylor indignantly inquired: 'How can we fail to rise to the occasion? This will be something special for our players.' Hagan concurred: 'Being 13th in the table could mean they are psychologically keeping something back.' The Saturday before the Portuguese champions arrived, Derby went down to Ipswich but Clough was on a rare spying mission in Portugal. What he saw did not frighten him, he claimed.

Derby welcomed back Archie Gemmill, out for two matches with a groin strain, and John O'Hare, who missed the Ipswich defeat with a bout of tonsillitis, while a slightly greying but barely slowing Eusebio was in the Benfica line-up. The Black Panther admitted to a deeper role but added: 'In Portugal, it is usual for players to retire at around 30 but I still feel a young man. Mr Hagan has helped us to discover strength in ourselves.' The former Derby man explained: 'I have stepped up the training and made 'em fitter and stronger, but I've always tried to preserve the rich skills which have been part of the side's make-up.' So was this a new, hardier breed of Latin opposition? And could Derby, in only their third European Cup-tie, handle one of the great clubs of Europe who were playing their 66th? A packed house could hardly wait to find out.

It did not take long to discover that Taylor was, as usual, spot on with his assessment: this *was* a different Derby and they tore at the Portuguese from the kick-off, O'Hare almost creating a chance for Hector in the opening moments. The pace did not slacken and it was the King's turn to be creator in the eighth minute when he set up the opening goal. Hector found Hinton on the left and the winger's cross was joyously headed home by the marauding McFarland. Taylor had already said: 'Roy is the greatest player I've ever seen,' and this goal did nothing to dent the defender's reputation. Derby were buzzing now and with Hennessey, McFarland, Todd and Daniel in total command at the back, Gemmill scurrying over every square inch of the famous ground and Hector, O'Hare and Hinton threatening at every turn, it took the Portuguese 15 minutes to get a look-in, 25 to fashion anything like a chance. And when they did, Baptista half-hit his shot which was deflected for a corner by Todd.

Two minutes later Hector put Derby two up with a sweetly struck volley that sailed under the angle after the Benfica defence had again been unable to cope with McFarland. It was a gem but the hero would have none of it: 'Alan's corner went over everybody and came to me. I just volleyed it,' he said. The Rams were rampant now and could have had more as Benfica reeled in the face of a sustained onslaught. 'We played out of our skins,' says Hector, 'and they never got a kick.'

Both Hector and O'Hare could have had more goals but Derby weren't complaining when McGovern added a third in the 40th minute. Again Hector was involved, nodding down Daniel's long ball for McGovern to rifle into the top corner. It was breathless, breathtaking stuff which was nigh on impossible to follow, the second half, in Hector's opinion, 'being a bit of an anti-climax. They tightened up and we couldn't quite match our first-half performance.' Eusebio did not have a look-in until late when he shot narrowly wide and hit the side netting before Boulton saved thrillingly from Graca. But no one from Derby went away disappointed and many good judges rated the first-half display as one of the best by a British side in Europe.

Malcolm Allison was among them: 'Derby were simply magic,' he enthused. 'And I can't see them dropping this sort of lead to any side in the world.' Clough said: 'We were absolutely brilliant but if I'd said we would win 3–0 as I honestly thought we would, who would have believed me?' Hagan admitted: 'I was very disappointed with our display in the first half but we are not without hope.' But they were, Derby comfortably holding them in the Stadium of Light. 'We did the job on the night,' says Hector. But it was the demolition job in Derby that is best remembered, and the night an unassuming Yorkshireman showed why he was 'the King'.

Derby County: Boulton; Robson, Daniel, Hennessey, McFarland, Todd, McGovern, Gemmill, O'Hare, Hector, Hinton.

Benfica: Henriques; Da Silva, Humberto, Messias, Adolfo, Graca, Nene, Toni, Baptista (Jordao), Eusebio, Simoes.

Jimmy Hill

FULHAM 4 NEWCASTLE UNITED 5
FA Cup fourth round: Craven Cottage, 28 January
1956.

Every so often in this cynical age we need to remind ourselves of how the game was once played: when the goals
flowed, when wingers were never more than 5'4" tall, had
bandy legs and could cross a ball with the lace away from
the centre-forward; when full-backs were built like brick
out-houses and would kick lumps out of anyone that
moved; when centre-forwards rattled in hat-tricks every
other week and caught the bus home. Those were the days
when grounds were full and the nearest thing to misbehav-
iour was a bit of banter with opposing fans; referees were
always right, the sun always shone, the right team scored
six . . . and there was always Hovis for tea. There was
also no *Match of the Day*, no umpteen camera angles and no
in-depth analysis – except by your mates in the pub that
night. And there was no Jimmy Hill. Don't be so sure.

The Fifties were perhaps the last time football even
faintly resembled the above idyll and there were certainly
plenty of goals. A glance at the scoreline suggests the
above game was one of those 'age of innocence' classics,
but no Jimmy Hill? 'I was playing,' television's top pundit
explains. 'And the only glimpse we saw of it afterwards
was on Pathe News! But it was the most memorable
match of my life. Anyone who was there will tell you that
it was the most exciting Cup-tie they ever saw, or in my
case, played in.' A glance at the papers of the time confirms his view. 'Frenzy at Fulham,' screamed the *Sunday*

126

Express. 'And no wonder after this fantastic, fabulous game, which was not only worthy of Wembley but had me alternately chewing my pencil in suspense or standing up in my seat roaring my tonsils out!' So said Alan Hoby. Roy Peskett, of the *Daily Mail*, asked his readers: 'Have you ever seen a pair of crutches hurled skywards at a football match? Well, I have . . .'

Yes, it was some game all right, with Fulham at their show-biz best with the likes of Bedford Jezzard and 'Tosh' Chamberlain, Hill, himself, and the legendary Johnny Haynes. For Newcastle, the Cupholders and five-times Wembley winners, there was Wor Jackie Milburn, Vic Keeble and Bob Stokoe. No wonder over 40,000 crammed Craven Cottage that winter's afternoon. 'Yet the game was almost over before it started,' recalls Hill. 'The powerful First Division side strolled to a three-goal lead after 27 minutes, and it looked as if the game had ended. Milburn scored first, Stokoe the second and Tommy Casey number three.' Milburn's was a fierce right-foot shot into the roof of the net from a Mitchell corner and four minutes later Stokoe's drive bounced off Wilson and beyond Black in the home goal. Newcastle delighted their army of travelling fans with a bewildering move involving Mitchell, Stokoe and Milburn before Casey sent in a scorching left-footer.

From then on all you could hear wafting across the Thames were incessant renderings of the 'Blaydon Races' as the holders revelled in the riverside mud, toying with their out-classed opponents. 'Just five minutes before half-time,' says Hill, 'Fulham scored what seemed to be nothing more than a consolation goal, but the way in which it occurred affected the rest of the game, and two players in particular, the scorer Tosh Chamberlain and his opponent, Newcastle's young full-back, Arnold Woollard. The move started on the right wing, Haynes' pass putting Jezzard on a run; Woollard moved in to intercept Beddy's low cross, missed it and there was Tosh on hand to slot it home. That incident,' claims Hill, 'put Tosh on a high and Woollard on a low, and as a bonus convinced Fulham fans that it might just be worth staying for the second half.

'From the kick-off, Chamberlain was inspired as he continued to torture Woollard. The game finished the young Bermuda-born full-back as a Newcastle player and he was soon transferred to Bournemouth.' It was 13 minutes into the second half when the other 21 players began to realise that they wouldn't forget the game in a hurry, either. Hill continues the story. 'I put Tosh through on the wing and he crashed an angled shot past Simpson; the ref pointed to the centre spot, but a young linesman, 25-year-old Jack Taylor, a Wolverhampton butcher [who became one of the world's most famous referees], kept his flag up and a goal was not given. George Hawley wrote in the *Daily Mirror*, "I, as one of the mystified 40,000, say linesman Taylor was wrong, terribly wrong in flagging Fulham out of the Cup with the worst off-side I can remember."'

Hill sportingly adds: 'My television experience since has convinced me that linesmen are far more often correct in their "offside" judgements than journalists, spectators, players or managers so I'm not complaining now, although I did at the time. The drama was only just beginning, though. Seven minutes later, Chamberlain, put through by Haynes, hammered a low shot past Simpson from an impossible angle and Fulham were only one behind. Newcastle were in a panic. Johnny [Haynes] and I swapped passes putting Tosh into a shooting position once more and could hardly believe that he beat Simpson, no mean 'keeper, for the third time. The stadium erupted, but it was nothing to what was to come. Just three minutes later, Tosh crossed from the left wing and Jezzard headed down towards the far corner of the goal. I could see that it was going to miss by inches and chased it, just managing to prod it over the line from no more than a few feet for what we all thought was the winner. For years,' admits Hill, 'I always remembered Beddy's header as a shot, until the Pathe film proved otherwise.' It was at this point that the *Daily Mail* witnessed the raising of the crutches.

'Never mind the crutches,' says Hill, 'more people lost their hats that day (everyone used to wear hats then) than come through the turnstiles in half a dozen matches now. What a fight-back! What drama! Sadly, though, for Fulham, more was to come.'

With the 'Blaydon Races' well and truly silenced, it looked as if Fulham had completed one of the great comebacks of Cup history but Newcastle treasured the old trophy more than most teams and would not give it up without one helluva battle. 'But,' claims Hill, 'it wasn't as if we threw the game away. Newcastle's equaliser, scored by Vic Keeble, which again changed the nature of the contest, was blatantly unfair. A picture reproduced in the *Daily Herald* shows that Keeble was nowhere near the ball and clearly pushing our 'keeper Ian Black, over the goal-line. Vic's arm is nowhere near Black's arm, either, but outstretched at shoulder height. The unfair goal destroyed Black's confidence and he misjudged the not-too-difficult cross from which Keeble, restored to life by an error of judgement, headed the winning goal.'

Keeble, who was suffering from the 'flu and should not have played, admitted: 'No one has ever been more relieved.'

Maurice Smith in *The People* summed it up: 'What do you want in a Cup-tie? Thrills? Great football? A hat-trick by a disappointed bridegroom? A grand rally and a grandstand finish? Well, it was all there at Fulham.'

Hill's answer is the last word: 'Well, nothing really, except a touch more justice.' 'Twas ever thus?

Fulham: Black; Wilson, Lawler, Smith, Brice, Lowe, Hill, Robson, Jezzard, Haynes, Chamberlain.

Newcastle United: Simpson; Woollard, McMichael, Stokoe, Paterson, Casey, Milburn, Davies, Keeble, Curry, Mitchell.

Roger Hunt

LIVERPOOL 2 LEEDS UNITED 1 (AET)
FA Cup final: Wembley, 1 May 1965.

Born in Golborne, Lancashire, on 20 July 1938, Roger Hunt became a natural target man. He represented the Army during his national service where he served in the Royal Artillery, then signed for Liverpool as an amateur in 1958 and as a pro a year later. A born goal-scorer and tireless worker, Hunt rattled in a club record 285 goals in his 489 matches. He lacked the finesse of Greaves and the flamboyance of Law, but was a team-mates' favourite. Fearless, and with a powerful shot in both feet, he was a regular in England's World Cup campaign of 1966. As unselfish as he was unsung, he brushed off his southern critics as easily as he did opposing defenders. Stronger than his 5'9" and 11st 10lb suggested, he won 34 England caps and was only on the losing side twice. A never-say-die competitor, he ended his career at Bolton, the team he supported as a boy, and now works in the family haulage business.

'Sir Roger', as the Kop labelled him, was Bill Shankly's sort of player. The soldier in him meant he was smart of appearance, disciplined, dedicated, could hit the target and, most important of all, was prepared, in football terms, to 'die' for the cause. Hunt took football almost as seriously as Shanks and soon endeared himself to the great man by notching 21 goals in their first season together. But no goal was more appreciated by the gaffer than Hunt's opener in the 1965 FA Cup final. Although Bremner equalised and St John got the winner, Sir Roger's strike paved the way to ending the Anfield Cup hoodoo.

To suggest that the Cup was a mere obsession at Liverpool is a monumental understatement and merely cast the grand old trophy in the same light as the next game – say, with Rochdale reserves. Every game was an obsession with Shankly but winning the Cup was in another stratosphere. Having taken over the manager's job on 1 December 1959 – four months after Hunt's first team debut – the Scot was well aware that the club, founded in 1892 and which he was so meticulously remoulding, had never laid hands on the most coveted of all trophies. Already he had captured both Second and First Division titles but still the twin towers remained elusive. Even such teams as Swansea, Southampton and Leicester had halted the Reds' Cup progress and when he looked a little further back, he would be told – in whispers by shamefaced assistants – that Liverpool had gone down to the likes of Southend, Gateshead and, heaven forbid, Worcester City! There were Merseysiders who thought there was some kind of jinx, and although Shanks was not one of them, Hunt knew how much landing that trophy meant to the boss and the bootroom. 'It's every player's ambition to win at Wembley,' he says, 'but for Liverpool the Cup was something special. It was amazing they had never won it with all their history.'

Hunt had been one of the mainstays of the side that had won the Second Division title, scoring a club record of 41 goals (including five hat-tricks), in 1961–62. With new signing Ian St John, he formed a devastating twin spearhead and with Ron Yeats also joining that season, the lynchpins of the magnificent mid-Sixties team were in place. 'We won the League the previous season and had by now established this great rivalry with Leeds,' Hunt remembers. 'But we still had trouble in the Cup, needing a replay against Stockport, who were bottom of the fourth, and another with Leicester. But we beat Chelsea in the semi-final and, with Leeds also making it to Wembley, the scene was set for this marvellous showdown.'

It could not have been more tantalisingly scripted: Lancashire v Yorkshire, Shankly v Revie, Bremner, Hunter and Charlton v Hunt, St John and Stevenson. However you looked at it, it was shaping up for a right royal Battle of the Roses. But it didn't materialise. Not for a long time, anyway. 'To be honest,' acknowledges Hunt, 'the 90 minutes were a disappointment. Even our fans were quiet for long periods. It was absolute deadlock and we seemed to cancel each other out. There was so much at stake, not just for us but for them, because we'd already won the League. But the real hero was Gerry Byrne who played on after breaking his collar-bone in the third minute.'

If anything, Liverpool may have edged the second half, in which Sprake had to make two fine saves as the outstanding Stevenson strolled through the driving rain with increasing authority. It was indeed the sort of situation where Shankly might have uttered those celebrated words, 'We murdered 'em 0–0.' But he didn't. He contained himself by convincing his men that they would win. 'Keep playing and it will come,' he told them.

It appeared to have come just three minutes into the first period of extra time and the gallant Byrne, who was taking pain-killers, had a hand in it. Hunt takes up the story: 'I remember Billy [Stevenson] beating about three men in a great run down the left and slipping it to Byrne on the overlap. Stevenson's run had left Leeds in disarray and Gerry had time to look up before sending over a waist-high cross. I was in a good position only about six yards out but can remember thinking: "What do I do? Do I side-foot it or do I head it?" When it came, I stooped to head it and in it went. Simple. We had broken the deadlock.'

Hunt wheeled away to scenes of jubilation that were unconfined. The sense of relief could not be explained even by the breaking of the cautious, gridlocked boredom of the first 90 minutes: no, it was as if the crowd had been waiting all of those 73 years. And as they let rip, one end of the old stadium was turned into a riotous sea of red while the white of the Leeds end was now almost ashen and motionless. Generations of Liverpool fans had despaired of this moment ever coming and the Beatle brigades were not going to spare the decibels. Of course, it was not over yet but the celebrations appeared justified as it always looked like the kind of game that one goal would decide. However, Leeds were never beaten until the final whistle and they kept battling. 'Even so,' says Hunt, 'their equaliser came out of the blue.' Norman Hunter, who had run himself into the sodden turf defending, eased forward to send a ball over to where Charlton nodded it down. Liverpool, with their longing for victory understandable after 206 fruitless ties, momentarily dropped their guard. It was enough for the lurking Bremner to lift his boot and batter a half-volley beyond the despairing dive of Lawrence. Relief for Leeds, despair for Liverpool. 'Oh, no,' Hunt thought. 'Not again.'

Wembley's foundations seemed to shake as these northern giants kicked off again. The stodge had long since been forgotten as a stirring finale unfolded. Yet Leeds, ever cautious, were afraid to commit themselves, allowing Liverpool to regain the initiative. With a European Cup semi-final against Inter Milan in four days time, perhaps they had the greater urgency to finish it and, with nine minutes remaining, they did. The redoubtable Smith sent Callaghan away down the right on one last gallop. The irrepressible England winger drifted by two Leeds defenders who had nothing left to give. With the Mersey roar mounting and the Yorkshiremen reeling, he could see his centre-forward advancing, ready to pounce. Ian St John was already the idol of the Kop; in another second he would be deified. 'I was at the far post when he prepared to cross,' he recalls. 'I knew he'd drop it short so I went to meet it. The goal looked like the Mersey tunnel as I headed it in.'

If St John had not connected, the ball may well have

gone in anyway – sucked in by some 20,000 Liverpool throats! But he did and those throats roared their adulation. Shankly had been right – victory had come eventually and for Sir Roger the satisfaction was two-fold: the cavalry had finished the job but the softening up had been done by the Artillery.

Liverpool: Lawrence; Lawler, Byrne, Strong, Yeats, Stevenson, Callaghan, Hunt, St John, Smith, Thompson.

Leeds United: Sprake; Reaney, Bell, Bremner, Charlton, Hunter, Giles, Storrie, Peacock, Collins, Johanneson.

Norman Hunter

LEEDS UNITED 7 SOUTHAMPTON 0
League: Elland Road, 4 March 1972.

Born in Eighton Banks, near Newcastle, on 29 October 1943, Norman Hunter first wielded his famous left foot with Birtley Juniors and Chester-le-Street before joining Leeds in November 1960. A lynchpin of the Revie era, he became a legend for his virulent tackling and formed a fearsome pairing with Jack Charlton at the impregnable heart of the United defence. He earned three Under-23 caps before making his full England debut against West Germany in February 1966 and would have won more than his 28 caps had it not been for the presence of the peerless Bobby Moore. He gained winners' medals in the League Championship (twice), FA Cup and League Cup, Second Division Championship and Fairs Cup, but the plethora of runners-up awards reflects the near misses the club experienced in those heady days. Hunter also had the distinction of being the first recipient of the PFA's Player of the Year award in 1973. A remarkably consistent performer who was an ever-present for Leeds for five seasons, he finally left Yorkshire for Ashton Gate in 1976, making over 100 appearances for Bristol City. He later managed Barnsley, Rotherham and Bradford.

The rich irony in Norman Hunter's selection of 'the Southampton match' is only surpassed by its poignancy: for the man whom Brian Clough unforgettably christened 'Bite Yer Legs' for the chomping nature of his challenges hardly made a tackle. 'In fact, I barely touched the ball,' he grins. Correction: *every* Leeds player touched the ball –

apart from 'keeper Gary Sprake – in those memorable, sweeping passing movements that gave the nation an all too brief glimpse of what the Revie era might have been. 'It was perfect football for 45 minutes,' adds Hunter. Indeed, in a career which spanned 543 appearances for Leeds, countless trophies and even more atrophies, it is telling that while some players opt for two-legged games and one a series of three, Hunter picks just a second half. And herein lies the poignancy.

For all his Yorkshire pragmatism, Revie was steeped in superstition and made as much use of psychology as he did his dossiers on opponents. He was, without question, a great manager, turning a near-moribund Elland Road outfit into one of the most feared in Europe. But his teams slipped so awfully and so frequently at the last hurdle that misfortune is a wholly inadequate explanation for their failings. 'We might have taken too much on at times,' admits Hunter, 'and were too tense at the death.' Indeed, that tension was a useful extra man for lesser opponents on numerous occasions. But Leeds not only gained less silverware than their talents deserved, they failed to win over the nation. Beyond Elland Road, they were often loathed, at best admired, but never loved.

Whereas Manchester United, Celtic and even Liverpool aroused adoration in other cities, Leeds were, for the most part, cynical when subtlety would have served them better, dour when a little dazzle was required and mean-spirited when the game cried out for magnanimity. And by the time they woke up to this, it was too late. Hunter was considered among the arch bad guys – even with his innocent smile. His reputation as a hard man was established early and it is said that when his mother accompanied him around the junior leagues, the two shared a joke. Mum would tell a friend: 'My Norman came home last night with a terrible leg, all covered in bruises.' 'Oh, yeah? Whose was it?'

In a delightful piece in *The Observer* Julie Welch wrote: 'Off the pitch, you'd never hear a word said against him.

On it, he had the reputation of a man who ate powdered glass sandwiches, chased his beer down with a paraquat and picked his teeth with a masonry drill. The harder he tackled, the more maniacally friendly the smile he bestowed upon his victim; in fact he gave the impression that after he'd broken both your legs he'd call a stretcher personally and ride with you in the ambulance.'

The legend was born and when Hunter bore down on an opponent, people would flinch – several rows back in the stand. Linesmen would inspect his studs with the nervousness of Dracula's dentist, while the only time he is said to have hesitated for a 50–50 ball was in a puddle . . . at a crocodile farm. As nice a guy off the field as he was formidable on it, Hunter relished his image and made light of his own playing abilities which were considerable. In spite of favouring his left foot – his right was in danger of wasting away from lack of use – he was a superb practitioner, a model of consistency and more creative than his critics would have us believe. He could thread a pass through the eye of a needle with his left foot but couldn't be guaranteed to hit a haystack with his right. Even so, he often linked with Giles and Bremner in the engine room of the Leeds locomotive. 'I even got involved in one of the goals against Southampton,' he claimed. 'And, actually, it wasn't a bad first half, either.'

When the Saints arrived in Yorkshire for this testing away game in March 1972, Leeds were at long last beginning to resemble the team whose colours Revie had adopted – Real Madrid. Looking a more mature and relaxed side than the frantic nearly men of previous seasons, their football was a joy to behold. They did not become cuddly overnight, however, and could still call upon the manacles when they were needed; but the possession game they were perfecting earned the accolade 'Super Leeds'. During a purple patch in the spring of that year, they were awesome. And against the poor, unfortunate Saints they surpassed themselves.

After dominating territorially, Leeds went in front

through Allan Clarke, who did much more than 'sniff' the first with a fierce angled drive after fine work by Jones and Gray in the 40th minute. When Lorimer rifled a second two minutes later, the contest was effectively over and the exhibition began. 'I thought we were doing well until the last five minutes of the first half,' said Saints' 'keeper Eric Martin, 'but then there was nothing we could do.'

His opposite number, Gary Sprake, observed: 'It was a wonderful exhibition by the lads.' Sprake need not have come out for the second half. Martin courageously kept Leeds at bay for 15 minutes but was again beaten by Clarke and then the floodgates opened. Lorimer snatched his second and Leeds' fourth in the 64th minute, his hat-trick in the 68th after intercepting Fry's suicidal back-pass. With loud *olés* greeting every Leeds player's touch of the ball, the home team were now lauding it over a broken side. And they were particularly pleased when the destructive duo of Charlton and Hunter combined for the sixth, Big Jack nodding home Norm's cross! There was still time for Jones to celebrate his 300th League game with a seventh from close range in the 78th minute.

It is significant that not just neutrals recall this match as frequently as any of Leeds' triumphs. Shown on *Match of the Day*, it was a glorious advert for the game and one in which Hunter was 'proud to have played a part'. In the end, they were pipped for the League by Derby but did land the considerable consolation of the Cup. Against Southampton, they simply won a lot of new friends. And for once the bark was worse than the bite.

Leeds United: Sprake; Reaney, Madeley, Bremner, Charlton, Hunter, Lorimer, Clarke, Jones, Giles, Gray.

Southampton: Martin; McCarthy, Fry, Stokes, Gabriel, Steele, Paine (Byrne), Channon, Davies, O'Neill, Jenkins.

Jimmy Johnstone

REAL MADRID 0 CELTIC 1
Alfredo di Stefano's Testimonial: Madrid, 7 June
1967.

---

*Born in Viewpark, Lanarkshire, on 30 September 1944, Jimmy
Johnstone graduated from Parkhead ballboy to become one of the
greatest Scottish wingers of all time. Just 5'4" and 9st 8lb, and
with a temperament as fiery as his flame-hair, 'Jinky' was a
caricature of a tartan wing wizard – a wee devil to his tumbled-
down socks. He joined Celtic in 1961 from Viewpark and, in 14
seasons with the green and whites, earned every available honour
at club level. Johnstone was a key member of the great Celtic
side which won nine Championships in a row (1966–74), five
Scottish Cups, five League Cups and, most memorably of all,
the European Cup in 1967. By comparison, his international
haul was relatively meagre, just 23 caps reflecting both his indis-
cipline and the serious competition for the right-wing berth – from
Rangers' Willie Henderson. But no one who saw Johnstone's
mesmeric dribbling – least of all a generation of left-backs – will
ever forget it. His acceleration was awesome, his tricks and control worthy of the circus, his courage straight from the trenches.
After leaving his heart at Celtic, he drifted among San Jose
Earthquakes, Sheffield United, Dundee, Shelbourne, Elgin
City and Blantyre Celtic – a confused postscript to a genius.*

When Paddy Crerand was asked to encapsulate a typical
Scottish footballer, he came up with: 'He would have great
natural ability, fight like King Kong and have a button
that he could press and destroy himself.' Apart from the

obvious discrepancy in build, Crerand might have been talking about Jimmy Johnstone. With his twinkling feet, ball-bearing hips and bristling red flag of temper, Wee Jinky was the archetypal Scottish winger, a defiant throwback to the days of the Wembley Wizards when the standard height was 5′4″ and the standard performance was to turn the full-back so many times he would lose his bearings. On too many occasions, however, it was Johnstone, who lost his way – frequently in less than salubrious bars and once, famously, off the Scottish coast in a rowing boat with just one oar.

If waywardness was an integral part of his make-up, Johnstone was a doughty campaigner on the field and diligent in practice. He perfected his craft by dribbling for hours round milk bottles as a kid, and was inspired by Stanley Matthews. But the greatest influence on his fledgling career was the European Cup final at Hampden in 1960. Johnstone watched bewitched by the magic of Gento, Puskas, Del Sol and di Stefano. 'It was a different game they were playing,' he says, still in wonder more than 30 years after the event. 'I had never seen fitba' like it.' So when – just seven years later – Celtic were invited to be Real Madrid's opponents for di Stefano's testimonial, Johnstone was determined to say 'adios' in style.

Even before Jock Stein's side had been crowned European Champions, a delegation from Real had asked them to grace the occasion, Celtic's uninhibited attacking style having won the Spaniards' admiration over more celebrated but cynical Latin alternatives. The Scots were honoured by the approach, if a little concerned that a fixture on 7 June would prolong an already long and arduous season. And there was the small matter of a fee, Stein not wishing his players to be undersold. Eventually, it was sorted out and, after a homecoming of epic proportions, Celtic set off for Iberia once more for what was supposed to be a friendly. Those who felt that the club had reached the pinnacle of European football with their 2–1 win over Inter Milan should have been in the Bernabeu on that balmy summer's evening. A full house of 130,000 Spaniards came primarily to salute di Stefano but also to remind the so-called new kings of Europe just who really did rule the continent. As for Celtic, a subordinate role was never in the negotiations.

'It was pure theatre,' recalls Johnstone. 'I'll never forget it. After 15 minutes the game stopped, the lights dimmed and a spotlight picked out di Stefano in the centre circle. There was a red carpet and he came off to receive a replica of the European Cup and a standing ovation. It was unbelievable. They treated him like a god.' Indeed, for Celtic the theatrical presentation made up for the somewhat shabby treatment at the end of the European Cup final, when the players' medals were stuck in a box and not handed out. But what really made it a night of nights was the match itself – and its frenetic tempo. 'It was some friendly, I can tell ya,' chuckles Johnstone at the memory of a game in which Auld and Amancio were sent off for a scrap that would have filled Madison Square Garden. 'It had everything,' he says. 'Besides the sendings off, the tackles were flying all night, di Stefano did his stuff and we played magnificent. And Bobby Lennox got a great goal tae win.'

Right from the kick-off, the pace was frantic, the tackling fierce. Both 'keepers had to make fine saves and Johnstone was made aware that his reputation had preceded him, being singled out for some special treatment. No sooner had di Stefano bid farewell, than Real were having to clear off their own line to prevent Celtic going in front. Then Real hit the bar. It was end-to-end stuff with Johnstone savouring every minute: he turned conjurer and the crowd loved him for it. Real's tackling was less than hospitable but Johnstone rode the worst of them and, with inspired counters, created havoc at the heart of the home defence. But Fallon had to be at his best to thwart Real whose adventures denied Celts their customary dominance of midfield. Velazquez hit the bar, Fallon twice tipped over and, at the other end, Junquera saved spectacularly from Gemmell.

Celtic were keeping commendably calm in the face of severe provocation but eventually the rough-house treatment in general, and of Johnstone in particular, lit their fuse. Auld broke through but when harassed by Amancio, the pair traded blows and both had to go after a memorable exchange on the hour. Shortly afterwards, Celtic scored. Inevitably, it was Johnstone who made it. With a dribble that left the entire Madrid defence sprawling, he went round five of them before releasing Lennox with an exquisite little ball. Lennox lashed home from 12 yards and Celtic toyed with them after that.

'It was a great goal,' acknowledges Johnstone. 'And the crowd – after a wee hush – really appreciated it. After that we just kept possession and tormented 'em – Real Madrid on their own ground. The crowd rose to us and Puskas put his arm around me. Then he kissed me! Di Stefano came up, too. It was amazing – the perfect follow-up to our win over Inter. If you'd done a film script, you couldnae hae done it better.'

Jock Stein agreed. 'I was tremendously proud of our lads for continuing to carry the flag for Celtic and Scotland. We played magnificently against a side determined to beat us. Puskas, Santamaria and di Stefano were all full of praise for Celtic's pace, skill, and professional approach to the game.'

The great man and Jinky had had their differences – not least over Johnstone playing keepie-uppie in training – but not tonight. Stein knew what courage he had in that wee frame of his and how many times he had been hacked down, only to get up and run at the man again. On this occasion, he could forgive him for his wee peccadilloes. On a brilliant night in the Bernabeu, he could forgive him anything – for Jinky had delivered: he had run round Real Madrid as if they were milk bottles.

Real Madrid: Junquera; Calpe, de Felipe, Sanchis, Pirri

(Pachin), Zoco, Serena, Amancio, di Stefano (Grosso),
Velazquez, Gento.

Celtic: Fallon; Craig, Gemmell, Clark, McNeill,
O'Neill, Johnstone, Murdoch, Wallace, Auld, Lennox.

Billy Liddell

ENGLAND 2 SCOTLAND 3
Home International: Wembley, 14 April 1951

Born in Dunfermline on 10 January 1922, Billy Liddell was the son of a miner and the eldest of six children. He used both the oval and round ball to great effect. A promising stand-off at Dunfermline High School, he played soccer for Lochgelly Violets where he was spotted by Liverpool. He signed amateur forms on the advice of a Presbyterian Minister as football was considered 'a risky occupation'. Liddell won 28 caps for Scotland and, along with Stanley Matthews, was the only player to represent Great Britain twice against the Rest of Europe. A sturdy left-winger who could also play on the right or at centre-forward, Liddell had 22 years at Anfield, where he logged 229 goals in 537 games, all while continuing his career as an accountant. After hanging up his boots at 38, he became a JP, a Sunday school teacher, a prison visitor and a staunch fan of his only club. A truly great player and a gentleman on and off the field, it was typical of his modesty when he said of his beloved Liverpool: 'They only became successful when I retired.'

William Beveridge Liddell didn't smoke, didn't drink, didn't swear and went to church as often as he trained. Compelled to play rugby at High School, his ambition was to be a chartered accountant. And even when he played football, he did so mainly on the left-wing – in spite of being right-footed. All this makes you realise what a player he must have been for Everton's neighbours to become known as Liddell-pool.

For all his undisputed status as a legend among Mersey-side Reds, Liddell could be a touch too individualistic for the Scotland selectors whose award of 28 caps for a player of such longevity was an insult. But Billy still enjoyed many magical moments in the dark blue shirt and perhaps there was no finer hour than when he snatched the winner against England in 1951. His countrymen were catapulted into paroxysms of joy for this victory over the auld enemy meant more than most, yet Liddell's abiding memory is of an accident to Wilf Mannion that reduced England to ten men.

The pre-match build-up lacked the Bannockburn intensity of 1967 when the clans claimed 'world champion' status after destroying the reigning World Cup holders. But for that gentler age the desire to duff the Sassenachs was more heartfelt than usual. England's narrow 1–0 win at Hampden had earned them the right to represent Britain in the 1950 World Cup in Brazil, where they completely blew it by going down 1–0 to the United States. Not only was that the greatest humiliation in their history but it also narked the Scots who naturally felt they would have done better. So it was with everything to play for – and a bit more to prove – when the teams met in the annual set-to in 1951, this time at Wembley.

What had made the USA defeat all the more unbeliev-able was that the England of those days contained far more maestros than mugs – Matthews (although he missed that particular game), Mortensen, Mannion, Wright and Finney were all in their heydey and it is a measure of Scotland's own strength and character that they approached the match with total confidence. Relying heavily on home-based players, the Scots headed south with a rare sense of purpose and it was a tribute to Liddell's status that he was the lone 'Anglo' in the side. At that time, the powerful Liverpool winger was arguably the most potent force in Britain.

At 5'10" and a little under 13 stones, the former Path-finder navigator could force his way through the tightest defence, and he was a fearsome sight when in full flow. Belying his nice guy image, he said: 'I enjoy playing against hard tacklers – I play hard myself.' Superbly fit even though he never trained on a full-time basis, possessing a screamer of a shot in either foot and the Lawtonian knack of nodding bullets from outside the penalty area, he gave the most resolute defender sleepless nights. The normally unflappable Alf Ramsey was saddled with marking him that day. Even at club level, he had never looked his usual composed self against Liddell. This knowledge only added to tartan confidence and they began the match as if still steaming into Kings Cross. Twice in the opening minutes, the visitors ripped through the England ranks and only the alertness of Williams kept the scores level. Ably led by Steel and with Reilly and Liddell torturing the home defenders, the tartan hordes roared in anticipation. Yet Liddell's strongest recollection is not one of this glorious opening – nor even of his clinching goal and hero status in a significant taming of the auld enemy – 'but poor Wilf Mannion. The game was barely 15 minutes old when Wilf and I went up for a high ball and collided. The back of my head hit Wilf's cheekbone and fractured it. He had to leave the field and I had a stitch put in a cut.'

Modesty prevents him from saying it had been at a corner, resulting from Williams' brilliant save from a fierce Liddell free-kick, that the accident occurred – after the 'keeper had twice previously thwarted the Liverpool man. But, as often happens to under-strength teams, England's ten men found a new spirit and took the lead in 25 minutes. It was a fine goal from debutant Hassall who fired home a square pass from Mortensen. But within seven minutes Scotland were level, Johnstone, also a newboy, making no mistake after receiving from Reilly. But England were to suffer an even more serious blow just four minutes later when Mortensen was concussed in another goalmouth skirmish. The Blackpool man stayed on the field until the half-time whistle but, badly shaken, had to be helped off by his team-mates. Only nine Englishmen returned to the fray.

It was certainly not enough and, in seven minutes after the break, Scotland appeared to have put the issue beyond doubt. First Reilly wriggled through for the second goal just two minutes after the re-start and, again showing his alertness five minutes later, the Hibs star whipped the ball away from Williams, who could not hold Steel's cross, for Liddell to ram home the third. 'The real credit for my goal must go to Lawrie Reilly, whose perseverance and quick reflexes paved the way for me to score,' said Liddell.

The Scottish legions were in full voice now but English hearts were lifted by the sight of Mortensen returning to the field. To the roars of the home fans, England rallied and, with the Scots scarcely believing what they were seeing, the white shirts laid seige to Cowan's goal. With almost half an hour remaining, the heroic Mortensen combined with Finney for the Preston plumber to draw the 'keeper and lob him superbly to make it 2–3. England came again and again but somehow the Scottish goal held. Finney said: 'For about 20 minutes in the second half, I thought we would win. Morty lifted us and deserved a medal for his bravery. But the winner could not have come from a nicer man than Billy Liddell.'

That man acknowledged: 'It was an important win for everyone connected with Scottish football because it restored our pride after the disappointment of the World Cup qualifying match defeat by England. We felt we had put the record straight. But if this match proved anything it was the need for substitutes being allowed. The game could have been ruined after Mannion's injury. Fortunately, England put on a great show with ten men and the match didn't lose anything in value. But this doesn't happen very often.'

When he retired and was visiting prisoners at Walton jail, Liddell talked of football being 'an international language'. It was seldom spoken more fluently than on this memorable, sunlit day at Wembley by a man from Liddell-pool.

England: Williams; Ramsey, Eckersley, Johnston, Froggatt, Wright, Matthews, Mannion, Mortensen, Hassall, Finney.

Scotland: Cowan; Young, Cox, Evans, Woodburn, Redpath, Waddell, Johnstone, Reilly, Steel, Liddell.

Gary Lineker

ENGLAND 3 POLAND 0
World Cup (Group match): Monterrey, Mexico: 11
June 1986.

---

*Born in Leicester on 30 November 1960. As a soft-spoken,
skinny kid Gary Lineker helped with his family market stall and
played snooker and cricket. At soccer, he was put on a steak and
milk diet to stop him being knocked off the ball. But the boy
Lineker possessed electrifying pace while, behind the camouflage,
lurked a deadly accuracy and a killer instinct: he carried a Smith
& Wesson in woolly gloves. A Leicester City season-ticket
holder at eight, he joined his local club as an apprentice in 1977,
turning pro in 1978. He made up for his lack of Schools and
Youth honours with goals by the lorry-load. Lineker signed for
Everton for £800,000 in 1985 and achieved superstar status in
the 1986 World Cup, where his six goals won him the Golden
Boot award – and saved England from an ignominious early exit.
He went to Barcelona for £2.75 million shortly afterwards and
became a hero of the Nou Camp. But his career suffered its first
hiccup with hepatitis before he fell out of favour with new manager Johan Cruyff. Eventually he returned home to Spurs where
his health and goals output were fully restored. He continued to
maintain a strike rate that was phenomenal for the modern game
and one wonders what England would have done without his 48
goals – one short of Bobby Charlton's all-time record.*

    *A model pro who was never booked, he was always able to
shrug off assassination attempts with a silent resolve to score even
more. He suffered an unhappy farewell to international football
when he was substituted in his final game during the European
Championships in Sweden, the one discordant note of a marvel-*

lous symphony. He opted to give his career a lucrative swansong by helping to launch a national league in Japan.

There was a sense of rare foreboding as Englishmen gathered around their television screens on that midsummer's evening in 1986. A national humiliation loomed as the hapless Bobby Robson sent his team out to do battle in the Mexican sun against Poland, a country which had been something of a *bête noire* to English ambitions in recent years. Some 20 million managed to bring themselves to watch but it might have been more – many could not face what they were sure would be unmitigated, unwatchable misery if it was anything like England's first two matches in the competition. And hopes had been so high – England had qualified impressively, had experienced world-class players with skipper Bryan Robson, 'keeper Peter Shilton and midfield maestro Glenn Hoddle just about at their peaks, while there did not appear to be an outstanding team in the finals. It looked winnable – which is how young striker Gary Lineker saw it: 'I always felt we had a good chance in this competition,' he says. Which only served to make the defeat by Portugal and the draw with Morocco even harder to bear.

If the campaign had been deliberately sabotaged it could not have got off to a worse start. Bryan Robson's shoulder had popped once too often, Ray Wilkins had been sent off and manager Bobby Robson was being harangued by the press for his team selection and tactics. The supporters, including those who brazenly wore the 'DHSS World Cup tour' t-shirts, felt let down. England might have been in Monterrey but to the folks back home it seemed like disarray. What was needed was a miracle; what they got was a more balanced team selection but it amounted to the same thing. Rumours still persist that the players 'picked the team' for the Poland match, rumours which Bobby Robson has fiercely denied. But a team meeting took place at which he was urged to bolster the midfield and in came the combative Peter Reid and Steve Hodge, with Peter Beardsley playing up front alongside Lineker.

'Everything was going against us,' recalls the Everton striker. 'We had had chances against Portugal but it had just been one of those games. And then with Bryan Robson injured and Ray Wilkins sent off, the pressure was really on. We were getting the papers faxed over to us and reading the reports about two days late. It was depressing stuff and not doing us any good. But even with the papers, you don't get the feeling in the country, you don't appreciate just how important it is to do well for so many people over there. As for me personally, I wasn't even sure I would be in the team – I thought I'd done enough in the first two games but you can never be sure. But one thing was clear – the knives were out. I had thought it was a chance in a lifetime thing to represent England in the World Cup and now we could have been on the next plane home.'

It took just eight more minutes for the nightmare to end. The fortified midfield was already encouraging optimism on the England bench and on those millions of armchairs back home. Then Hoddle's well-flighted pass was nodded down by Lineker to Beardsley. The pair exchanged passes before the Evertonian slipped it inside to club colleague Trevor Steven. Waiting for Gary Stevens to arrive on the over-lap, Steven passed to the right-back whose cross was swept in by Lineker. The build-up was powerful and precise, the finish stunning. Suddenly, the skies of doom lightened and Bobby Robson's perpetual frown gave way to a smile.

But the night had only just begun. Six minutes later Sansom's ball down the line to Beardsley was played on to Hodge whose accurate centre was hit home with the ruthless efficiency of a hired killer. Lineker 2 Poland 0. And there was more. 'Peter Beardsley and I just struck up an understanding,' says Lineker. 'I found that I had more space in the penalty area and we seemed to know where each other was. I scored most of the goals but he created the space.'

England were rampant now and there could have been further goals but, in the 35th minute, nobody was complaining and comparisons were being made with a certain Geoff Hurst. Steven's corner slipped through the hands of Polish 'keeper Mlynarczyk and Lineker gratefully accepted his place in history. 'If I hadn't scored in this game, I may not have played for England again for a while,' he says modestly. 'Every time the ball went in the net was a second of sheer ecstasy. There's absolutely nothing to compare with it. It not only transformed England's World Cup, it transformed my career. It put me on to a new plateau, I got the Golden Boot award and went to Barcelona soon afterwards. Nothing I have done since has surpassed it.'

England did not score again but contained Poland comfortably in the second half, even though Boniek hit a post and Fenwick was booked. A place in the second round was secured and Paraguay were beaten 3–0 – this time Lineker managed only two, with Beardsley getting the other. It set up the first meeting with Argentina since the Falklands War, a meeting which was lost thanks partly to Maradona's infamous 'hand of God' goal. Lineker pulled one back to bring his personal tally to six but England were out. However, the skinny kid from the Leicester market stall, had well and truly arrived in the world's market place – as the game's undisputed top striker.

'Those goals against Poland were the most valuable I ever scored,' he acknowledges. 'We owed that performance not just to ourselves but to the people back home. People had been having a go and the best way to answer them is to do it on the field.' Referring to the switch from 4–3–3 to 4–4–2, Lineker paid tribute to the Everton connection. 'We'd been playing that way at Everton with Peter Reid, Trevor Steven and Gary Stevens and it worked well for England, too. It was the greatest day of my life.'

The only disappointment in that Poland game? 'The manager asked me for four but I only managed three . . .' He chuckles and then adds thoughtfully: 'I suppose it changed my life, really.'

England: Shilton; Stevens, Butcher, Fenwick, Sansom, Hoddle, Steven, Reid, Hodge, Lineker (Dixon), Beardsley (Waddle).

Poland: Mlynarczyk; Pawlak, Majewski, Wojcicki, Ostrowski, Komornicki (Karas), Matysik (Buncol), Urban, Dziekanowski, Boniek, Smolarek.

Ally McCoist

RANGERS 3 CELTIC 2 (AET)
Scottish League Cup final: Hampden Park, 25
March 1984.

---

*Born in Bellshill, Lanarkshire, on 24 September 1962, Ally
McCoist wanted to play for Rangers ever since choosing a Light
Blues' jersey as his prize in a newspaper competition. 'I was
about six and wore it for weeks,' he says. For all that, he was a
long time in getting to Ibrox and when he finally arrived, the fans
did not take to him – not for a while.*

*McCoist impressed as a junior with Fir Park Boys Club but
joined St Johnstone where he made his debut as a bairn of 16.
Two years later, he slotted 23 goals in a season and went to
Sunderland, whose £400,000 bid was a cool £100,000 more than
Rangers had offered. But it did not work out at Roker where he
was always in a struggling side, and he eventually landed at
Ibrox for a knock-down £185,000 in 1983.*

*Wiser but no less bubbly, Coisty still found goals hard to come
by, scoring just nine in the League in his first season and could
not even find the net against Valetta – when Rangers won 8–0 in
Malta! 'It took me a lot longer to settle at Ibrox than I expected,'
he says. 'About two years I reckon, and I was nearly on my way
in the middle of all that.' Hard to believe in these days when he
can't miss, but the net was an elusive target in the early Eighties.
He also had to put up with 'about 15 different partners' – most in
the first few years – and changes in the manager's seat. John
Greig, who signed him, quit five months later, opening the way
for the return of Jock Wallace. Then came Graeme Souness and
then Walter Smith. Meanwhile the goals went from a trickle to a
mighty flood.*

Few players in Scottish football have achieved cult status. The man they simply refer to as 'Super', however, must be the president of that exclusive club. Ally McCoist is the darling of Ibrox, the hero, and, in Glasgow, as close to a living legend as you are ever going to get. He can be relied upon to get goals in anyone's company; relied upon never to give a pass in the penalty area; and always relied upon to turn up late for everything from training to personal appearances. But although he is now the king of Ibrox, things were not always so bright. In fact, at one stage, McCoist was on the way out – unfancied by his manager, unwanted by the fans.

Anyone who scores against Celtic is a hit down Ibrox way. McCoist's performance, grabbing a hat-trick and a trophy for the Gers over their deadly Old Firm rivals was the thing that turned the Light Blue tide in his favour. McCoist would be the first to admit that he was anything but flavour of the month during his early days at Ibrox. McCoist was looked upon as someone who had turned his back on the Glasgow club when the then boss, John Greig, first made the approach for the St Johnstone youngster. Instead, Sunderland was McCoist's choice and only when that move didn't work out did he accept a move to Glasgow.

Pleasing Rangers fans is difficult enough. Doing it after having snubbed them left McCoist with a real popularity mountain to climb. However, the first domestic Cup final played on the Sabbath gave McCoist his chance. 'I wasn't accepted at all by the Rangers punters,' he says. 'They were against me totally. Anything I did just wasn't good enough. Sandy Clark and I were taking some stick, there was a story going around about the two big lassies playing up front for Rangers – Sandra Clark and Alison McCoist. If chances were missed, it was my fault. If they were not created it was my fault. And if the defence was caught sleeping, you've guessed it. There were all sorts of things being said. That I was going to Cardiff City, that I was going full stop. Even though I turned out to be the hero against Celtic, I wouldn't have been a starter had it not been for others being suspended or injured. We played Linfield on the Tuesday night in a warm-up game and because Ian Redford and Robert Prytz were banned, I was played in midfield and was handed the same role against Celtic on the Sunday. You know, the gifted maestro, the ball player, the midfield general. Anyway, Big Jock Wallace was the manager and fancied me there, so that's where I started and was lucky enough to get the opener.

'Davie Cooper started things off on the left, where else? Coop slipped the ball through to Bobby Russell, who could always find anyone on the park. Bobby slipped the ball through Murdo McLeod's legs and Murdo repaid the compliment by tripping Bobby. So when the penalty was awarded, I walked up. The nerves did begin to go but I just hit it low and left and Packy Bonner went the other way. Big Jock made a substitution in the second half and I was pushed up the park to play alongside Sandy. Then big "Gas Meter", Peter McCloy, launched a long kick upfield. Sandy challenged Roy Aitken and the ball was coming down with snow on it. "Shirley" pushed Sandy's head into the ball and it came across for me to slide under Bonner. Then I just went away for a wee celebration at the Rangers end.'

However, the game was far from over. McCoist goes on: 'Celtic scored a brilliant goal – it hurts to say it – and it was a sore goal to lose. Tommy Burns flicked a free-kick over the wall and Brian McClair volleyed it home. Then with two minutes to go Celtic got a penalty. It was never a penalty. Never. Murdo McLeod dived. Dropped like a stone. Never a penalty. I felt sorry for the guy who gave it away. He played the ball, definitely played the ball. I saw him.' At this point, McCoist's rant breaks into a big laugh – it was McCoist who conceded the penalty! And Mark Reid converted.

'The whistle sounded for full-time,' he continues. 'We were all sitting around the centre circle and I felt great Just kidding. This was typical of my luck. Get a goal, then give away a penalty. The gaffer was out, waving the fist, getting some fire back into the bellies of his troops. When Big Jock was bellowing at you, you tended to listen. Anyway, things had a happy ending. In the first period of extratime, Jimmy Nic (Nicholl) dinked a wee pass forward on to the edge of the box. I can't remember if I actually got to the ball but big Roy came, clattered into me from behind and Mr Valentine pointed to the spot. You can sense why big "Shirley" was the candidate for so many Rangers Supporters Clubs' "Player of the Year" awards after that.

'Anyway, I stuck the ball on the spot again and even when I was running up, I hadn't decided where I was going to put it. Again, like the first, I hit it low and left, but this time Big Packy got down and pushed it out. Even now, it's amazing just how much you actually take in during what is only a split second. When he saved it, the Celtic fans behind the goal suddenly went up, all noise and colours. And they were still on their way up when I got to the rebound first and knocked it home. It was amazing: one second they were rising up, the next shooting back down again. And as that end was going quiet and the scarves and flags were coming down, this massive whoosh came from behind me, where the Rangers fans were celebrating the goal.'

Rangers: McCloy; Nicholl, Dawson, McClelland, Paterson, McPherson, Russell, McCoist, Clark (McAdam), MacDonald (Burns), Cooper.

Celtic: Bonner; McGrain, Reid, Aitken, McAdam, McLeod, Provan (Sinclair), McStay, McGarvey (Melrose), Burns, McClair.

Frank McLintock

ARSENAL 4 ANDERLECHT·3 (ON AGGREGATE)
Fairs Cup final (two legs): Brussels and Highbury, 22 and 28 April 1970.

Born in Glasgow on 28 December 1939, Frank McLintock graduated from that renowned inner city academy, the Gorbals, to Shawfield Juniors, Leicester City, Arsenal and QPR. He was capped only nine times, a modest reward for a magnificent defender and an inspirational skipper. Like club-mate Gordon Banks, McLintock was destined for greater things after being on the losing Leicester side in two FA Cup finals (1961 and 1963). He became the rugged central pillar of Arsenal's revival, which culminated in the Double in 1970–71, before ending a 20-year career at QPR. Typically, he was the most influential figure in the west Londoners' challenge to Liverpool in 1976, leading a less-gifted side to within just one point of the club's first-ever Championship. He is now a respected commentator on the game.

For Arsenal, *the* team of the Thirties, the late Fifties and Sixties were barren days. As the Manchester United of Matt Busby, the Liverpool of Bill Shankly and, most irritatingly of all, the Spurs of Bill Nicholson, stole the glory, the brow on the bust of Herbert Chapman is said to have furrowed, while the echoes of the marble halls had a hollow ring. 'When I signed in 1964, I was immediately made aware of how desperate the club was for success,' says McLintock. 'They had been *the* team, *the* Arsenal, for so long before the War but had won nothing since Joe

Mercer had led them to the League in 1953. And they were suffering. They had tried everything from changing the strip, the socks, the style of play. But still they couldn't win. But when I went, I felt they had the makings of a decent team.'

Although there were central defenders around of greater international and club pedigree than McLintock, the Scot was arguably Highbury's most significant acquisition since Alec James. At 5'10" and 11 stones 4 lb, he was hardly towering in the mould of Jack Charlton or Ron Yeats, and he lacked the exquisite craftsmanship of Bobby Moore or the dynamism of Dave Mackay. But the Glaswegian was just the tower of strength the marble halls' masonry needed. Possessing masterful timing and a terrific spring, he was dominant in the air, unflagging in spirit and a superb organiser. He was also one of the most consistent performers in the game. Still, it was six years before he was able to get rid of his jinx. Being in a modest Leicester side that went down to Spurs and then United was nothing to be ashamed of but footballers are superstitious types and, although McLintock was canny enough to dismiss the idea that the major prizes were destined to elude him, he completed a reluctant quartet of loser's medals when Arsenal were runners-up in the League Cup in successive years. And when it was said that the Fairs Cup, with its two-leg format, was the most difficult European trophy to win, he could be forgiven for thinking that Europe did not offer the easiest route to breaking his duck.

Perhaps the most enduring vision his many fans have of McLintock is of him racing up for a last-minute corner when the cause seemed lost. Countless times when the referee would look at his watch and the faithful were making for the turnstiles at one or even two goals down, the dark-haired Scot would arrive to bolster his attack. And once the danger had passed, he would sprint back to resume his defensive duties to counter any quick break. Quite simply, he never gave up. And when Anderlecht took a 3–1 lead in the first leg of the Fairs Cup final of

1970, he did not tell his troops, he implored them: 'We can still win this.'

They would not have expected anything less, even though it had taken a late Ray Kennedy goal to breathe new life into them. Two devastating strikes inside five minutes in the first half had tested even McLintock's mettle. 'The continental sides didn't bombard you like British teams,' he remembers. 'Their build-up was much more patient yet before you knew where you were, you could be two or three down.' After containing the home side for 25 minutes, Arsenal suddenly found themselves two down to goals from Devrindt and Mulder. The Londoners recovered their poise in the second half but in the 77th minute fell three down to a 'killer' goal from Mulder.

Manager Bertie Mee took off a badly buffeted Charlie George and brought on Kennedy, a strapping 18-year-old Geordie, who couldn't wait to join the fray. Four minutes after being introduced and with his first touch, Kennedy met an Armstrong cross and headed powerfully home. After the match, Mee conceded: 'Kennedy's goal was vital to us as it means we can face the second leg with confidence.'

McLintock remarked: 'We had spotted the weakness of the Anderlecht defence and I had seen enough to know that we could win the return with a packed Highbury behind us.'

More than 51,000 fans assembled, it must be said more in hope than expectation, as Arsenal set out to write a new chapter in their post-war history – and exorcise the ghosts of their recent past. However, those 17 fallow years wore heavily on the players in a nervous opening and it took a goal out of the blue to break the deadlock. An Armstrong corner had been partially cleared when Kelly sent a glorious half-volley soaring over a Belgian defensive wall. 'I didn't have time to take aim,' said Kelly. 'I just let go and hoped for the best. I could have jumped out of the stadium when I saw it go into the top of the net.'

The relief around Highbury was tangible but the job

Martin Peters – for once not ten years ahead but right on time – as he heads past Scotland's Bobby Clark to score for England at Wembley

The unflappable Alf Ramsey converting a penalty – England's third goal in their 6–3 humiliation by Hungary at Wembley in 1953. Grosics is the goalkeeper

A typical piece of early Peter Shilton excellence as he dives to thwart John Toshack of Wales at Wembley in one of his record 125 appearances for England

*Affectionately known as 'The King', Kevin Hector is in thoughtful mood
before one of his record 581 games for Derby County*

*One occasion when the ball is not 'tied' to Liam Brady's left foot as the
Arsenal midfield maestro tussles with Middlesbrough's Craggs*

Ian St John celebrates Jim Baxter's goal for Scotland against England at Wembley in 1963 as his Liverpool colleague Gerry Byrne (No. 3) looks on. As ever, the Saint was in position for the rebound

Jimmy Greaves, the 'Fagin of the penalty area', snatches a hat-trick in a six-goal win over Forest at White Hart Lane in 1962

Frank McLintock in characteristically combative mood, tangling with Bobby Moore in an England-Scotland international

was only half done and McLintock told his men to be patient. 'We couldn't go on all-out attack as they were a skilful side – they'd shown that in the first leg – and continentals were always capable of the counter-attack. So we just had to concentrate 100 per cent. The strain was enormous as we still needed two more goals to be sure but couldn't afford to let them score. I told them to just keep at it – for the whole 90 minutes. It was a difficult task but I knew we could do it.'

As the Gunners found their range, the anxiety that had hitherto inhibited their every stride was suddenly lifted and a series of telling moves soon had the Belgian defence rocking. But they refused to panic and, with Trappeniers a defiant figure in goal, must have felt they could hold out when they reached half-time with just one goal conceded.

In the second half, Anderlecht continued to play neat, if seldom threatening, football and Arsenal took the game to them. However, if the Gunners appeared in control of the match, the Belgians were still in charge of the tie – and time was ticking away. Anxiety crept back into the Londoners' play, passes went astray again and hearts stopped when Swedish international Nordahl hit Bob Wilson's post. As in the first period, Arsenal needed a goal and just when it looked as if it might elude them – and the faint-hearted began to feel they would be brave British losers – it came. With just 20 minutes to go and both full-backs pushing forward in an increasingly frantic Arsenal onslaught, McNab crossed and Radford rose to power home a header. The North Bank was in heaven and the Belgians visibly wilted. Even the faint-hearts fancied Arsenal now and when Charlie George produced a spot of magic to put Jon Sammels through two minutes later, it was all over. Highbury rejoiced.

McLintock paraded the trophy around the ground and, recalling the scenes of jubilation and his own overwhelming sense of relief, remembers 'being jostled like a rag doll. It was all good-natured stuff but we were so knackered, we had no strength left to resist and it was quite frightening.' But once in the dressing-room, he recovered his poise and let the achievement sink in. 'It was a magnificent non-stop performance – absolutely unbelievable. At last I'm able to get rid of that feeling that I'm a jinx player. This was my fifth major Cup final and the first time I've finished on the winning side. I'm overwhelmed.'

For Highbury as well as McLintock, the long wait was over and there were those filing past the bust of Herbert Chapman that night who could have sworn he was smiling.

Brussels

Anderlecht: Trappeniers; Heylens, Velkeneers, Nordahl, Kialunda, Cornelis (Peeters), Desanghere, Devrindt, Mulder, Van Himst, Puis.

Arsenal: Wilson; Storey, McNab, Kelly, McLintock, Simpson, Armstrong, Sammels, Radford, George (Kennedy), Graham.

Highbury

Arsenal: Wilson; Storey, McNab, Kelly, McLintock, Simpson, Armstrong, Sammels, Radford, George, Graham.

Anderlecht: Trappeniers; Heylens, Maartens, Nordahl, Velkeneers, Kialunda, Desanghere, Devrindt, Mulder, Van Himst, Puis.

Billy McPhail

CELTIC 7 RANGERS 1
Scottish League Cup final – Hampden Park, 19
October 1957.

*Born in Glasgow on 2 February 1928, like his brother John,
who played for Celtic and Scotland, Billy McPhail first showed
his paces with St Mungo's Academy before joining Queen's
Park. After four years with the amateurs, he went to Clydebank
and finally to Celtic. The injury-prone striker recalls the move:
'Bob Kelly had always wanted me but I warned him that I only
had one leg – I had had so many knocks. He insisted and asked:
"Can you do a job for us?" I said I could, hit a hat-trick against
Rangers and packed up the following year.'*

Almost as traditional as the sectarian clamour and intensity
of passion that accompany Old Firm games is the knife-
edge equilibrium of the contest. In the late Forties and
Fifties, no matter what the League positions, the narrowest of wins over the other half of Glasgow would be sufficient to illuminate the Stygian darkness of the pit or
make a long, cold winter in the shipyards almost bearable.
'There was never much in it,' says Billy McPhail. 'One
goal was often enough and if you went two-up, you were
away. That day we were on top and the ball was running
for us, but we did not feel relaxed as the other team always
got such a lift when they levelled. So what really did it for
us was Neil Mochan's goal just before the break. To go in
at half-time 2–0 up was unbelievable.'
In spite of winning a League game at Ibrox for the first

time since the War just a month earlier, Celtic had taken the field as underdogs. Since the end of the 1940s Rangers had won four League titles, two Cups and, unlike Celtic, had experienced European competition. Under the Czarist regime of Bill Struth and later under Scott Symon, the Light Blues were pre-eminent in Scottish football. McPhail, however, was unimpressed. 'It was a familiar story for us and we were quite relaxed about it. But it was always important for me to start well as I had scored inside ten seconds on my debut for Clyde.' McPhail didn't even get one in the first half at Hampden but he wasn't to be too upset about that – by the end of the game, time would stand still for him and all Celtic fans as Rangers would painfully discover.

Before an assembly of 82,293 the opening was tense – and scrappy. 'We had the wind behind us,' recalls McPhail, 'and had the better of it to begin with.' But having survived the first 15 minutes of Celtic dominance, Rangers at last began to assert themselves. However, there had already been misunderstandings at the back where Valentine, an untried Highlander, suddenly found himself in a distinguished line of succession as Rangers centre-half – and out of his depth.

George Young had retired and Willie Woodburn had been suspended *sine die* so in came Valentine. An early foul on McPhail caused referee Mowat to have a word in the youngster's ear and he appeared reluctant to go near the Celt after that. Equally worrying for the Gers, Celtic's Willie Fernie was taking charge. 'He reached perfection that day,' McPhail claims. 'And I just felt he would win it for us. At times he tried to do too much but early on he crossed and I got my head to it but hit the bar. Even so, I had this feeling that he'd do it for us.'

Fernie was superb but the real job was done by McPhail whose superiority over Valentine gave Celtic, as one reporter put it, 'as much room to roam as the Russian satellite'. It was after one such orbit in the 23rd minute that McPhail headed down for his partner, Sammy Wilson, to rifle home the opener from 12 yards. But despite the space which Fernie was now utilising and the force the whole half-back line was exerting, the Celts had to wait until a minute before half-time for the second. Mochan squeezed it in after gliding past two defenders on the by-line. The angle was impossible, Rangers disappointment profound.

McPhail admits it was a long time ago and his memory does not match his modesty, but he scored the third, 'getting my head to it before Valentine'. That was in the 53rd minute as Rangers, he recalls, 'collapsed'. If that is putting it kindly, it is typical of the hat-trick hero that he continually plays down his own role. 'Perhaps the man in the middle was not as good as he should have been,' is as far as he will go in criticising an opponent. But he did not allow that to halt the rampage – especially after Simpson had reduced the arrears just before the hour. Rangers briefly roused their blue and white legions but were soon blunted by McPhail's second – and his team's fourth. 'I can recall this one,' he says, 'but only thanks to a photo of about five Rangers defenders lying on the ground after my first attempt had come back off the bar.'

Sixty-seven minutes had gone and the Celts were 4–1 up. It was the stuff of dreams but there was more, much more to come. With the green and white hordes now in full cry, Fernie running the game and McPhail rampant, the Greens did not let up. With a quarter of an hour to go, Mochan crashed in his second and, five minutes later, McPhail achieved immortality when he capped a magnificent performance with a brilliant solo goal. Rounding the hapless Valentine, he raced on to sweep the ball past Niven with one of Hampden's finest. But modest to the last, when he was upended in the last minute, he refused the chance to make it four from the penalty spot. 'Charlie Tully came up to me and said, "Take it, Billy. Nobody's ever scored four against Rangers." But three was enough – if I'd missed it might have taken a bit of the shine off everything.'

Fernie stepped up to take Celtic into their Seventh

Heaven and the hat-trick hero was left to contemplate more personalised headlines like 'Bill Never McPhails'. When the whistle sounded, the humiliation was too much for many Gers fans whose response was to shower the pitch with bottles, leap from the stands and start running fights with whoever was in their path. It was a sad end to a sensational game but was not the reason McPhail remembers the immediate aftermath being a bit of a let-down. 'It was the biggest ever Old Firm win and yet it took a long time to sink in. I left the field with a sense of anti-climax.'

His disappointment was not eased by an amazing blunder by the BBC, who were televising the match. It afforded some consolation to one half of Glasgow but for the other, instead of being able to savour the highlights that night, they disbelievingly had to settle for watching just the first half. Camera-work was less sophisticated in those days and less efficient – at the start of the second half someone had forgotten to take the lens cap off! But the Celts had their revenge: even months afterwards in the streets of Glasgow, Rangers fans were wary of asking the time. For Celtic, whatever the hour, it was always 'seven past Niven'!

Celtic: Beattie; Donnelly, Fallon, Fernie, Evans, Peacock, Tully, Collins, McPhail, Wilson, Mochan.

Rangers: Niven; Shearer, Caldow, McColl, Valentine, Davis, Scott, Simpson, Murray, Baird, Hubbard.

Wilf Mannion

PORTUGAL 0 ENGLAND 10
Friendly International: Lisbon, 27 May 1947.

Born in Middlesbrough on 16 May 1918, Wilf Mannion wanted to become a shipyard worker but possessed a refinement more suitable for Swan Lake than Swan-Hunter. Robust but with a poise worthy of the ballet, he was an artist with a football, his deft brush strokes illuminating the bleak landscape of the industrial north-east. Soon hailed as the best boy footballer since Cliff Bastin, he was snapped up by 'Boro as if he was the Kohinoor diamond.

Mannion first revealed his sublime skills with South Bank St Peters and signed amateur forms for 'Boro in September 1936, turning pro the following January. Of a generation for whom the outbreak of War could not have been more untimely, the 'Golden Boy' made his mark immediately hostilities ceased. Having won four 'wartime' caps, he linked with other similarly deprived legends to earn just recognition and rave reviews in the post-War era. He scored a hat-trick in a 7–2 win over Northern Ireland in his first 'full' international and notched two for Great Britain against the Rest of Europe. But 26 caps was scant reward for an undoubted genius and said more about his brushes with authority than the quality of his rivals.

At 5' 6" and 11 stones, he boasted one of the best shots in the game, while his perception was almost psychic; his passing being so accurate and perfectly weighted he could find his colleagues in a crowd – and suddenly they would have space. After retiring prematurely in 1954, he had a second coming with Hull City six months later before winding down in the unlikely outposts of the lower leagues.

167

'Mannion is Mozartian in his exquisite workmanship,' wrote Donny Davies, of *The Guardian*, memorably. 'His style is so graceful and so courtly that he wouldn't be out of place if he played in a lace ruffle and the perruque.'

With locks as golden as his first touch, he was bound to be eulogised but for Wilfred J. Mannion the white shirt of England and the company of fellow maestros were quite enough. Alongside Messrs Matthews, Mortensen, Lawton and Finney, Mannion felt completely at home and this fabulous five were probably the finest forward line ever to wear the three lions. However, when they played together for the first time – against Portugal in Lisbon – the portents were not good.

'It was an end-of-season tour and we had just been beaten by Switzerland,' Mannion recalls. 'England were not supposed to lose to anybody in those days so you can imagine the stick we got from the press. Stan [Matthews] had had one of his rare off-days and the reporters had really got on to him.' The team for the Portugal match was picked on the plane – over the Pyrenees – and Finney came in for his debut, replacing Langton who had a knock. 'In Lisbon,' remembers Mannion, 'we met an Englishman, Bob Kelly, who had been helping the Portuguese and he warned us that they had their best side for many years. He said they were "very quick and clever", and also told us that we might struggle in the intense heat.' As if that were not enough, it was felt that both Matthews and Lawton would be up against it – their respective markers reputedly being measured at 6'2" and 15 stones.

As the teams came out, the setting could hardly have been more spectacular: a magnificent natural amphitheatre whose marble steps were teeming with a 65,000 crowd. Clad in the colours of the kaleidoscope, they were full of anticipation as the old masters took their bow. But there had already been drama, with England manager Walter Winterbottom concerned that two members of his team had soaked up too much of the festive atmosphere. Mannion remembers: 'Tom Finney and I had been sitting on the beach at Estoril in the boiling sunshine while the others had been sheltering under umbrellas. Walter disapproved. He said: "It's for mad dogs and *not* footballing Englishmen to go out in the midday sun." Nor did he take kindly to our excuse that we were used to it after serving in the Middle East and Italy in the Eighth Army! But neither Tom nor I felt any effect and in 13 seconds we went in front. And I had laid it on.'

With the shirt-sleeved crowd still settling, Mannion crossed for Lawton to hammer home. This goal was scored with the 'heavy' British ball and the England party looked on in amazement when it was replaced by the lighter, larger continental ball. But that was not the only thing that was changed. Heartened by his goal and relishing his partnership with Mortensen, Lawton put the Blackpool man through for the second, a terrific right-foot drive, after eight minutes. Three minutes later, Lawton went through on his own and in the 21st minute Finney opened his international account following a clever move down the left.

'After this,' chuckles Mannion, 'they changed the goalie – without telling anyone, not even the ref. Walter went to the touchline and skipper George Hardwick protested, but the ref did nothing. At 4–0 up, we weren't too bothered and Frank Swift said: "Well, you'll just have to put another four past him." Before half-time, Lawton had got three himself, and we might have eased up after that but when we went in at the break, we got a dressing down. Old Iron Man, Wilf Copping, a real disciplinarian, told us: "No slacking. Herbert Chapman always used to say that slackers never got anywhere. Keep on until their net is full of goals."'

That message and the lessons of Switzerland sank in. Instead of weaving pretty patterns which got them nowhere, England delivered a powerful punch at frequent intervals, demoralising the home side into further unsanctioned substitutions before they were finally counted out. No one enjoyed their football holiday in the sunshine more than Mannion, who prized open the home defence at will, while Lawton was a revelation alongside Mortensen, both players collecting four goals. Matthews, who made four, added one himself and ran the home defence ragged.

'Everybody scored but me,' says Mannion, 'but I played deep behind Lawton and Mortensen to collect the loose material and keep the link between them. We were unstoppable and even had two goals disallowed. It was a marvellous performance, one of the best ever by an England team. But old Kelly was right – the Portuguese *were* clever and quick, and never gave up. It was just masters against pupils.'

Portugal: Azevedo; Cardoso, Feleciano, Amaro, Mereira, Ferreira, Correira, Arajuo, Peyroteo, Travassos, Rogeiro.

England: Swift; Scott, Hardwick, Wright, Franklin, Lowe, Matthews, Mortensen, Lawton, Mannion, Finney.

Alex Miller

RANGERS 0 HIBERNIAN 1
Skol Cup semi-final: Hampden Park, 25 September
1991.

---

*Alex Miller was born in Glasgow in 1949 and played for his
school team before joining the Under-17 team Clydebank Strol-
lers at the age of 14. He signed provisional forms for Rangers in
September 1966 and joined the Ibrox club in January 1967, just
a few weeks before their ignominious and notorious Scottish Cup
defeat at the hands of lowly Berwick Rangers. He won three
League Championships, two Scottish Cups and five League
Cups before leaving Ibrox in January 1983 for a short stay in
Hong Kong with the South China team. In July 1983 he
returned to Scotland as player-manager for Greenock Morton
before moving on a few months later to manage St Mirren. In
December 1986 he was appointed manager of Hibs and in 1991
brought a trophy to Easter Road in the form of the Skol League
Cup.*

'All we asked of Alex Miller at the start of the season,'
said Hibs chairman Douglas Cromb, 'was that the team
showed a gradual and steady improvement.' If that sounds
more like a medical bulletin than a mid-term report, it
unconsciously reveals the trauma of the previous year at
Easter Road. Hibernian FC were recovering from a spell in
intensive care and reaching the first major final of the
season was nothing short of a miracle for a patient whose
condition had recently appeared terminal.

Edinburgh, the cultured capital of Scotland, had never

shared Glasgow's tribal passion for football, never engendered the hatred among the hordes nor hosted clashes between its rival clubs that seemed like rehearsals for Armageddon. Compared to the Old Firm legions, followers of Hearts and Hibs were few and far between and their proportionate lack of success encouraged the view that Edinburgh was not a football town. It certainly looked that way when Hibs' gates fell to 5,000 and, to anyone outside the Lothians, claims of 'latent support' appeared distinctly dubious. But in the city itself they should have known better. Especially at Tynecastle.

By 1990, Hibs, for all their fine traditions, were in the football and financial mire. Too long in the shadow of Hearts, the trophy room was gathering dust while debts piled up like dirty washing. A takeover seemed inevitable but what was never envisaged was that it would come from Tynecastle. And constitute a death warrant. Wallace Mercer, the high-flying Hearts chairman, offered just over £6 million for a controlling interest in Hibs, his intention being to incorporate them with Hearts, shut down both grounds and shift to a new site near the Glasgow motorway. He now knows what it is like to light a bonfire on an ammunitions dump.

The explosion of outrage that greeted Mercer's proposal was not confined to the Hibernian half of the city, nor even to the East of Scotland: Hearts' fans were also incensed but what was truly staggering was the incandescent rage of Hibs fans from Easter Road to Easter Island. Hibs' latent support was world-wide, pledges of undying loyalty to the club being backed by lumps of international currency from the four corners; supporters clubs from Australia to Canada were mobilised while hate mail for Mercer was delivered by pantechnicon. The Hearts chairman attempted to explain: 'There is considerable merit to Edinburgh and the Lothians of combining together the two principal clubs to try and create one unit which could compete at the highest level with clubs from the West of Scotland, and also have the opportunity of competing at the highest level in European football, should the situation ever arrive of a European League.'

His attempts at justification only fuelled the flames: 'Sadly, I appreciate there is going to be a considerable amount of emotional distress . . .' As far as Hibs were concerned, Mercer's·merger was the combining of the cannibal and his victim – and would be resisted with every possible means. The massive mobilisation of public support was a major factor, of course, but it was the subsequent backing of big business that ensured the club's survival. Mercer managed to raise his sums too, but, disturbed by death threats from the lunatic fringe, he abandoned his scheme. Hibs survived but, like Waterloo, it had been a close-run thing.

Miller, meanwhile, had had to steer his playing staff through these turbulent waters and, for him, even the rescue did not guarantee salvation. 'It had been a horrific time,' he says. 'And the word was that my job was on the line. So at the start of the 1991–92 season I told the directors if they wanted rid of me to say so. But they confirmed they were behind me. I had a year of my contract to go but I felt it was more important, with the changeover at the top, that everything was cleared up. There was a lot of pressure when the club was strapped for cash but we sold £2.5 million worth of talent to keep afloat, and were in the black when we kicked off in August. But all heads were on the block, only people who were prepared to muck in were to be kept and I was still under a great deal of pressure.'

From having to convince players they would get their wages, Miller then had to persuade them that they could win matches – not easy with an influx on the field to match that of the boardroom. But helped by his clear-the-air approach with the new gaffers and a special knack with youngsters, he was making progress. The £500,000 purchase of Keith Wright (made possible by the sale of Paul Wright and Keith Houchen) also helped, the striker scoring in every round of the Skol Cup and, by late September, Hibs had still to lose a game and were facing Rangers, Miller's old club, in the semi-final. 'It's a one-off game and we can cause an upset,' said the former Ibrox defender, who was well aware of the Light Blues' awesome record in the competition.

Rangers had only lost once since Hibs beat them in the semi-final in 1985–6 season. 'We know what we've got to do,' added Miller. 'I had already been to Hampden ten times and eight times came away a winner, but my players hadn't experienced that. I had to instil confidence into them and impress upon them that nobody wants to leave Hampden a loser.' Rangers boss, Walter Smith, agreed and refuted Miller's suggestion that his side might become 'complacent'. But even Smith reflected football's genuine joy that a great institution had survived: 'It's great to see them up near the top and featuring in a semi,' he acknowledged. 'Their unbeaten run makes them as dangerous opponents as we could get.' But even Miller admitted that his men would need a bit of luck to dislodge the holders and overwhelming favourites. 'We've been having the rub of the green lately and just hope it continues,' he said.

Rangers were surprised by Hibs' cool, measured approach from the outset. Given their opponents' recent history and their rampant desire to reach a landmark final, the Gers looked to be expecting a more frenetic opening from Miller's rag-tag outfit of youngsters and old hands. Oldest hands of all belonged to veteran 'keeper John Burridge whose bulging, Shiltonian presence between the posts was always a reassuring sight. 'John has worked like a bear and earned another year's contract – at 39,' said Miller. 'Murdo McLeod's experience was also a big factor in motivating the other players,' he added. Against Rangers, it was felt that the first half hour would be vital. And it was: 30 encouraging minutes had gone when Goram's punch landed at the feet of Weir. The midfielder glanced at goal and, seeing Goram stranded, lobbed over him for Wright to head home. The two Rangers defenders on the line were unable to stop it and all 11 were just as helpless when it came to fashioning an equaliser. Clearly stunned by the reverse and lacking the guidance of injured skipper Richard Gough, the Light Blues could not get back on terms. With both Mo Johnston and Mark Hateley well manacled and Hibs' confidence growing visibly, the holders struggled. A rare fumble by Burridge almost brought them level on the stroke of half-time but McGinlay booted away Johnston's effort. Lacking their customary fire and with their passes going astray, it did not look Rangers' day and when Johnston hit a post in the 70th minute, Hibs' dream drew closer. 'I thought we always looked the more likely winners,' said Miller. 'We deserved it. No question. And what really pleased me at the finish was that the players wouldn't do their lap of honour without me. Walter Smith and Archie Knox also looked me out and wished us all the best. After all we'd been through, it meant a lot to get such respect.'

Completing the fairy-tale journey from near oblivion to a major title, Hibs did what they failed to do six years earlier with a 2–0 victory over Dunfermline in the final. As a game, it never really fired but that did not matter to the hordes of Hibernian fans who gave the team a reception that surpassed anything seen on the other side of Scotland and compared with Celtic's homecoming from Lisbon in 1967. But even that, euphoric though it was, was not inspired by the desperation that made the Hibs' rise unique. No sooner had the Fifers been tamed than the celebrations began and the most difficult obstacle Hibs faced all season was the masses blocking the route back to Edinburgh. When the team coach finally made it through the wildly cheering tens of thousands, the gates of Easter Road were thrown open and scenes of unbridled joy engulfed everyone. Joe Baker was just one of many former greats who kissed the ground. Hibs had survived to fight and win another day and one half of Edinburgh and much of football rejoiced. Said Cromb: 'Who could have believed how well things have gone?' Miller added: 'It was the Rangers game that made us.'

Whatever made them, Miller had played a huge part and in future all football Phoenixes would have to go some if they were to match the rise of Hibernian FC in 1991.

Rangers: Goram; Stevens, Robertson, Brown, Spackman, Nisbet, McCall, Durrant, Hateley, Johnston, Huistra (McCoist).

Hibernian: Burridge; Miller, Mitchell, Hunter, McIntyre, McLeod, Weir, Hamilton, Wright, McGraw, McGinlay.

Stuart Pearce

COVENTRY CITY 5 NOTTINGHAM FOREST 4
Rumbelows Cup fourth round: Highfield Road, 28 November 1990.

Born in London's Shepherd's Bush on 24 April 1962, Stuart Pearce is a late developer at top level. Pearce played low-voltage, local football into his early twenties while pursuing his trade as an electrician. He represented Wealdstone where his strong tackling and fierce determination were spotted by Coventry City who paid just £25,000 to take him to Highfield Road in 1983. For all his prodigious commitment on the field, however, the Londoner remained fully earthed off it, continuing to ply his other trade until he'd made his name. He joined Forest in a double deal (worth £450,000) that also took Ian Butterworth to the City Ground in 1985. Under the tutelage of Brian Clough, Pearce honed his technique, adding explosive free-kicks and cavalier runs to his burgeoning repetoire. He soon became a cult figure in Nottingham where he is known affectionately as 'Psycho'. He replaced Kenny Sansom in the England side after just one appearance at Under-21 level and has not looked back. With his refreshingly old-fashioned view of playing for his country, he was 'honoured' to be asked to take over the captain's role from Gary Lineker in 1992.

With thighs like the twin towers, the courage of a cavalry officer and a shot like an artillery shell, Stuart Pearce is a chilling sight – even in the pre-match kick around. On the charge, opponents have been known to fall back before he's crossed the half-way line. And then fall down. Graham Taylor rewarded his commitment by making him captain of his country. 'I saw his face when we were struggling in a match against Turkey,' recalls the England manager. 'And it was almost wild. I need that.' Brian Clough needed it, too, as ballast for his team of neat-passing, non-combat choirboys. Yet the most feared defender in football of his day could still pass for a cherub – from the neck up. The blond mop of hair, the thin face, even the chest – which is hardly Schwarzennegger – are not what opponents expect to see in the man whose tackle has just deposited them in the twelfth row of the stand. But one look at those legs and they want to swap their shin pads for railway sleepers.

Being marked by Pearce is akin to enduring a survival course, with each tackle rating a mention in dispatches. Yet the man himself is deceptively soft-spoken: a strong, silent type whose London vowels are just another bit of camouflage for the Nottingham hard man. The enigma in him is confirmed by his choice of a defeat as his most memorable match. 'You seem to remember them more, somehow, don't you?' he asks.

With over 50 England caps and a belated haul of club honours, he has plenty of video material to choose from. So just what are we to make of him opting for not merely a reverse but one in which Forest let in five? And, if that's not enough, he reminds you: 'The bloke I was marking got a hat-trick!' As Brian Clough knows better than most, it confirms that his 'number three' is nothing if not honest.

For successful campaigners, failure is always going to be felt like a violent jolt to the solar plexus. But seldom can defeat have left a player more badly winded than Coventry's victory did Pearce that night. Forest were the holders, having won the Cup twice in successive seasons and not lost in the competition since November 1987. In that time they had won 22 successive matches while sustaining long runs in other knock-out events. If the League title remained elusive, Clough's team had acquired a belief in their near-invincibility in sudden-death situations. And for Pearce, the tie at Highfield Road contained the added poignancy of returning to his first League club. Terry Butcher, the Sky Blues' new player-manager, had dropped himself, abandoning a flirtation with the sweeper system in favour of a conventional back four, and settled down to watch just his third game in charge. Butcher, of course, had seen everything in a distinguished career with Ipswich Town, Rangers and England. Or so he thought. He had still to see his new side win and he watched . . . open-mouthed.

Forest made a strangely subdued start and had great difficulty dealing with corners. As Coventry's confidence grew, Forest wobbled even more at the back and soon found themselves two goals down. Kevin Gallacher, the home side's most expensive signing at £900,000, poked in the first after Hodge had hooked Speedie's header off the line and, just 76 seconds later, the former Dundee United winger's attempted cross looped over Crossley for a second. The Sky Blues were now rampant and, in the 29th minute, went further ahead when, of all people, Forest's England defenders got into a tangle. Des Walker and Pearce allowed the alert Livingstone to effectively seal the match – or so Coventry thought. Brian Clough, for whom clean sheets could be middle names, shook his head in disbelief when Gallacher completed a memorable hat-trick in the 34th minute, once again capitalising on Forest's inability to clear a corner. But the home side had reckoned without the Reds' unquenchable spirit – epitomised by their captain.

Inspired by Pearce's refusal to lie down – or was it the thought of what their manager might say to them at half time? – Forest stormed forward. And, sure enough, it was the manager's son who pulled a goal back. Nigel Clough had scored just three all season but gratefully reduced the deficit with a 20-yarder in the 36th minute. Forest began to scent survival when Nigel notched a similar effort six minutes later after good work by Jemson. 'We definitely thought we had a chance,' said Pearce, 'as it was already one of those games. Every time somebody attacked, they looked like scoring.' With Pearce now making more frequent sorties, Forest's confidence grew as Coventry's drained, and it was from Pearce's cross that Clough completed the second hat-trick of the night two minutes before the break. His goals had come in just eight minutes and, after having had the luxury of contemplating the quarter-final draw, Highfield Road was suddenly hushed – and in panic. Even Butcher admitted: 'As the goals began to fly in I wanted to be out there – not watching from the bench. I was so wrapped up in it that I kept hitting my head on the roof of the dug-out.'

When the teams reappeared, it was Forest who continued to rampage forward and an equaliser looked inevitable. It came when Garry Parker drove home in the 53rd minute and at that point few would have backed the home side. However, having somehow kept Forest at bay for ten minutes, Coventry remembered their opponent's weakness and counter-attacked. They were rewarded when, after Gynn's flag kick had not been cleared, Livingstone knocked in his second in the 63rd minute. It might have finished some teams but Forest rallied again, Hodge having a 'goal' disallowed for pushing at a corner, and Pearce, at his battling best, blasting a 25-yard free-kick at Ogrizovic. Parker and Jemson went close, too, but the home side hung on, the sigh of relief from the 16,304 fans being heard all the way across the Midlands.

'Heart-breaking,' admitted Pearce. 'We felt we'd get something after all that effort.' As for Brian Clough, he quipped: 'I'm lucky to still have a job after that defensive performance.' Gallacher said: 'It's one thing to score a hat-trick but I couldn't believe it came so quickly,' while Butcher claimed, tongue in cheek: 'I always knew we'd win 5–4.'

Clough stayed in his job and Pearce led his side to Wembley the following year – where he scored the opening goal in the FA Cup final defeat by Spurs. He had also missed a penalty in England's semi-final defeat to West Germany in the 1990 World Cup. But none of those could compare with the bizarre goings-on at Highfield Road that November night.

Coventry: Ogrizovic; Borrows, Edwards, Gynn, Billing, Peake, Gallacher, Speedie, Regis, Livingstone, Smith.

Nottingham Forest: Crossley; Laws, Pearce, Walker, Chettle, Hodge, Crosby, Keane, Clough, Jemson, Parker.

Steve Perryman

TOTTENHAM HOTSPUR 2 AC MILAN 1
UEFA Cup semi-final, first leg: White Hart Lane, 5 April 1972.

Born in Ealing on 21 December, 1951, Steve Perryman joined Spurs as an apprentice in 1967 after impressing with Middlesex, London and England Schoolboys. He turned pro two years later and became a White Hart Lane legend, making 655 appearances, many as inspirational captain. A cherubic 5'8" and 10st 10lb, he did not look like a strongman but was a tiger in the tackle and a dynamo in midfield. In international terms, he was perhaps a victim of his own versatility, playing anywhere for Spurs but winning only one full cap for England after earning Youth and Under-23 honours. His longevity at the top is illustrated by his capture of two UEFA Cup winners' medals 12 years apart – in 1972 and again in 1984. He played for the FA Cup-winning teams in 1981 and 1982 and was a UEFA Cup finalist in 1974. He won League Cup honours in 1971 and 1973 and was a runner-up in 1982. Converted with great success to full-back later in his career, he finally left Spurs for Oxford United in 1986. He entered management at Brentford, where he continued to play before joining Watford.

For a 'baby-faced killer' dissatisfied with his strike rate, there had never been a better time to hit the target. Twice. AC Milan, brazenly exhibiting the cynical face of Italian football, had just taken the lead. It was the home leg of the UEFA Cup semi-final at White Hart Lane and, as everyone in North London was aware, you simply did not score at the San Siro. Spurs had to get a couple here or they could forget it. Forget the tantalising prospect of an all-English final as Wolves were in the other semi, and forget the chance of landing the club's first piece of European silverware since the celebrated Cup Winners' Cup triumph of 1963. But it was not looking good: Spurs' formidable strike force of Martin Chivers and Alan Gilzean was finding it tough against the customary *catenaccio* defence and inclement tackling. But they were getting little protection from the referee and frustration was not helping Spurs find a way through. Even the ghostly Peters could not penetrate the massed Milanese ranks.

'Of all the big European nights at White Hart Lane,' recalls Perryman, 'the AC Milan game was the one I remember most. The crowd was terrific, we had a great team then but Milan were real giants. They had won the European Cup in '69 and had people like Schnellinger and Rivera. You had only to look at those black and red stripes and you had a shiver down your spine.' The Italians were intimidating, alright, yet the same could be said of Spurs: England, Chivers, Gilzean were of impressive build and pedigree. Mullery and Peters were masters. But when Milan saw Perryman they might have been forgiven for thinking he was the mascot!

However, when Spurs were stunned by a 25th minute goal, it was Perryman they looked to as much as skipper Alan Mullery. 'We had said that whatever we did, we must keep a clean sheet,' he remembers. 'We knew they would come to defend and thought that if we just went forward the goals would come. What we hadn't bargained for was going a goal down.' To be fair to Milan, they were always on the look out for a breakaway goal and, in Rivera, possessed one of the finest creative talents in the game. And, sure enough, it was the brilliant midfielder who set it up for Benetti to gleefully snaffle. 'I always remember the deathly silence when it went in,' says Perryman. 'To be behind on your own patch to them, of all people, looked hopeless. But it meant that I found myself going forward more and that's how the equaliser came.'

Perryman was always critical of his goals output but then, as his later years proved, he was probably a better defender than attacker. Perhaps he did not get into as many scoring positions as he might but he more than made up for that by the sixth sense he frequently displayed in his own box. On this occasion, however, the cause was desperate and he found himself on the edge of the Italian penalty area. Knowles, Peters and Gilzean combined and the Scot laid it back. Perryman hit it with all he had and the ball soared high into the Milan net. 'Gilly set it up for me and I just let fly. It put us back into the match and we had loads of pressure, but still couldn't find a way through. It was like coming up against a brick wall.'

Besides Perryman, Mullery was also an inspiration. Having been farmed out to Fulham to help with his rehabilitation from a pelvic injury, he had been recalled to the Tottenham squad, it could be said, in the nick of time. Milan protested about his eligibility right up to the kick-off but manager Bill Nicholson ignored them and so did the referee, UEFA having approved his playing on the morning of the match. The returning skipper received a tremendous roar of welcome when he turned out and now appeared hellbent on lifting a trophy after languishing at Craven Cottage. Indeed, all Mullery's leadership qualities were needed on a night when Milan seemed to be as interested in Oscars as European medals. Spanish referee Mariano Iglesias said: 'There was a lot of acting by the Milan side, but I ignored it.' Spurs' forwards wished he hadn't and felt that the Italians were getting away with murder. On they would press only to be thwarted by a cynical lunge and thespian dive. But on the hour the cynicism sank to a new punishable low and Sogliano was giving his marching orders. 'For twice refusing to move back to allow a free-kick to be taken,' said the ref. Ten men meant a chink in the armour, a crack in the wall.

Spurs had renewed hope. Four minutes later they were in front.

In spite of playing their 60th match of the season and their sixth in 12 days, the Londoners showed no signs of fatigue. They did, however, tire of the constant play-acting and childish antics of their opponents. Perryman is not far off the mark when he says: 'Hitting long shots from outside the box was probably the only way we could score. The second goal came when a corner was headed out of the area. It bounced and then I managed to control it. I just hammered it and in it went. Before that I had the feeling that it might have been one of those nights.'

But a 2–1 lead over such arch-spoilers and counter-attackers as Milan was hardly enough to instil confidence in the Tottenham ranks – as Perryman confirms. 'We were slightly disappointed as a 1–0 defeat over there meant we were out. But,' he concedes, 'it was a lot better than losing or even drawing, and we felt we had a good chance. And I was happy with my own display. I was saddled with the tag of being a hard-working midfielder so to score both goals against AC Milan was really something. I was even a hero with Milan's arch-rivals Inter – as we discovered when we stayed at the hotel complex in their training ground for the return leg. We had real VIP treatment there.' But according to AC's coach Nereo Rocco, that would be all Spurs would get. 'I'm delighted,' he said after the first leg. 'Now we only need one goal and we're in the final.' They got their one goal, alright, but Mullery's 'goal of a lifetime' secured a 1–1 draw and meant that Spurs were in the final.

Wolves beat Ferencvaros and the two English First Division teams duly slugged it out over two legs. Spurs won 3–2 on aggregate with two goals from Chivers at Molineux proving decisive. But no one will forget the two unstoppable drives by the young midfielder against Milan. The kid who claimed he couldn't shoot straight had broken down the brick wall.

Tottenham Hotspur: Jennings; Kinnear, Knowles, Coates (Neighbour), England, Naylor, Gilzean, Perryman, Chivers, Peters, Mullery.

AC Milan: Cudicini; Sabdini, Zignoli, Anquilletti, Schnellinger, Rosato, Sogliano, Benetti, Bignon, Rivera, Golin (Zazzaro).

Martin Peters

MANCHESTER UNITED 1 TOTTENHAM HOTSPUR 4
League: Old Trafford, 28 October 1972.

Born in Plaistow on 8 November 1943, Martin Peters played for Dagenham, Essex and London schools before enjoying the classic international apprenticeship: representing England at schoolboy, Youth and Under-23 levels, then winning the first of his 67 caps in 1966. Signed as a pro for West Ham in 1960, he made his name in the club's most illustrious 'firm' of Moore, Hurst and Peters and collected a European Cup Winners' Cup medal in 1965. Scorer of the second goal in the World Cup final triumph over West Germany, he captained his country four times and broke the British transfer record in 1970 when he left Upton Park for Spurs in part-exchange for Jimmy Greaves. Valued at £200,000, he handsomely repaid Bill Nicholson, helping the club to the Fairs Cup in 1972 and the League Cup twice (1971 and 1973). A UEFA Cup finalist in 1974, he joined Norwich City in 1975, and then Sheffield United where he was player-coach. He later worked in insurance with old pal Geoff Hurst.

For a man supposed to be 'ten years ahead of his time', Martin Peters coped admirably with being one minute short of immortality. Having justified Alf Ramsey's famous remark by putting his country on the road to apparently certain victory in the World Cup final of 1966, the West Ham midfielder had to settle for a place among the also-scoreds. West Germany's Weber robbed him with that controversial equaliser 60 seconds from time and then

187

a club colleague brusquely commandeered the rights to deification. Geoff Hurst acknowledges that his hat-trick 'changed my life' but Peters remained unaffected, continuing to play like a man from another decade. The honours and accolades rolled his way with conveyor-belt regularity, three Cup-winners' medals in successive years assuaging the memory of another World Cup game against the Germans – and that mortifying defeat in Mexico. 'But the game that stands out for me, the World Cup final apart,' says Peters, 'is when I scored four at Old Trafford. Not many people do that.'

Lesser players than Peters might have baulked at being asked to fill the boots of Alan Gilzean, a cult figure at White Hart Lane and among the game's greatest predators. But when the gangling Scot damaged an ankle before the clash with Manchester United, Peters did not hesitate to step up among the strikers – even though his normally deft touch had temporarily deserted him. 'I had gone nine games without scoring and had even missed the same penalty twice, so I was beginning to wonder where the next goal was coming from,' he admitted. But following in goal-den footsteps was nothing new for the Tottenham captain – he had not taken much persuading over that part-exchange with Jimmy Greaves. And as if that were not an onerous enough burden, Peters was saddled with being one of Britain's most expensive players with a value of £200,000.

Although he was never meant to slot into Greavsie's striker's role, the goals Peters regularly notched were a major influence in Nicholson's strategy – midfielders who could find the net were becoming priceless as defences tightened – so the Spurs boss had no qualms about asking his costly disciple to play up front alongside Martin Chivers. United, even with Law, Best and Charlton still in the side, were in decline and Spurs still conjured hopes of a Championship challenge when the two giants clashed at Old Trafford in the autumn of 1972. So was this, after years of mysterious ghosting, at long last, a straightforward role? 'Well, not quite. I sort of floated on Chivers's right, playing inside and more forward than usual,' Peters explained. But the cultured East Ender, whose long white sleeves and swivel of hips accentuated his leanness, did not do anything so inelegant as to run through defences: he glided through them, swaying one way and then the other as the tackles came, seldom hurrying but moving, like a ship in the night, with silent purpose. For Frank O'Farrell's beleaguered legends that day, he was as lethal as a nuclear submarine.

Peters remembers: 'We knew United were on the wane but you never go to Old Trafford thinking it's a formality. Certainly not when you've got players of that calibre against you. And we had not won there in the League for donkeys years, either. But it was one of those days when everything goes right – even if it felt strange not being in midfield.'

United's increasingly distraught defenders also found it strange and played him throughout as if they believed the mythology. There was always a certain mystique about Peters which Ramsey had perpetuated. Even when Malcolm Allison had tried to puncture the myth with his irreverent 'If he's ten years ahead of his time, we've got to wait ten years for him to come good' comment, the Peters aura survived. There were occasional mutterings about workrate, but generally he rode smoothly over them – like he did over those 'non-existent' tackles.

'I was saddled with all that rubbish about fading out of a game for half an hour and then suddenly ghosting in,' he says. 'But that's because people saw the two runs when the ball arrived but didn't notice the hundreds when it didn't.' No, he was too smart for his colleagues some of the time and it was this 'extra-sensory' perception that led to him being labelled as 'the ghost' – and why Ramsey claimed he had arrived on the scene a decade too soon. But for United it was a case of 'call the exorcist'. Drifting away from his 'marker' with the ease of the Invisible Man, Peters combined the elegance of Hoddle and the control and timing of Cruyff to single-handedly destroy what, on paper at least, was a powerful line-up. Relishing his freedom, he roamed and tormented a hard-pressed defence and then, after 20 minutes, he pounced. With the visitors already in total command, a long ball from Cyril Knowles eluded both Chivers and Sadler, and when Stepney came out, Peters, who had characteristically appeared from nowhere, found his first shot blocked. 'But I got a lucky rebound off Stepney and hooked it in,' he recalls.

With Spurs continuing to play superb football, he struck again four minutes later. Jimmy Pearce collected from Ray Evans and crossed, Ralph Coates mis-hit a shot and Peters knocked it home. 'Through Alex's legs this time, I think,' he chuckles. Pearce, chasing a 'lost' cause, gathered on the left and laid on the hat-trick goal – another close-range effort – in the 35th minute. 'I managed to creep in behind everyone,' Peters explains modestly.

United were now in disarray and Spurs were taunting them with their sweeping football – and their skipper could hardly believe that it was not yet half-time and he had scored a hat-trick. 'It was not the first I got but I couldn't believe I'd done it at Old Trafford,' he said.

United could not believe it either, and although they showed more spirit in the second half, Spurs were always going to halt their run of nine successive League defeats on the famous ground. Indeed, they took to strolling and were punished when Charlton pulled a goal back just before the hour. Peters decided to restore the Cockerel's strut and nodded a Knowles' cross past Stepney from 12 yards. 'That was nice,' he said. 'I'd never scored four in the League before. I might not have got any if Gilly had been fit. But I'll be happy to move back into midfield when he is. I have played better games but it's hard to top that for a memory. United fans were reduced to a stunned silence.'

Spurs had justified their manager's bold new attacking policy away from home and it was left to Law to sum up Peter's performance. 'This man takes up positions better than anyone else in football.' And then he shook his head.

The ghost allowed himself a smile – Old Trafford had been well and truly haunted.

Manchester United: Stepney; Watson, Dunne, Law, Sadler, Buchan, Morgan, MacDougall, Davies, Best, Charlton.

Tottenham Hotspur: Jennings; Evans, Knowles, Pratt, England, Dillon, Pearce, Perryman, Chivers, Peters, Coates (Neighbour).

Michel Platini

FRANCE 3 WEST GERMANY 3 (AET) WEST GERMANY WON 5–4 ON PENS.
World Cup semi-final: Seville, Spain, 8 July 1982.

Born in 1955 in Joeuf, the grandson of an Italian immigrant, Michel Platini began as a centre-forward at Nancy, where his father was coach. He played for France in the 1976 Olympics and won his first full cap the same year. He notched 98 goals in seven seasons before moving to St Etienne in 1979. He dropped back to midfield but still continued to find the net, his free-kicks being the most feared in the game. This potent weapon, allied to exquisite control and rare perception, made him the world's leading footballer in the early 1980s.

Juventus paid £1.2 million for him in 1982 and went on to win three League titles in four years. Platini scored the penalty that pipped Liverpool in the fateful 1985 European Cup final in Heysel. He was European Footballer of the Year three times in a row (1983–85) and eclipsed Juste Fontaine's scoring record before retiring with 41 goals in 72 internationals. He played in the final stages of three World Cups (1978, 1982 and 1986) but enjoyed perhaps his finest hour when he led France to the European Championship, scoring in every match (including two hat-tricks) in Paris in 1984.

Any doubts about who the good guys were in the semi-final of the 1982 World Cup in Seville were removed when France were awarded a penalty in the 27th minute. Forster held Rocheteau, the whistle sounded and up stepped Platini to kiss the ball before sending the 'keeper the wrong way. 'I did it for luck,' he explained. Most neutrals and all romantics were already in the French camp while the lacklustre Germans had let down their followers by losing to Algeria and then contriving a 1–0 win over Austria. This farce ensured that both nations advanced to the second phase – and that Algeria didn't. It also caused one German fan to burn his national flag in disgust, while FIFA 'regretted the tactical and technical behaviour of the teams concerned'. The timing was unfortunate: football was suffering from a growing cynicism and a creeping malevolence besides running out of goals. It badly needed a good World Cup but what it was getting was stodge and a bitter taste. France, with a more than a hint of garlic, were providing much of the palatable fare and their cavalier football was as popular as the Brazilian samba. It was very good – and very Gallic.

Platini knew that his French side needed luck against the Germans. Jupp Derwall's side were not playing well and had injuries and illness to worry about. Their star striker, the great Karl-Heinz Rummenigge, was being nursed along on hot pepper poultices and pills, Breitner had sun stroke and, without worthy successors to the masterly likes of Beckenbauer and Muller, they struggled to justify their positions as pre-event favourites. But as Platini was well aware, they were never beaten until the final whistle. He only had to think of England in 1966 and 1970 to know that.

The Frenchman also knew that fortune had been against his country in the previous World Cup when they had outplayed eventual winners Argentina in a group match but had been on the wrong end of several bizarre decisions. It had looked as if it might be going wrong again when they went down 3–1 to England in their first encounter in Spain. They had looked the classier team but never overcame Bryan Robson's strike in the 27th second. Later they did get their act together and were surprised to find themselves being held by an improved West Germany after the first half-hour. Having shaken off their stomach

bugs and self-doubts, the Germans played their most positive football of the tournament and deservedly took the
lead through Littbarski in the 18th minute.

France were shaken. After 15 games between the two
countries with five wins apiece and five draws, they felt
the time had come to nose in front. They were altogether
more fluid than their opponents and possessed a mobility
and penetration that matched the Dutch 'Total Football'
masters of the previous decade. And if there was no
Cruyff, there was a worthy successor in Platini. Shirt outside shorts, dark locks dangling over collar, deft sway of
the hips, delicate control, he caressed the ball in one move
and dispatched it like an Exocet in the next. He lacked
lightning pace but hardly needed it when he could beat a
man with no more than a Gallic shrug.

Platini's penalty lifted France and they had the better of
the rest of the half, preferring subtle water colours to the
sweat of their opponents. It was fascinating stuff and 1–1
at half-time was a fair reflection of the endeavours. And
Platini felt the luck was turning – Littbarski having rattled
the French bar just before the break. But five minutes into
the second-half, Genghini limped off to be replaced by
Battiston as France sought to take command. Ten minutes
later, Battiston was being given oxygen as he was carried
off on a stretcher – the most infamous foul in the history of
the game had turned the Championship.

There was a strut and a purpose to Platini's play as he
pierced the German defence once more with a stunning
through ball. Battiston, sensing the opening that could put
his country into its first final, latched on to it and sent a
drive past Schumacher. But Battiston did not see it rattle
the outside of the post and go harmlessly wide for a goal-
kick. He did not see it because he was unconscious. Sensing the danger, Schumacher had raced from his line, but
instead of diving at Battiston's feet to grab for the ball or
up-ending him and hoping for the benefit of the doubt in
the ensuing tumble, the 'keeper resorted to a brutal fore-
arm chop. It would have been illegal in karate and hard to

justify in an alley-way, let alone in a World Cup semi-final. Four years before Maradona's notorious 'Hand of God', here was a cold-blooded mugging and, like the Argentinian's punch over Peter Shilton, it went unpunished. Dutch referee Charles Corver gave a goal-kick and did not even caution Schumacher whose act of shame most Frenchmen felt merited not just a sending off but a lengthy suspension – preferably in the Bastille.

So France were not only deprived of a just penalty but also numerical advantage, and it would have been hard to imagine even the Germans overcoming a double blow of this magnitude. However, from the way Platini was running the game from midfield, it looked as if the good guys would still triumph – even though Amoros's 25-yard drive rebounded off the German bar in the last minute. Two minutes into the extra period France went in front when Tresor volleyed home following a free-kick by Giresse. When Giresse rifled in a third off a post six minutes later it seemed all over – even though the half-fit Rummenigge had now been pitched desperately into the fray.

But France, intoxicated by their own vintage attacks, eschewed defence and, unbelievably, did not close the game down. Barely 20 minutes away from immortality, it was the strategy of the Light Brigade and they poured forward with same abandon as those ill-fated cavalrymen. Rummenigge, hamstrung and hurting, still retained his machine-gunners' eye for the target and was able to turn in Littbarski's centre at the far post. At that the proud cockerel panicked. The strut was now a totter and the Germans, sensing that they could escape from the dead yet again, came forth in numbers. But when the equaliser came it still took the breath away, Klaus Fischer effecting an over-head bicycle kick so stunning that it would have won a design award at Raleigh. It also ensured the World Cup's first penalty shoot-out.

A shaken France now not only had to come to terms with their own hari-kari tactics which had brought them to this unworthy climax but had to hide their resentment at the continued presence of Schumacher in goal. A novice might have survived a period of open play but the harshness of the shoot-out would surely expose all but a 'keeper of the highest class. The odds favoured Germany so when Giresse sent Schumacher the wrong way with the first kick, France were entitled to feel relieved. But then, amid tension more suited to the nearby bullring than the Sanchez Pizjaun Stadium, Kaltz levelled, Amoros made it 2–1 and Breitner brought it back to 2–2. Then it was Rocheteau and 3–2 to France. Then Stielike and the first miss! The German looked as if he wanted the ground to swallow him – until Schumacher saved a weak shot from Six. Littbarski equalised and then both Platini and Rummenigge scored. It was 4–4 from the mandatory five penalties apiece but now it was sudden death.

A time for heroes to become villains . . . and villains to become . . . Bossis hit his shot firmly but Schumacher dived – and made a marvellous save. It was up to Hrubesch. Hollywood would not have let it happen but when he sent Ettori the wrong way, the good guys had lost.

The tears did not stop in France – most romantics were crying for football although the Germans deserved credit for their latest and most remarkable resurrection. Platini said: 'I'm sure the world knows that the best team lost. But in a way we have only ourselves to blame. If the Germans had led 3–1 they would have closed the game up. But it is not in our nature. We like to be adventurous. Perhaps this is one time when we should have defended.'

France: Ettori; Bossis, Janvion, Tresor, Amoros, Tigana, Giresse, Platini, Genghini (Battiston [Lopez]), Rocheteau, Six.

West Germany: Schumacher; Kaltz, Stielike, K-H. Forster, Briegel (Rummenigge), Dremmler, B. Forster, Breitner, Magath (Hrubesch), Littbarski, Fischer.

David Platt

Born in Chadderton, near Oldham, on 10 June 1966, David Platt was six weeks old when England won the World Cup. He first played rugby league – not football – and wanted to become a jockey but his appetite would not allow it. Having switched to the round ball, he developed a craving for goals which he sated as a teenage centre-forward. At 17, he quit his studies at Oldham Tech to join Manchester United on a £25-a-week YTS course, but after failing to get into the Reserves he was given a free transfer to Crewe. Ron Atkinson later confessed: 'I don't make too many mistakes but that was definitely one of them.' Under the guidance of Dario Gradi, he had a spell on the wing – still scoring regularly – and attracted '57 offers' before Graham Taylor's £200,000 took him to Villa. The fee was a Fourth Division record but soon looked a bargain as Platt earned England Under-21 and 'B' honours before making the senior side within 30 months of his departure from Crewe. Nicknamed 'McDonald' for his penchant for fast foods, he played in the Villa side which gained promotion to Division One and then there was a small matter of the World Cup. Afterwards there came the inevitable lira-strewn path to Italy, first Bari for a British record £5 million then Juventus and, equally inevitably in many eyes, the England captaincy.

David Platt is one footballer who will never mind changing at Crewe. Shunted into what must have seemed like the ultimate siding from his beloved Manchester United, the Lancashire lad came close to quitting the game before discovering the main line to fame and fortune. Lesser characters than the mature and eminently sensible kid from the Pennine foothills might literally have gone off the rails but not this second son of *The Guardian* production director. In 18 months at Old Trafford, Platt had not got past the third team and with five centre-forwards lining the tracks in front of him, his career faced nothing but delays with few apologies. Crewe changed everything. 'He was not obviously exceptional at anything,' said Gradi, 'but he was good at everything, especially timing his runs into the penalty area.'

Bryan Robson had been pretty good at that, too, and when the England skipper of the late Eighties began to show his age, Platt's knack of scoring and all-round talents were viewed with gathering interest. The Villa man was increasingly seen as a possible replacement for the irreplaceable, but he had to get into the team first. However, the timing of his run was as immaculate as ever: making his full England debut against Italy in November 1989, at the age of 23, he earned selection in Bobby Robson's squad for the 1990 World Cup. Although not an established member of the 'first XI', it was a glorious opportunity to arrive.

'I don't think Bryan's situation necessarily strengthens my chances,' said Platt when Captain Marvel's fitness was once again in doubt months before the squad for Italy was chosen. 'And it's wrong to write him out of the World Cup at this stage.' He was right – both Robson and Platt were selected but England had made their characteristically stumbling start to Italia 90. Robson was injured yet again and the pundits were writing off both the skipper *and* England. But somehow they muddled through their group games to find themselves jousting with Belgium for a quarter-final berth. Gazza was beginning to show, Mark Wright and Des Walker were holding the defence together and victory did not look beyond them. But Belgium were a good side and the consensus was that it would be a close-run thing. Even team selection would be agonising and Platt did not make it – partly because he was just the kind of player managers love to have up their sleeves and partly because Bobby Robson did not know him as well as his two previous club managers did. 'He gives us a footballing intelligence,' said Taylor soon after he'd taken him to Villa. 'He influences the whole team.' Gradi said: 'He has a great willingness to run. The work he did on the wing, up and back in a 4–4–2/4–2–4 formation for us, helped create the stamina that he has now.' Taylor added: 'I knew when I signed him that he could play anywhere. He's not quick but quick at the right time. He's not great in the air but he scores with his head. Timing. He continually exceeds his talent. When I go to sleep on a Friday night, I don't worry about David Platt.' Bobby Robson wasn't worried either but kept his options open. Platt takes up the story.

'Sitting on the bench in any game is not what a footballer wants,' he says. 'However, when it is in a World Cup and you only made your debut for the national side eight months earlier, there is some sort of recompense, especially when five unlucky people are not even on the bench and Bryan Robson had already returned home due to an injury. Watching was difficult. Jan Ceulemans was a hair's breadth away from opening the scoring for Belgium when his shot struck the outside of a post, but this was cancelled out when John Barnes' legitimate "goal" was ruled out for offside.

'The second half was no easier, the manager and substitutes on the bench being right behind Enzo Scifo's curling shot which thumped against a post but came back out to safety. After 75 minutes, I made my entrance as substitute for Steve McMahon. Fourteen minutes later with the score still at 0–0, a cross from Chris Waddle was helped on by Gary Lineker and I met it with a swift shot that just missed the outside of a post. And so it was that we entered into extra time with the manager already having nominated his penalty takers in the event of the game being a draw after the extra 30 minutes. I was to be one of the "lucky" ones".'

Platt did not know just how 'lucky' he was going to be. He continues: 'Extra time was a drab affair with both sets of players feeling the effects of a gruelling 90 minutes.' Indeed, the tense, hard-fought contest between two evenly matched teams wore on with neither side looking capable of a breakthrough. England certainly appeared resigned to the lottery of a shoot-out as Platt confirms. 'Everyone thought it was going to go to penalties, including me,' he acknowledges. 'However, in the last minute something happened which not only changed the game but also the life of David Platt. Paul Gascoigne broke free and was stopped by a foul about 40 yards outside the Belgian goal line. Paul took the free-kick himself and as it floated down inside the box I had lost my marker well enough to be able to meet it on the volley as it came over my shoulder. It was one of those that 99 times out of 100 you either do not connect with or the ball goes way over the bar. This one didn't, and before I knew it, I was racing away with my arms aloft after seeing it nestling in the back of the net.'

And that is how a modest man describes one of the most dramatic goals in World Cup history. It ignited England, captured the doubting Thomases at home and alerted the world to the possibility that Bobby Robson's men could actually land the trophy. In a memorable quarter-final with Cameroon, England came from behind to reach the semi-final and that epic encounter with Germany. That time it did go to penalties and Platt, one of the 'lucky' ones, was one of England's scorers. But it is doubtful if he will ever score a more amazing goal than the bicycle kick that sank the Belgians. As his old Crewe boss might have put it: 'He's not great at anything but bicycle kicks . . .'

England: Shilton; Pearce, Walker, Butcher, Parker, Wright, Waddle, McMahon (Platt), Gascoigne, Lineker, Barnes (Bull).

Belgium: Preud'homme; Gerets, Clijsters, Demol, Grun, De Wolf, Van der Elst, Scifo, Versavel (Vervoort), Degryse (Claesen), Ceulemans.

Sir Alf Ramsey

TOTTENHAM HOTSPUR 1 BLACKPOOL 2
FA Cup semi-final: Villa Park, 21 March 1953.

Born in Dagenham, Essex, on 22 January 1920, Alf Ramsey played for Essex Schools, Five Elms FC and for the Army during the War. He signed amateur forms for both Southampton and Portsmouth but turned pro with Saints in 1944. He had already guested for them as a mature-looking private in the DCLI and, confirming his late development, made his debut for England when almost 30. He joined Spurs for £21,000 in May 1949, and, exuding calm assurance, helped the Londoners to the Second Division title in 1950 and the League Championship the following year. Entrusted with penalties for club and country, he survived the two greatest shocks the England team suffered, losing to the USA in 1950 and to the Hungarians in 1953, but still managed to convert a spot-kick against Puskas & Co. An astute reader of the game with a fine positional sense, he was as imperturbable as he was single-minded, refusing to smoke, being reluctant to drink and always doing things his own way: solid, trustworthy and not unpopular, but definitely not one of the boys. When invited to an evening on the town, he would decline in his inimitable, clipped tones: 'Most certainly not.'

After retiring in 1955, he took over at Ipswich, then in the Third Division, and was told he would have to buy. He refused and took them to the Second Division the following season. Again he was implored to bolster his playing strength – or face relegation. He acquired a couple of players cheaply and eventually led them into Division One. Now, conventional wisdom decreed, he really did have to strengthen the squad. He did not. They won the League Championship in 1961–62. His reward was the England job and, uncharacteristically, he promised: 'We will win the World Cup.' He was knighted for doing so. With what was generally considered an even better side, he was unfortunate to bow out in Mexico in 1970 and was harshly dismissed in 1974 after losing just 17 times in a 113-match reign. Much loved by his players, he had the courage to leave Jimmy Greaves out of the 1966 World Cup final – and was rewarded when Geoff Hurst scored a well-documented hat-trick. He became a board member at Birmingham City in the mid-Seventies but his name will be forever associated with England's finest footballing achievement: not only did they win the World Cup, they did so playing his way.

Whether he was being coaxed into celebrating a glorious victory by a delirious bench or consoled after an agonising defeat, Alf Ramsey kept his head while all about him were losing theirs. John Arlott wrote that 'he can watch his side lose without a shout, an anguished gesture or even the slightest nibble at his nails'. The two most memorable matches in his managerial career, England's 1966 triumph and 1970 disaster against West Germany, were perfect examples of his legendary unflappability. But his recall of a much earlier match, as a player, is perhaps even more illuminating.

A semi-final defeat is the most demoralising of all, such occasions frequently seeing dressing-room doors slammed shut as the dream of a showpiece final is dashed for another season and, in some cases, forever. It is not unusual for grown men to shed the odd tear, for youngsters to be beside themselves and for managers to require much more than the chairman's vote of confidence before they can face the world, let alone the press. All this is bad enough if you simply belong to the losing side but if you have contributed significantly to their downfall by scoring an own goal or presenting the ball for the opposition's winner, it can mean a busy night for the Samaritans. Only Sir Alf

'The Unruffled' would choose such an occasion as the match of his life.

Forgotten now as an eventful precursor to the 'Matthews final', the 'Matthews semi-final' was, says Sir Alf, 'an absolutely marvellous game of football. It really stands out even today,' he insists. 'Of course, the World Cup final was a special achievement but as a football match, the game against Blackpool would be hard to beat.'

Contrary to what his critics might think, Ramsey reveals a rare human weakness: 'It was a very sad occasion, too, as I rather made a mess of things . . .' Not only that, he did so with his last touch, when a replay seemed certain! But he is still happy to recall the game's more uplifting moments. 'I can remember it being a very fine match and having the best of everything,' he says. 'It was one of those unusual occasions when almost everybody seemed to get the best out of himself.' *The Times* agreed, beginning its match report: 'Every sport at one time or another will throw up a dramatic highlight that will live vividly in the mind always.' And this was before the national desire for Matthews to land a Cup-winners' medal had gathered momentum.

With respect to Bolton and Everton, who were disputing the other final berth at Maine Road, the North-South clash looked the more fascinating contest: Spurs, after all, had been champions two seasons before and were famous for their push-and-run style while Blackpool, besides Matthews, boasted Mortensen and Mudie in a magnificent forward line. Against them was the redoubtable Roy Burgess, Ted Ditchburn in goal and, of course, the unflappable Ramsey.

If the rest of the country had not yet woken up to the fact that Matthews was nearing his elusive prize, the wing wizard himself seemed well aware of it as he produced a truly dazzling display. And it was from his precise corner in the sixth minute that Perry headed the Tangerines into the lead. But for all Matthews's mastery, it was Tottenham who took charge, as *The Times* noted, 'once Ramsey, cool and masterful, had reminded his colleagues of their true stature and artistry'. On two occasions, the Lancastrians had the woodwork to thank for preserving their lead, McClellan brushing a post after a length-of-the-field move begun by Nicholson on the half-hour and then, shortly afterwards, when Baily nodded Duquemin's free-kick against the bar. It was not one-way traffic, however, as Matthews would have Spurs on the hop whenever he had the ball. But the Londoners were level five minutes after half-time, Duquemin slotting home after intelligent play by Baily.

Even though Bennett was a helpless passenger on the left wing, Spurs appeared the more likely winners – except that luck was still against them, McClellan again hitting an upright with Farm beaten in the 65th minute. Blackpool seemed spent – but for Matthews – and even the normally indomitable Mortensen was not himself, shooting straight at Ditchburn when put through. But somehow Blackpool raised their game and the spirits of their temporarily downcast supporters as they threw everything at Tottenham in a frantic last ten minutes. Matthews found yet more magic to set up Perry but the South African's shot was headed off the line by . . . Ramsey. It drew applause from his relieved team-mates and added to his burgeoning reputation. The man looked almost inhumanly calm . . . until, with the crowd at a rare pitch of excitement and a replay looking inevitable, a linesman flagged for hand-ball against Baily who appeared to control the ball with his chest as another Tottenham attack was in the making.

The free-kick was quickly taken by Kelly who made a short pass to Taylor. There were only seconds remaining and Spurs sensed no danger. The ball was hoisted hopefully toward the Tottenham penalty area and Ramsey, facing his own goal, tried to bring the high, spinning punt under control. Harassed by Perry, the England full-back saw Ditchburn advancing and, as ever, eschewed the wild clearance in attempting a short pass back to his 'keeper. He had made this type of pass 1,000 times in his career, could probably do it in his sleep or while fastening his collar stud but on this occasion he slipped as he made contact. The pass was short alright, too short for Ditchburn to gather, and the perennially alert Mudie intercepted. The Londoners looked on in horror and Ramsey picked himself up. Ditchburn dived despairingly but Mudie's low shot sped past the 'keeper's outstretched hand. There was barely time for Spurs to kick off, the whistle sounded and the Matthews final was on.

Debate would rage about the validity of the hand-ball decision but by such fine margins are legends made. Spurs were distraught but Samaritans? 'It was disappointing,' acknowledged Ramsey. 'Very disappointing.'

Blackpool: Farm; Shinwell, Garrett, Fenton, Johnston, Kelly, Matthews, Taylor, Mudie, Mortensen, Perry.

Tottenham Hotspur: Ditchburn; Ramsey, Withers, Nicholson, Clarke, Burgess, Walters, Bennett, Duquemin, Baily, McClellan.

Lawrie Reilly

ENGLAND 1 SCOTLAND 3
Home International: Wembley, 9 April 1949.

Born in Edinburgh on 28 October 1928, Lawrie Reilly attended a rugby-dominated school but had already acquired enough skill with the round ball to get a 'double first' in keepie-uppie. He had honed his talents in the back streets of Gorgie, a Hearts area of Edinburgh, but was destined to beome one of Hibs' all-time greats. He played for Edinburgh Thistle before signing on at Easter Road where he became the club's most capped player, representing his country 38 times. A member of the Famous Five forward line that lifted the League title in 1951 and 1952, at 5'7" he was not tall for a striker but made up for his lack of height with power and directness. Centre-forward for Hibs, his only club, but usually outside-left for Scotland, he was a prolific goal-scorer and earned the nickname 'Last Minute' Reilly for leaving it late.

To aficionados of the Famous Five, to fans of Scotland's Jimmy Cowan and, perhaps most surprising of all, to thousands of early departees who changed the habits of a lifetime to 'wait' for Lawrie Reilly's last-minute goals, the '49 international at Wembley might seem a strange choice. It was, of course, not a Hibs game, it will always be remembered as 'Cowan's match', and, most surprising of all, there was a good 20 minutes remaining when Lawrie Reilly scored! Closer scrutiny of the occasion, however, makes his selection perfectly understandable: it was, after all, his first appearance at Wembley, he scored the third goal, Scotland won not only the match but the Home

207

International Championship and, if that were not enough, the dark blues were rewarded with a cruise to America!

Crossing the Atlantic was the last thing on Reilly's mind as he lined up before the kick-off on this memorable day. 'It was a special moment for me,' he recalls, 'as my Mum and Dad were there as well as a lot of dignitaries, and we were introduced to royalty. We were the underdogs and the England team of that time seemed like gods . . . Matthews, Finney, Carter, Mortensen, Swift in goal . . . They were heavily odds-on.' Yet skipper George Young told his forwards: 'Just get on with the scoring – we'll hold these fellahs without your help.'

England were a bit useful in those days and had not been beaten, home or away, by any country since the War ended. In contrast, Scotland had not won the Home International series since 1936 while they had not managed to defeat England, Wales and Northern Ireland in the same season for 20 years. But opening the domestic campaign with seven new caps, including Reilly, against Wales, the Scots were in the rebuilding phase after enduring a torrid continental tour. Only an optimist – or a George Young – would have believed the dark blues would triumph on this occasion.

Perhaps the Scottish Football Association secretary, George Graham, had his doubts too, or maybe he just felt the boys needed a little more incentive. He came up with the tempting carrot of a seven-week voyage on the *Queen Mary* to the United States – if they won. No Scot had ever needed a farthing's worth of bait to beat the auld enemy but Graham tossed in £50 spending money as well. However, from the way England began, it looked as if the Sassenachs were on a sizeable incentive, too – perhaps the Crown Jewels! Their anticipated onslaught was sustained for a full 20 minutes. 'We were overwhelmed,' says Reilly, 'but Jimmy Cowan had a magnificent game. Some of his saves were unbelievable.' Young had been right though: the defence had kept those fellows out and now it was up to the forwards.

After playing what *The Scotsman* described as 'copybook football', England fell back to catch their collective breath and to contemplate just how to breach this particular Hadrian's Wall. Mortensen shook his head at his failure to score, being repeatedly denied by Cowan's acrobatics, while Matthews and Finney seemed bewildered by their inability to get past Cox and Young. If the full-backs were having blinders, up front the Scots were finding their feet too, Reilly looking a handful and Steel a constant source of torment to an England defence which lacked its customary composure. Even Swift was not his usual commanding self and the Scots sensed that the match was swinging their way. 'Once we had weathered that early storm,' said Reilly, 'we were always in with a chance. And when we scored just about on the half-hour, it really settled us.'

Reilly had a hand in the goal, exchanging passes with Steel before crossing for Third Lanark's Mason to side-foot home off the post in the 29th minute. With Woodburn nullifying Milburn – it was more a case of Where? than Wor Jackie – and even the normally tireless Mortensen waning, England's threat diminished after the break. 'I remember Willie Waddell really turning it on in the second half,' says Reilly. 'He'd had a quiet first-half but he was brilliant in the second.' Derby's Howe had a nightmare while Manchester United's Aston fared little better against the sturdy Reilly on the other flank. But the second and decisive goal came from Steel, who slid home a loose ball created by the challenge of the burly Houliston, the only player from Queen of the South ever to be capped, who gave Swift an uncomfortable afternoon.

But the third goal was the best, and the one ten thousand Scottish fans savoured as much for its quality as for putting the match beyond England's reach. 'Again it was Willie Waddell who started it,' says Reilly. 'He just went past Howe and sent over a perfect cross. I had come in from the wing and got on the end of it. Beautiful – 3–0 over England at Wembley.' It was Reilly's centre-forward's instincts that finished the job, a splendid header from a lovely centre from the right. Not bad for a left-winger.

To their credit, England never gave up and Milburn snatched a consolation goal 17 minutes from the end after Finney had finally eluded Young. For a few minutes, the white shirts threatened a revival, both Matthews and Mortensen looking dangerous, but the Scottish defence, marshalled grimly by Young, held firm. And with Waddell, Reilly and Steel lightning on the break, England's hard-pressed defenders could never relax.

At the whistle, thousands of Scots invaded the pitch and lifted their heroes shoulder-high. Cowan came in for special treatment and, after receiving a buffeting from his admirers, was glad to reach the sanctuary of the dressing-room where he declared: 'Oh Lord, save us from our friends!' The unfortunate Morton custodian missed out on the cruise when his mother fell ill but for Reilly the game had only happy memories. 'I didn't want it to end,' he says. 'I was enjoying it so much.'

For the Hibs man, the match was really the beginning as his goal was the first of six in seven games against England – and came before the last-minute legend was born. No, you can't blame him for choosing Jimmy Cowan's match – even if it was in his 'early' period.

England: Swift; Aston, Howe, Wright, Franklin, Cockburn, Matthews, Mortensen, Milburn, Pearson, Finney.

Scotland: Cowan; Young, Cox, Evans, Woodburn, Aitken, Waddell, Mason, Houliston, Steel, Reilly.

Peter Shilton

NOTTINGHAM FOREST 1 HAMBURG 0
European Cup final: Madrid, 28 May 1980.

Born in Leicester on 18 September 1949. Since dangling from the banister with his mother holding his legs as a boy, Peter Shilton has always believed in stretching himself. He had to settle for six feet in height but reached the zenith of his profession during an extraordinary career that spanned a quarter of a century. He earned England honours at Schoolboy, Youth and Under-23 levels before becoming his country's most capped player with 125 caps. He made his First Division debut for Leicester at 16 and was the world's most expensive goalkeeper when sold to Stoke for £340,000 in 1974. Joining Forest in 1977, Shilton was a major factor in their amazing run of success – winning the League Championship, two European Cups and the League Cup – before he left to go to Southampton and then Derby. He continued to be England's 'keeper until the 1990 World Cup in Italy. He left Derby to join Plymouth as player-manager.

Among the countless eulogies of Peter Shilton's goalkeeping, David Miller's in *The Times* is the most irresistible. Instead of contenting himself with extolling Shilts's legendary athleticism, courage, command of his area and shot-stopping abilities, Miller wrote: 'He is to any opposing team what Moscow was to Napoleon and Hitler.'

You can come across football people who feel that Shilton was not the greatest 'keeper of all time. They are entitled to their views. There are those who say that he was not even the greatest *English* 'keeper and cite both

Banks and Swift as his superiors. Former England manager Ron Greenwood, the man without whose dithering Shilton would have had closer to 200 caps, preferred Ray Clemence. And there are those who have the temerity to suggest that because he never played for one of the 'big' clubs, his greatness is somehow diminished. No such debate can ever be settled, of course, but a candid insight into his worth can be gleaned from the followers of Nottingham Forest, many of whom are prepared to admit that their club's halcyon days at the end of the Seventies simply would not have occurred without the awesome impregnability of their last line of defence. A late spring evening in 1980 at the Bernabeu Stadium was one of those occasions.

To some observers, Forest's appearance in the European Cup final for the second successive year confirmed that lightning *can* strike the same place twice. The continent's respect for Brian Clough's team was grudging at best: true, they were not to be compared with the Real Madrids, the Benficas, the Celtics and the Manchester Uniteds but they had out-Liverpooled Liverpool, whom they most closely resembled, and had a spirit and organisation that made them a side nobody wanted to meet. And they had the best goalie on the planet.

When Forest reached their second European Cup final, Shilton admits: 'It was at the end of a very long and hard season. A lot of people wrote us off but we always felt we could win it again.' Assistant manager Peter Taylor, a renowned optimist, was among them but Clough was not so sure. 'I confess my conviction was not that strong,' he said. The Reds had not quite recaptured the form of the two previous seasons and were unlikely to in Spain without their most inspirational players. Archie Gemmill, the midfield dynamo, and Trevor Francis, their brilliant £1 million striker, were injured, while the mercurial Stan Bowles, who may not have played anyway, did little for pre-match harmony by walking out days before. 'I can't take any more. I've never had a chance,' he whinged.

Most neutrals would have given little for Forest's

chances against the German sophisticates, Hamburg, whose all-round talents were harnessed by that redoubtable European campaigner, Kevin Keegan. 'I am just not interested in the feeling that a Forest win would be a great boost for English football,' said the former Liverpool man. 'Nobody is a bigger believer in England's cause than me but this is not England, it is Forest. There are no divided loyalties in my mind. Believe me, there'll be nobody more pleased if Hamburg hammer Forest.'

That was how the build-up went, people talking of how many Hamburg would score . . . and they didn't know about Shilton's injury scare while training on the morning of the match. Without their play-maker, their star striker and the 'joker' in their pack, Forest had little option but to funnel back, rely on counter-attacks for a breakthrough and fight for their lives. It was not going to be pretty but who could blame them? They were defending the European Cup. Shilton was going to have a busy night.

His first significant save came in the ninth minute, when he flung himself to his left to reach Magath's low drive. Two minutes later he had to come out to grab a through ball from Nogly that had ominously pierced the Forest defence. No signs of worry there. But Forest were already heavily under the German kosh and their 4–5–1 strategy had retreated to 9–1, with Garry Birtles ploughing a lone furrow up front. Keegan was buzzing but then Keegan always did.

Twenty minutes had gone and Hamburg were not getting anywhere. But Forest were. In a brief respite, Gray pushed forward, passed to young Mills who laid it on for Robertson. The winger cut inside Kaltz, exchanged passes with Birtles and hit a low drive that went in off the far post. 'It was just the lift we needed,' recalls Shilton, 'and came at exactly the right time.'

Keegan, ever the fighter, redoubled his efforts and a minute later fell offside when Reimann netted. A minute after that he was brought down by Burns who was booked. There were those already doubting if it was to be

Keegan's night. But Hamburg kept coming. Keegan again breached the thin red line and when Milewski shot on the volley it looked like the breaththrough. But Shilton took off, twisted his body and turned the ball away. Forest were heartened and mounted a few attacks of their own. Could the worst be over? The champions enjoyed half-time more than the challengers who decided to gamble on giant striker Hrubesch for midfielder Hieronymous.

With those redoubtable centre-backs, Lloyd and Burns, at their trench-like best, O'Neill harrying and covering every blade of grass, Birtles battling and Anderson having one of his finest nights at right-back, Forest were difficult to break down. And every time Hamburg pierced the wall, there was still the massive figure of Shilton standing in their way. Whether diving like a demented acrobat to reach a rasping drive, leaping to snare a tantalising centre or looming like an on-coming express to derail advancing strikers, Shilts was in command. Never had his ability to 'fill' the goal been more apparent, never had his reflexes been so razor-sharp. One minute as massive as the Michelin Man, the next as lithe as a gymnast, he was alternately bawling at his defenders and bewildering his opponents. As the Hamburg attacks became more frantic, Shilton surpassed himself. He had to – the worst was not over and the siege of his goal had only just begun.

But Forest were still capable of the occasional break-out, Mills and Robertson both going close and, in the 57th minute, justified claims for a penalty were ignored when Birtles was sent tumbling by Buljan. Unsung heroes McGovern and Burns both had to hack clear but in the 67th minute a Kaltz piledriver finally beat them all . . . only for the post to intervene. Goal-kick. A minute later O'Hare replaced Mills, an older, wiser head to help Forest hang on. But they had soaked up more than most teams do in a season and though the spirit was willing, the flesh was weary. Gunn had to take over from Gray and Hamburg upped the tempo even more. Shilton and Shilton alone stood against a Hamburg breakthrough. He had to fly

214

through the air to thwart a blockbuster from Nogly, rush off his line to smother from Hrubesch, beat out another effort from Magath. And two more from Keegan. Anderson had to head over his own bar, Hamburg's appeals for hands in the area were turned down and then Birtles, in a solo break, almost made it two.

Back came Hamburg for one final effort. Gunn got in a crucial header. The whistle went and Forest began to celebrate. But it was only the ref ordering Hamburg to retake a throw-in. More agony. And finally, it was over – Forest had flummoxed a continent for the second year in a row. And even Clough admitted: 'We defended for 84 of the 90 minutes.'

As for Shilton, he simply shrugged and said: 'I made two or three decent saves.' He made thousands more, of course, but at his best, it took something special to get past him. Maradona did it years later in Mexico with two kinds of magic, yet you suspect that if Shilts had been faced with 'the Hand of God' that night in Madrid, he probably would have shaken it – and then turned the ball round the post for a corner.

Nottingham Forest: Shilton; Anderson, Gray (Gunn), McGovern, Lloyd, Burns, O'Neill, Bowyer, Birtles, Mills (O'Hare), Robertson.

Hamburg: Kargus; Kaltz, Nogly, Jakobs, Buljan, Hieronymous (Hrubesch), Keegan, Memering, Milewski, Magath, Reimann.

Ian St John

LIVERPOOL 3 INTER MILAN 1
European Cup semi-final: Anfield, 4 May 1965.

Born in Motherwell on 7 June 1938, Ian St John first showed his worthy touch playing for the local Bridge Works FC and Douglas Water Thistle, joining 'Well in August 1958. A year later he made headlines by scoring a hat-trick in two and a half minutes against Hibs and four for the Scottish League against the Irish League. He earned two Under-23 honours and the first seven of his 21 full caps while at Fir Park.

At 5'7", he lacked height for a centre-forward but that did not deter Liverpool who paid £37,500 for him in 1961. He was Bill Shankly's first signing and, along with centre-half Ron Yeats, provided the formidable spine of the first great Liverpool side of the modern era. He formed a lethal partnership with Roger Hunt and was worshipped by the Kop as much as he was feared by awkward, gangling centre-halves whom he would often turn into tailor's dummies. Not only could the Saint leap as if on spring heels but he was sturdy enough to stand the roughest treatment – and mete out some of his own. As tenacious as he was talented, St John often forced his way through defensive thickets by sheer will power. Short enough to be looked on as an underdog, good enough to be a king, he donned the red of Liverpool over 400 times, notching 118 goals. He won medals in the Second Division Championship, First Division (twice), FA Cup and was a finalist in the European Cup-winners' Cup. The Saint retreated gracefully to midfield when his legs began to fail him. He moved to Coventry in 1971 and tried his hand in management (at Portsmouth) before becoming a TV personality – and establishing another great partnership – with Greavsie.

'Jesus Saves!' proclaimed the hoarding. Alongside someone had scrawled: 'But St John knocked in the rebound.' It said it all – both about the Saint's sharpness in front of goal and his celestial status in the city. Maybe it had something to do with his stature for crowds love a good littl'un; maybe it was his spiritual sobriquet or perhaps it was just his instant success . . . a hat-trick on his debut against Everton in the Liverpool Senior Cup! Whatever it was, the Saint did not merely have a rapport with the fans, he had a communion with the Kop. The sturdy, crew-cut Scot, who signed from modest Motherwell when Liverpool were still in the Second Division, came to be deified. So it is appropriate that he has chosen the match that Shankly, himself, rated as 'the greatest of all games'. No matter that Liverpool lost the return leg 3–0 amid dark rumours about the ref, let us savour that magical night at Anfield. It was an occasion when the Kop surpassed itself for sheer, unbridled passion and Liverpool, three days after winning the Cup for the first time in their history, ripped the masters of defence to shreds in an unforgettable display of flowing, surging football.

'It was some night,' says St John. 'The whole of Liverpool – oh, well, half – seemed to be jam-packed into Anfield and had been for hours. The gates had been locked since four o'clock and we could have filled the ground twice. Three times. People were still celebrating our win in the Cup final on the Saturday and now we had Inter Milan, the holders of the European Cup. They had superstars in every position and still, at that time, no British club had ever won the trophy. You could not have staged it better and Shankly, ever the showman, milked it for all it was worth – for our benefit.'

Not content with merely having the crowd welcome the heroes home a second time – they had already been royally received on a tour of the city – Shanks cunningly turned the show into a huge psychological boost for his team and Inter must have wondered what had hit them. Anfield-watchers say that neither the sense of anticipation, which seemed to course through the city like the Mersey in flood, nor the decibel count has ever been greater – and in 28 years there has been severe competition. The official figure was 54,082 and by the kick-off they had been there for three and a half hours. Shankly saw that they were rewarded – even before the start.

'Shanks,' recalls St John, 'had Gerry Byrne, who had his arm in a sling and was the hero of Wembley, and Gordon Milne, another regular who was out, come out with the team and parade the Cup around the ground. It got the crowd into a frenzy. The atmosphere was incredible and we hadn't kicked off!'

But while the city had been in tumult for three days, the players had been oblivious to it – Shankly having taken them off to Blackpool for a spot of rest and recuperation. 'He was a master,' says St John. 'So when we turned out in front of that crowd, we had got our breath back from the final – and were ready.' Buoyed by the tumultuous reception, Liverpool tore straight for the heart of Inter. 'We just went for them,' St John remembers, 'and were one-up after a few minutes.' Ian Callaghan took the ball from Strong, raced down the line and centred perfectly for Hunt to steer it past Sarti. Four minutes. But the jubilation did not last long. 'Inter were not European champions for nothing,' adds the Saint, 'and they came back at us with one of their classic breakaways.' Ron Yeats, of all people, the pillar whom Shanks introduced by inviting people to walk around him, had made an invitation of his own – and paid dearly. Missing a crucial ball, Yeats had seen Piero race past him and set up the equalizer for Mazzola. 'It was a killer blow,' admits St John. 'A very clinical finish and out of nothing.'

Liverpool did not stay deflated for long – just until the re-start. But the Italians now felt confident enough to strut their stuff before the home side, lifted by the furious exhortations of the crowd, came at them again and again. 'It was thrill a minute action,' says the Saint, who led the line with his customary dash, an indomitable battering ram against the finest defence in Europe. It cracked again in the 34th minute. St John recalls: 'Much to Shanks' annoyance we would laugh about how hopeless we were at free-kicks. So when we were awarded one just outside the box, we all stood around like a card school and nobody could make up their minds who would take it. Finally, Ian Callaghan ran over it, Billy Stevenson stuck it to Roger Hunt who side-footed it to Callaghan. He put it into the net. It was a classic!'

Inter were reeling now and could have rocked six minutes later when Lawler had what looked a perfectly good goal disallowed. 'It was a blow and we couldn't see anything wrong with it,' says St John. But Liverpool had only themselves to blame for not going to half-time with a two-goal cushion, Hunt hitting the 'keeper when it seemed easier to score. Then a Yeats header brought a stupendous save from Sarti.

The Reds continued to dominate after the interval but the goals that would provide insurance for the return leg still refused to come. The crowd's anxiety grew but, in their hour of need, they should have known who to look for. Again Callaghan was the instigator from the flank and he found Smith who fed Hunt. The striker's powerful drive hit the 'keeper – and St John was on hand to stab it home.

'We want four,' a delirious Anfield demanded but, for all their pressure, the Reds could not oblige and Inter, badly shaken though they were, somehow hung on. Smith and St John were both denied by the agile Sarti, Thompson met his match in the electric Burgnich and, at the other end, Strong and Moran almost put through their own goal. Liverpool had to be satisfied with a 3–1 margin over the champions but had, for much of the game, out-played and out-classed them. At times, the Italians were reduced to panic-stricken rabble and though they recovered the deficit and retained their trophy with a win over Benfica, they will not have endured a more uncomfortable passage than this one.

'Even though we would lose the tie,' says St John, 'we did a lot for British football that night.' And no one did more than the Saint – who had knocked in the rebound.

Liverpool: Lawrence; Lawler, Moran, Strong, Yeats, Stevenson, Callaghan, Hunt, St John, Smith, Thompson.

Inter-Milan: Sarti; Burgnich, Facchetti, Tagnin, Guarneri, Picchi, Jair, Mazzola, Piero, Suarez, Corso.

Nobby Stiles

MANCHESTER UNITED 4 BENFICA 1 (AET)
European Cup final: Wembley, 29 May 1968.

Born in the footballing hotbed of Collyhurst on 18 May 1942, Nobby Stiles played for Manchester, Lancashire and England Schoolboys before joining the United groundstaff in 1957. Short of sight and stature – a mere 5'6" – he had lost his teeth but not his biting tackles, the timing of which improved with contact lenses. Vilified abroad, he became a national hero for his never-say-die approach for club and country. He achieved a dream double of World and European Cups in the late Sixties and was capped 28 times. He moved to Middlesbrough in 1971 and then Preston, whom he also managed, then he had spells at Vancouver Whitecaps and West Brom before returning to Old Trafford in his favourite role as youth coach. He is married to Kay, sister of former Leeds star Johnny Giles.

The Argentinians called him 'El Bandito', the Portuguese 'the Butcher of Madrid'. And when Bobby Charlton compared him to 'a sheepdog constantly rounding up the sheep that got out of line and putting them firmly back in the pen', he was not just talking about opponents! At United and England, players soon learned that being in the same team as Nobby Stiles did not mean immunity from his snapping at heels. Or any loss of sharpness in his fangs. Poor covering or a misplaced pass could lead to public admonishment and it was no good looking at the referee. Even his fans cringed at some of his flying tackles but the nation forgave all when he danced his joyous, toothless jig after the Germans had been vanquished in 1966.

For most of the England team, winning the World Cup was the pinnacle of their playing careers and Stiles was no exception. The erstwhile 'villain' savoured the triumph more publicly than anyone, sinking to the Wembley turf in a relieved embrace with George Cohen at the whistle and then, Jules Rimet trophy held aloft, cutting his ridiculous capers. But for Stiles and for Charlton, there was other business to attend to. 'The European Cup was still left to be done,' he says. 'And right from being a kid I knew how much it meant to United.'

Unlike Charlton, Stiles had not climbed from the wreckage and slush of Munich in 1958 but heard the horrific news in stunned disbelief at home. A groundstaff boy, having signed the previous September, he was very much in awe of the great Busby Babes. And very much in the shadows. But when eight of that side, which had maintained its thrilling assault on the European Cup with a 3–3 draw in Belgrade, died in the crash, Stiles, like many other United youngsters, experienced a swift promotion. It was to be a difficult apprenticeship. 'We were struggling in the League yet still people talked about the European Cup,' he says. 'I'm sure we would have won it in '58 and, even before Munich. I knew how much that trophy meant to the club. After Munich, we just *had* to win it.'

By 1964–65, with Matt Busby recovered and back at the helm, Stiles firmly established and the likes of Denis Law, George Best and Paddy Crerand gloriously augmenting the existing genius of Charlton, comparisons were inevitably made with the tragically mortal Babes. The First Division title was won and the European Cup beckoned once more. Nineteen sixty-five looked to be the year and when Benfica were destroyed 5–1 in Lisbon by a refulgent Best, it seemed pre-ordained. But Busby was to have his dreams dashed once more – in the semi-final by Partizan Belgrade. United could manage only fourth place in the League that season and time appeared to be running out. But in 1966–67, the defence bolstered by the purchase of goalkeeper Alex Stepney, United won the League to secure another shot at the elusive prize. European progress was made but after a narrow 1–0 home win over Real Madrid in the first leg of the semi-final, Busby must have wondered if it was simply not to be when the Spaniards led 3–1 at half-time in the return. But against the odds and against history, United courageously levelled to claim their date with destiny.

Benfica were again the opposition but United's greatest danger was the daunting burden of expectation. After Munich, Sir Matt had silently vowed to win the trophy for those who died, while the current squad had similarly pledged themselves to do it for *him*. Laudable though these motives were, such dedication – however private – can become an onerous millstone for the broadest of shoulders, especially when so recently loaded with tragedy. And with the match at Wembley, it was not just England that expected: the whole football world outside Portugal was willing United to victory. Stiles and Charlton had won the World Cup on the same ground and for them failure was too awful to contemplate. Never has a team been so burdened or so motivated than the men Charlton led on to the lush turf that humid, electrically charged evening.

The tension affected the Portuguese, too, and the opening was as scrappy as it was ill-tempered. With Law in hospital and replaced by birthday boy Kidd, United lacked fluency while Benfica were more bothered about emasculating Best, their tormentor in Lisbon, than taking advantage. Even Eusebio lost his cool and both sides were grateful for the sanctuary of the dressing-room after a goalless first half. But Stiles, hero of '66, was not dismayed: 'We had their measure, we always did well against Portuguese teams – whether for club or country – and I felt we had gained from our disappointments. Like losing to Partizan. We thought we could take them in the second half.'

Although saddled with the 'impossible' task of man-marking Eusebio, Stiles had the spirit and experience to lift the younger players around him. And as the second half began to the roars of their red and white legions, United took command. Three scoring chances were spurned before Charlton, the man for all occasions, sent the crowd into ecstasy with a header from Sadler's cross. With Best rampant and Aston playing the game of his life, the Red Devils went for the kill. But somehow the Portugese goal survived and then, 11 minutes from the end, Stiles, of all people, allowed his prisoner a chink of light. For the lethal Black Panther a chink was enough and when he slipped the defence for Graca to pound an equaliser past Stepney from a narrow angle, Stiles groaned: 'Oh, no, it's the World Cup final all over again.'

Minutes later, it was almost all over as a revitalised Eusebio again bore down on the Manchester goal. But somehow Stepney blocked it, clutching a cannonball shot that seemed powerful enough to have taken him with it. 'That was the moment we won it,' claims Stiles. 'It was a fantastic save and just the bit of luck we needed. But God knows how he stopped it – even Eusebio patted Alex after that one. But if the game had gone another ten minutes, we would have lost. We were on top but when they scored it knocked the heart out of us.'

The full-time whistle blew and on strode Busby, knowing that his life's work could rest on his next few syllables. Stiles remembered Sir Alf Ramsey in similar circumstances two years earlier and expected something equally uplifting. He was not disappointed. 'Keep attacking,' Busby told them. 'Make every pass count and don't give the ball away. Play football again and you'll win.' He had stuck to his principles. Stiles admits: 'We were knackered alright but so were they. And I remember thinking British clubs always find something extra in these situations, but I didn't know where it would come from.'

But Busby had not panicked and neither would his team. As it had in Lisbon in 1965, the spark came from Best. Latching on to a long kick from Stepney, he ghosted past his full-back before rounding the goalie as if it were a training session. With Wembley already in a frenzy of anticipation, he casually turned the ball in. The roar almost razed the twin towers and United just could not lose after that.

Kidd then gave himself the ultimate birthday present by heading home after his first effort had rebounded off the bar. Now there was tumult in the stands. Even Charlton did a backward somersault and Kidd made it back to the centre circle with tears staining his red shirt. But there was more. A now delirious, seething crowd saluted the master, Charlton, who volleyed home a glorious fourth that wrapped up a fairy-tale finale. Stiles recalls: 'What I remember most is the relief, the unbelievable sense of relief. We had done it for Busby – *and* the Babes.'

Manchester United: Stepney; Brennan, Dunne, Crerand, Foulkes, Stiles, Best, Kidd, Charlton, Sadler, Aston.

Benfica: Henrique; Adolfo, Umberto, Jacinto, Cruz, Graca, Coluna, Augusto, Eusebio, Torres, Simoes.

Alec Stock

YEOVIL 2 SUNDERLAND 1 (AET)
FA Cup fourth round: 29 January 1949.

Born in Peasedown St John, near Bath, on 30 March 1917, Alec Stock played for Charlton and QPR before the War when he served in the Royal Armoured Corps with great distinction. In 1946 he became the youngest player-manager in the game, beating 60 applicants to the Yeovil job. Sometimes director-general, sometimes dogsbody, he was Yeovil and a famous managerial career was launched. From deepest Somerset, he went on to Leyton Orient, Arsenal, Roma, QPR, Luton, Fulham and Bournemouth, with QPR's Rodney Marsh-inspired comeback to beat West Bromwich Albion in the League Cup final his second most memorable achievement. The first?

'Player managership,' Alec Stock was fond of saying, 'is violent exercise on top of a pile of worries.' Having what he called 'an average' season in the Southern League, Stock was spared the pressure of his big–club counterparts but then he was expected to do the books, deal with the mail, help the groundsman, talk to the press, pick the team and play in it. So when his part-timers, whose total wage bill was barely £60 a week, drew Sunderland, whose 'Bank of England' team had cost £60,000 to assemble, in the fourth round of the FA Cup, Stock would have been forgiven for resorting to a shrink. Instead, he turned psychologist himself, and it was Sunderland who had the pile of worries.

Stock knew that he had to use every weapon at his

226

disposal if his motley bunch of triers were to topple the mighty aristocrats from Roker. The visitors boasted some of the legends of the game including Len Shackleton, who had cost £20,000 alone, cricketer Willie Watson and Jackie Robinson, whereas Stock had to make do with 'chaps who worked for a living'. But there were no mugs and Stock knew that he had a few things in his favour: the closeness of the fans, the fact that extra time would be played after 90 minutes (because of post-war travel restrictions) and, not least, that the pitch had a ten-foot slope. He had also had a trial run against League opponents in the third round. 'We had beaten Bury 3–1 and were beginning to fancy our chances,' he recalls. 'The Bury performance was the best we ever played.'

When the draw had been made, Yeovil were the focus of national attention. Gaumont British News cameras were there for the game, special coaches were laid on and 13,500 people crammed the Huish ground. Fleet Street's finest came to the West Country for feature stories and when Stock was asked for a new angle, he could always oblige. 'Not much had been written about the slope,' recalls Stock mischievously, 'so I told them the pitch went down about ten feet at one end. Every time a new piece appeared in the paper, the reporter had added a couple of feet to it so by the time Bury arrived, they were convinced we played on the north face of the Eiger!'

Stock knew that the pitch's influence was mainly psychological although he did acknowledge that Yeovil knew how to use it. For years afterwards, visiting teams, especially nervous League sides, hopped off their coaches expecting to have to wear crampons. In 1948–49, Cup fever, skilfully fanned by Stock's public relations, spread throughout the West Country. People were hanging from rooftops and clinging to walls outside the ground, while the whole nation tuned in – and that was against Bury! By the time Sunderland pulled into town on the Thursday before the kick-off, Stock was a household name, the slope steeper than Ben Nevis and the odds against the only surviving non-League club winning the Cup cut from 5,000–1 to 500–1.

'It's a queer thing, a Cup-tie,' recalls Stock. 'It affected the whole town. The place came alive, shop windows were painted green and white and there was a real gala atmosphere. The opposition were already frightened of our reputation and every available space was taken. I don't know how we got them all in.' That doyen of commentators, Raymond Glendenning, was there and so were thousands of others, many perched on beer crates and happy to pay heftily bumped-up prices. Sunderland felt that everything was against them but remained calm as a public holiday was declared.

The Geordies were accustomed to passionate crowds but had seen nothing like this. Jack Stelling, Sunderland's right-back, recalls: 'I remember running out and there were people sitting on the touchline. We weren't used to this sort of thing.' But Stock, too, had his problems. 'During the week, our 'keeper, Stan Hall, had dived on a bottle top and injured his knee. I had to call up his replacement, Dickie Dyke, who worked in the local solicitor's. He played a blinder.' Tactics? 'Well,' chuckles Stock, 'the team didn't need motivating. I said: "Let's have a bit of a go," but I did devise a sort of working man's 4–2–4 which was mainly because I couldn't get upfield quickly enough! Yes, you could say we invented push and run.'

Yeovil's opening salvo was not that sophisticated and the non-Leaguers simply charged at their illustrious but apprehensive opponents from the kick-off. Mapson had to save twice in the first three minutes, once from Stock, and Sunderland soon knew what they were in for. With the crowd barely able to contain its excitement, Stock's men pushed and ran – straight for the heart of the Wearsiders' defence. They had the ball in the net but it was disallowed for a handling offence and then Mapson turned miraculously to beat out a Bryant effort that seemed destined for the goal. 'They gave us hell,' admits Stelling. 'We knew it was going to be a difficult game but it turned out worse than expected.' The inevitable breakthrough came in the 28th minute. Hickman's free-kick was headed on by Wright and there, 'with no time to think' but in the right place at the right time, was the player-manager. 'I just whacked it – and prayed,' he recalls. The roar told him the rest.

At half-time, Sunderland knew they were facing perhaps the greatest humiliation in FA Cup history. But they did have the slope in their favour in the second half. And they had the class – or so they tried to convince themselves. All around the ground, the crowd sensed that history was in the making. Glendenning was able to tell the nation but the scribes were not so lucky: in the ramshackle Press-box where they were perched, there were no phones. David Foot, now a distinguished journalist, was one of the young cubs positioned to help them. He recalls: 'I phoned my sports-editor's copy from between the lamb-chops in a butcher's shop across the road. This was after it had been lowered by string to where I was standing – in the gents' urinals.'

Sunderland knew they were similarly placed and came out for the second half fighting. Dyke must have been wishing he was back poring through his articles as his goal was continually peppered. The bar was hit, he was hit, his defenders cleared off the line. But he held firm – until he dropped a shot from Ramsden on the hour and the Wearsider followed up to level. One might say there was a hush over the Huish as tension mounted. Yeovil lost their early coherence and were frequently caught off-side but there were no more goals and the game went into extra-time.

Fog descended as the part-timers rediscovered their touch, knowing that Sunderland would have been overwhelming favourites in a replay. Then they saw a glimmer of light as Shackleton's pass was intercepted. Wright slipped it to Bryant who beat Mapson with ease. Pandemonium broke out in this, the 114th minute, but Sunderland were still not finished. Petrified of returning to the wrath of Wearside, they staged a grandstand finish. Stock will never forget it. 'The clock seemed to stand still and then the whistle went for a free-kick with about three minutes to go. The crowd thought it was all over and rushed on to the pitch. They took some convincing that it wasn't and the next few minutes were agony. The free-kick was just outside our penalty area and everyone knew this was it, their last chance. Up stepped big Barney Ramsden to take it. We lined up our wall and I threatened anyone that moved with the sack. You could hear a pin drop. But Barney stubbed his toe and we cleared it. Into the allotments, I think. It was all over.'

The celebrations went on for weeks, telegrams poured in from around the world, Stock remained a household name and the slope had entered the folklore. Wearside was in mourning. Yeovil were drawn against Manchester United in the fifth round and, before 81,565 people at Maine Road (Old Trafford was still under repair from bomb damage) United won 8–0. But Yeovil were cheered off the field. They had had their day and the FA Cup legend was all the better for it. 'Beating Sunderland stuck with me for ever,' said Stock.

Yeovil: Dyke; Hickman, Davis, Keeton, Blizzard, Collins, Hamilton, Stock, Bryant, Hargreaves, Wright.

Sunderland: Mapson; Stelling, Ramsden, Watson, Hall, Wright, Duns, Robinson, Turnbull, Shackleton, Reynolds.

Ian Storey-Moore

NOTTINGHAM FOREST 3 EVERTON 2
FA Cup sixth round: City Ground, 8 April 1967.

Born in Ipswich on 17 January 1945, Ian Storey-Moore served a relatively undistinguished apprenticeship, playing for Scunthorpe Schools and Ashby Juniors (Scunthorpe). He signed as an amateur for Forest in 1961, turning pro a year later. The Nottingham club soon realised it had acquired a star of the future when Storey-Moore scored with the regularity of a centre-forward – from the wing, either wing. Powerfully built (5' 10" and 12st 7lb) for his position, he was a handful for central defenders as well as full-backs and, with 105 goals from 236 League games for Forest, he made a dramatic impact in the late Sixties. Manchester United paid £200,000 for him in 1972 but he was forced to quit the game with a leg injury in December the following year. A distinguished member of England's one-cap club, he would surely have graced many more internationals but for his premature retirement.

Tall, dark and double-barrelled, Ian Storey-Moore stood out among footballers of his age: he was a goal-scoring winger who blasted with both feet. A powerful runner, good in the air, he would have made a great centre-forward if he'd not been an absolutely lethal winger. But lurking on the flanks, he possessed the element of surprise and was, for a while, a kind of secret weapon who moved in for the kill when defences assumed the danger had passed. Half-clearances would suddenly be returned with interest, while no one could relax when he launched himself on a run, even when he started well inside his own half. He was truly a different type of player, the like of which has not been seen since his career was tragically curtailed in 1972.

Storey-Moore's finest hour came during a sixth round FA Cup-tie with Everton at the City Ground. Under the quiet tutelage of 'Gentleman' Johnny Carey, their pipe-smoking Irish manager, Forest had assembled the most formidable team in their 102-year history and were chasing the Double. Although acknowledged as a skilful side, Carey's men were dismissed early in the season as lacking both the resilience and the cutting edge to hand off the heavy brigades of Manchester and Liverpool. But it was now April and they were on United's shoulder in the League and at home to holders Everton in the quarter-final of the Cup. Forest had pursued both trophies with a flair and relentlessness that earned the respect of the nation and caused barely disguised panic among their rivals. 'We sensed that we could really do something,' said Storey-Moore, 'as we had gathered a very, very good side.' With Welsh maestro Terry Hennessy coolly organising the defence, Henry Newton a dynamic influence in midfield and Joe Baker the most exciting centre-forward in the game, they had players of the highest class. But it was on the left wing where they hid their trump card.

Often referred to as plain Ian Moore, his was a name that was whispered uncertainly by full-backs. And it wasn't just because they rarely mentioned both barrels that they didn't tell the full story. Conventional methods of dealing with wingers had been found to be hopelessly inadequate against a man who could waltz around his marker on either side and unleash a pile-driver from 30 yards in the same movement. But Everton could take some comfort in being as well-equipped to deal with his menace as anyone – in Wright and Wilson they possessed two of the best backs in the game. In Labone they also had a man who could take care of Baker, who, significantly, had limped off during the previous match. To Nottingham's immense relief, Baker passed himself fit, as did Newton, while Wilson, who had also been hurt, lined up for the visitors. But Everton's redoubtable 'keeper West was out with a broken hand and Andy Rankin deputised. The *Nottingham Evening Post* lamented the lack of noise at Forest's last home game – '37,000 watched in silence', it claimed. But when the teams came out on that second Saturday in April, they were greeted by an ear-splitting roar.

Less than two minutes had elapsed when the moment the majority of the 47,510 fans had dreaded actually happened – Labone clattered into Baker and the city's biggest hero since Robin Hood hobbled disconsolately off. Bravely he returned later but as little more than a passenger and, after 35 minutes, he accepted the inevitable, Hinton replacing him. But Baker had barely reached the dugout when Everton, with the timing of champions, struck. Alan Ball split open the home defence with a splendid 60-yard pass for the teenage Husband to strike past Grummitt. Buoyed by their success, the holders turned on the style and might have wrapped it up immediately after the break through the lively Husband, but Grummitt saved brilliantly with one hand. Sensing that their 'keeper had given them a lifeline, Forest poured forward, driven on by Hennessy, Newton and Barnwell. It was high-octane, Cup-tie football at its best and the crowd roared for a breakthrough.

The burly Wignall, determined to put one over his former club, was waging war with his old mates and sent a fierce cross-cum-shot which Rankin could not hold. It went to Storey-Moore who did the rest. 'It was the simplest of tap-ins,' he says, 'and it was Frank [Wignall] who had been causing all the problems. He really meant it against his old club and played better than me.'

With the crowd baying for a second, Everton began to wilt under the pressure and it was the Wignall-Storey-Moore combination that put Forest in front. 'John Barnwell began the move and Frank gave me the perfect opening. I hit it with my left foot and, in spite of all the later publicity, it was easily the best goal of the three.' It was certainly good enough to have booked a semi-final berth but Everton were not Cup-holders for nothing and showed tremendous character to come back and level with just eight minutes left. Sandy Brown, in an unaccustomed role up front, rounded the home defence and squared for Husband to joyously stab the equaliser.

The images of relief on the Everton faces would have stayed with the crowd for a long time were it not for the unforgettable drama to come. The ground was now in tumult as both sides, like winner-take-all prize fighters, slugged it out for a decider. 'I've never known an atmosphere like it,' recalls Storey-Moore. 'It was super-charged and the football was ferocious end-to-end stuff. We didn't want to go to Goodison for a replay but they kept coming as well.' In one memorable thrust, Grummitt heroically thwarted Morrissey while, at the other end, Harvey had to head off the line from McKinlay. But with the minutes ticking away and the realisation that they would be favourites at Goodison finally dawning on them, the Toffeemen tried to keep possession. Forest, without the stricken Baker and facing a daunting trip to Merseyside to save their double dream, grew desperate. The crowd willed them on but Everton were superbly organised at the back and looked like holding on. Forest needed a super-human effort – and they got it.

Storey-Moore suddenly broke through the blue line. This is how he tells it: 'My first shot hit Ray Wilson and it came back to me. I hit it again and this time the 'keeper's legs got in the way. But it came back to me again. Bouncing. I headed it. It looked to be going in. But it hit the bar.' At this point, the crowd could not take any more but the Forest winger could. With his last drop of energy, he lunged for the ball once more – the fourth time – and somehow headed it over the line. The roar that greeted it was more of relief than triumph but still might have caused the Trent to burst its banks. The crowd had been carried on a yo-yo of emotion and could scarcely believe what they had seen. Nor could his delirious team-mates who swamped the hat-trick boy as the normally sedate City Ground for once rivalled the Kop in its jubilation. The Everton players, as the *Nottingham Evening Post* graphically put it, 'slumped around the penalty area like piles of blue washing'. England full-back Wilson was so distraught that he fell to the ground without bothering to put his hands out to stop himself.

For Storey-Moore, the joy had yet to be tempered by having to spend the rest of his life re-telling it. He was like a man who thought he was throwing his last dice, only for it to keep coming back, again and again. The BBC's Sam Leitch voted it one the greatest goals he had ever seen – 'for tenacious endeavour', while no one who witnessed it – and a good many who didn't – will ever forget it. Modestly, the hero says: 'Don't ask me how many bites I had or how I managed to have so many – I didn't even know where the ball came from, I was too busy trying to pop it into the net.'

Nottingham Forest: Grummitt; Hindley, Winfield, Hennessey, McKinlay, Newton, Lyons, Barnwell, Baker (Hinton), Wignall, Storey-Moore.

Everton: Rankin; Wright, Wilson, Hurst, Labone, Harvey, Young, Ball, Husband, Brown, Morrissey.

Mike Summerbee

ATLETICO BILBAO 3 MANCHESTER CITY 3
European Cup-winners' Cup: Bilbao, 17 September 1969.

Born in Preston on 15 December 1942, Mike Summerbee is the son of one pro and nephew of another. Mike played with Cheltenham Schools, Baker Street YMCA and Bristol City before joining Swindon as an amateur in August 1959, turning pro the following December. He made his name as an aggressive winger-cum-centre-forward, notching 39 goals in 218 League games for the Wiltshire side. He was still with Swindon when they were the visitors to Maine Road for what is widely considered the nadir in City's fortunes, a derisory 8,000 turning up for a Second Division match.

He joined the Blues for £32,000 in 1965 and soon helped bring about a revival. Along with Colin Bell and Frannie Lee, Summerbee formed one of the game's most devastating triumvirates, their dynamism and élan being sufficient to cause any defence a triple by-pass in the late 1960s. Summerbee won one Under-23 cap and one League cap but played for England seven times, scoring once, with a rare header. He was a key cog in the swashbuckling Allison-Mercer machine that swept all before it, winning the Second Division (1966), First Division (1968), FA Cup (1969) and both League Cup and Cup-winner's Cup in 1970. He wound down his career with Burnley, Blackpool and Stockport.

As de Coubertin put it, 'It is not the winning but the

taking part.' The good baron's laudable sentiments are no longer even laughed at in the cynical Olympic arena but at Maine Road they should be carved over every turnstile and flashed on the electronic scoreboard: so often have City snatched defeat when even Houdini would have settled for a draw. And in the halcyon days of the late 1960s, when victory was a more common occurrence, it was never a foregone conclusion. Not when leading 3–0 with five minutes to go, not when drawn against no-hopers in the European Cup.

City sampled the cruel hangover of complacency in the autumn of 1968. 'We are going to conquer Europe,' boasted Big Mal, and when Turkey's Fenerbahce were paired with the English champions in the first round of the European Cup, he could barely conceal his delight. But City made the most ignominious of exits and Mike Summerbee still winces at the pain: 'It hurt us badly,' he says. 'Winning the League in the spring and then going out at the first hurdle the following autumn was very hard to take. So for me, one of the most satisfying performances, both personally and for the team, was this away leg at Bilbao. You can imagine how we felt going two-nil down after about 10 minutes?'

It looked like a repeat of the Turkish roasting when Arguita and Clemente rattled in those telling strikes in the ninth and eleventh minutes. With Corrigan uncharacteristically nervous and Booth being given the run-around by the lively Arieta, City were on the rocks – and could have been sunk without trace had the Basques been steadier in front of goal. 'We were having a terrible time,' says Summerbee, 'and nothing was going right – the training pitch had been flooded so we had not prepared properly – and we were just not in the game.'

City had travelled to the ground in a fleet of taxis, the coach driver refusing to take them, and Allison, lambasted for his lack of preparation against the Turks, cut a miserable figure. The trench coat seemed to sag and even the Fedora lacked its usual jauntiness. But Big Mal was angry:

'I never expected these tactics to be used here,' he stormed, 'but should have known better from the way Joe Mercer and I were treated when we came over to watch Bilbao in San Sebastian. We were given seats behind the goal with a great pillar in the way.' He must have longed for something to block his view on this occasion as the skilful Spaniards threatened to rip City apart.

Allison, as ever, had stuck his neck out, forecasting a 3–2 win for City. 'We will not make the same mistakes this time,' he said. After 11 disastrous minutes, he must have wondered how he would explain this one away. He need not have worried. When he and Mercer recruited players, they did their homework on their characters and were seldom let down.

On this occasion, it was Summerbee and Book who rallied the rest when all seemed lost. Book was magnificent, sealing the early haemorrhage and making recovery possible. Summerbee inspired it: 'It was one of those nights when I really felt as if the full-back was in my pocket,' he says. The former Swindon winger was physically strong enough, at 5'10" and 11st 4lb, to lead the line, and, mentally, was prepared to scrap. He led the counter attack. Not only did he torture poor Igartua, he took on the entire Bilbao defence and lifted City by doing so. But having played half an hour without shipping any more goals, Mercer's men needed one themselves. It came three minutes before half-time when Neil Young's shot deceived Spain's international 'keeper Iribar.

'We felt we were back in the match and the tie at half-time,' says Summerbee, who was relishing the fight and revelling in the atmosphere. He unveiled his complete repertoire on that memorable night and his class, allied to that touch of arrogance, galvanised his colleagues as it must have shaken his opponents. Turning inside, outside, dashing to the by-line and sending over hard low crosses, cutting in himself to unleash powerful drives, he was the chief tormentor and looked capable of salvaging it for City single-handedly. But just as the Fedora had assumed its rightful tilt, Arguitia scored a third – in the 57th minute. Back to square one? 'Not really,' declares Summerbee. 'We knew we could beat them and *they* knew it. So we just had to keep battling.'

The City spirit, developed under the benign gaze of Mercer and fostered by the tactical and inspirational genius of Allison, simply would not be extinguished on this difficult night in the Basque country. With men like Mike Doyle and Frannie Lee, Colin 'Nijinsky' Bell and Alan Oakes to support the efforts of Book and Summerbee, they possessed players who would have walked across the Pyrenees clad only in their club colours – if necessary. And they kept coming at Atletico who, unaccustomed to such indefatigable opponents, did not know how to cope. Midway through the second half, Booth, shrugging off his nightmare start, went up for a corner and reduced the deficit again.

'At 3–2 and with two away goals, we were in the box seats,' says Summerbee, 'but we just kept pressing.' Five minutes from time. Colin Bell – who else? – chased a Book pass down the right and crossed. It was turned into his own net by Echeverria. 3–3.

Allison said: 'I tell you this – I'm proud to be British tonight.' Peter Gardner, of the *Manchester Evening News*, wrote: 'Salute the magnificent men of Manchester City.' Summerbee, ever the pro, said: 'It gave me a lot of pleasure as we proved a point. It was also job satisfaction.' For City fans, it was one of those nights when they sympathised with their rivals – Houdini could not have done it better. They won the return and the Cup. Summerbee did not play in the final – he was injured – but he was awarded a winners' medal anyway. After Bilbao, it was the least they could give him.

Bilbao: Iribar; Saez, Igartua, Larraure, Echeverria, Arganguren, Arguitia, Uriante, Arieta, Clemente, Rojo.

Manchester City: Corrigan; Book, Pardoe, Doyle, Booth, Oakes, Summerbee, Bell, Lee, Young, Bowyer.

Mickey Thomas

WREXHAM 2 ARSENAL 1
FA Cup third round: Racecourse Ground, 4 January
1992.

---

*Born in Mochdre, near Colwyn Bay, on 7 July 1954, Mickey
Thomas played for Clwyd and North Wales Schoolboys, joining
Wrexham as an amateur in 1969. He became a pro in 1972 and
made 217 appearances before going to Old Trafford for £300,000
in 1978. At 5'6" and 10st 6lb, he was pocket dynamite on and off
the field but seldom stayed anywhere long enough to produce the
consistency to match his talents. After 90 games for Man United,
he moved to Everton for whom he made just ten appearances, but
still commanded £350,000 in a switch to Brighton. Just 18 games
for the Seagulls saw his value drop to £200,000, which is what
Stoke paid for him in 1982. After 57 games for the Potteries club,
Thomas's career went through one continuously revolving door,
but he totted up a half-century of caps for Wales before coming
'home' to the Racecourse Ground in 1991.*

Two decades of midfield combat had taken Mickey
Thomas from Colwyn Bay to Kansas – and back. One of
the most gifted players to come out of North Wales, he
had won 51 caps for his country, while at club level he'd
experienced the whole gamut: starting as a whippet-like
15-year-old with Wrexham, he had a dream move to Manchester United but couldn't handle the pressure; at his
beloved Everton, he had walked out. In a dizzy, Docher-
tyesque whirl, he found himself at Brighton, Chelsea,
Stoke, Derby and West Brom. Somewhere in between he

241

was a Wichita line man. He could torment managers as effortlessly as he did defenders and there were scrapes, rows, drinking, disappointments. But he had his moments, too, gracing Wembley and being voted the Most Valuable Player for the Wichita Wings in North America. A nomad, a character and a self-confessed 'daft person', the phrase 'wayward lad' might have been invented for him. But now he was back home, living in Colwyn Bay and in his second spell with Wrexham. His career had encompassed more highs and lows than most clubs experience and now it seemed that there were no headlines left to write as he entered the twilight of his playing days. But as his literary namesake, Dylan, might have put it, Thomas would not 'go gentle into that good night'.

Among others, he had scores to settle with Arsenal. Twice the Gunners had cruelly dashed his dreams of Cup glory: once in the final when, after he'd helped haul Manchester United back from the dead at 0–2, they had knocked in a late, heart-breaking Wembley winner in 1979; and the season before when those same Londoners had defeated a Thomas-inspired Wrexham 3–2 in the quarter-finals. Now the odds were even greater as Arsenal were back at the Racecourse Ground as League Champions while Wrexham had finished 92nd.

Typically, Thomas was undeterred. 'Every year there's a shock,' he said before the match. 'Like Sutton beating Coventry. We just have to believe it could be us. We have some great youngsters.' For their part, Arsenal were involuntarily boosting hopes of an upset: humiliated by Benfica in Europe, bundled out of the Rumbelows Cup, haunted by their disciplinary record, without Wright, Limpar and Bould, and losing touch in the League, the Gunners were currently firing blanks. They were there for the taking, it seemed. But by Wrexham? It was still going to need one of the great Cup upsets and Arsenal were niggardly enough to spoil the most fanciful script – as they had done before. And Thomas knew it. After supping his obligatory pint of Guinness on the eve of the match, the 37-year-old got down on those wounded knees of his and prayed. 'I've been doing this since I was a kid and don't mind who knows it,' he said.

For a long time, there was no hint that those prayers would be answered – in spite of Thomas's class and tenacity in midfield, in spite of Arsenal's own obvious anxieties and the passionate exhortations of the bulk of the 13,343 people present. It was Arsenal who created the chances and held an obvious technical superiority over the eager but largely unsophisticated efforts of the young Wrexham side. Thomas was everywhere, harrying, harrassing, fetching, carrying, scheming, tackling, shooting, defending . . . in a magnificent throw-back to the sort of performances that persuaded Manchester United to pay big money for him 14 years earlier. But Arsenal only had their own profligacy and the enduring excellence of another veteran, Vince O'Keefe, in the Wrexham goal, to blame for not putting the issue beyond doubt in the first half-hour.

Their frustration was palpable and growing. If Wrexham could hold on until the break and then stage a storming finish . . . such thoughts were enough to warm the crowd on a chilly January afternoon. But the Welsh defence was becoming increasingly desperate and Smith eventually breached it, sliding home following a marvellous run by Merson on the left – in the 44th minute. 'It couldn't have come at a worse time for us,' admitted Thomas. Indeed, at the interval, the second half looked a routine stroll for Arsenal. The opposition were clearly out-classed, the Gunners had a 1–0 lead and had scored at a psychologically devastating moment. What's more, the old heads of Wrexham, Thomas and Davies, were in their thirties and, surely, would not last the pace.

But Thomas continued to forage in midfield as Davies probed for openings. The striker claimed: 'I never thought they would pull away from us and they were complaining amongst themselves. Although they kept the ball, they

243

never really got at us in the second half.' Thomas, too, was encouraged by Arsenal's inability to finish them off, while the crowd were heartened by the never-say-die spirit of the home side. Better still, Winterburn walloped the underside of the bar with an angled drive early in the second half. The ball came out . . . to safety. The fans began to sense that the game was not lost and Seaman was forced into frantic action to thwart Thackeray. Arsenal began to sense it, too, Adams, Winterburn and Dixon all being booked as their apprehension mounted. But still Wrexham needed a breakthrough.

It came when O'Leary was controversially penalised for 'climbing' on Davies. 'He was all over me like a rash,' said the former international. O'Leary pleaded his innocence. 'Mysterious,' was how George Graham put it. But the outcome was all too plain as Thomas tore up to the ball and smashed the free-kick ferociously past Seaman from 25 yards. An absolute pearler. Pandemonium! 'I've scored some great goals,' he beamed, 'including a 30-yarder against Liverpool, but that has to be the best of all.' Certainly, none could have been more beautifully struck or received more passionate acclaim. And as the crowd urged the Fourth Division minnows on, Arsenal's anxiety was as visible as Wrexham's confidence.

'Once we scored,' said Thomas, 'I thought we'd get a goal every time we went forward.' Two minutes later, Davies broke on the right and crossed, Adams made a hash of a clearance and there was Watkin to prod home. Disbelief on the faces of *both* teams, delirium in the stands. Arsenal looked ashen, Wrexham hysterical as the awesome weight of Cup history dawned on both sets of players. The crowd were in a frenzy and whistled for time. 'They'll score, they'll score,' wailed an anguished Welsh voice above the tumult. He and some 11,000 others thought they had when Carter netted, but the linesman's flag was already raised. There were still another couple of minutes of barely endurable agony. And then it was all over. The final whistle was heard only for a split second before being drowned by an eruption of sound that rolled around Wrexham and out to distant valleys. Arsenal hung their heads in shame. The famous club had suffered celebrated humiliations at York, Peterborough, Northampton, Bradford and Walsall. And now Wrexham had to be added to the list. 'It's a big blow,' was all Graham could muster in his summing up.

For Thomas it was headlines again – for the right reasons. 'In all my career and over 50 caps with Wales, this win gave me the most satisfaction. You just can't beat it. The sort of thing you dream about.'

Brian Flynn, Wrexham manager, said: 'When Mickey Thomas came to us for his second spell with the club, he did not have a deal. You could say he was on trial but he played himself into a contract and he's been our most consistent player most of the season. If he was ten years younger, I'd be able to sell him for about £5 million.' To borrow from the poet again, Mickey Thomas had 'raged against the dying of the light'.

Wrexham: O'Keefe; Thackeray, Hardy, Carey, Thomas, Sertori, Davies, Owen, Connolly, Watkin, Phillips.

Arsenal: Seaman; Dixon, Winterburn, Hillier, O'Leary, Adams, Rocastle, Campbell (Groves), Smith, Merson, Carter.

Jock Wallace

BERWICK RANGERS 1 RANGERS 0
Scottish Cup: Shielfield Park, 28 January 1967.

Often known as 'Rock Wallace', if seldom to his face, this former King's Own Scottish Borderer did his national service in the jungles of Malaya and ran his teams with military discipline. As a goalkeeper, he played for Airdrie before joining West Bromwich Albion for £8,000 in 1959. He went on to Bedford, Hereford and Berwick before becoming coach at Hearts and then Ibrox. In 1972 he took over as Rangers' team manager and embarked upon a legendary stewardship that saw the Light Blues achieve the treble – twice! He shocked football with his resignation in 1978 when he went to Leicester, then later to Motherwell, then Rangers again, Seville and Colchester. A remarkable career for a remarkable man – he was both a tough taskmaster and a brilliant tactician.

As Cup upsets go, they do not come greater than this. It was the result that was queried by every copy taker, that left sports desks around the globe incredulous, while the wires themselves crackled in disbelief. When you heard it you expected 'correction' to follow immediately because it could not possibly be true. No way, not the mighty Rangers. Their fans could only adopt Bill Shankly's stance in defeat and insist: 'It never happened.' But it did and the *Sunday Post* screamed: 'This is the most fantastic story of the century.' What about the First World War? The Second World War? Hiroshima? The *Titanic*? Kennedy's assassination? No, Berwick toppling Rangers beat them all, it seemed.

Of course, there had been no hint of such an epoch-making event in the build-up. The Rangers players were pictured in the *Daily Record* on the eve of the tie, looking cool and unconcerned about the trip to the Tweed. They spent the night at Dunbar and the caption read, 'There's an air of Cup confidence about the Ibrox Rangers . . .' Why shouldn't there be? Berwick were one of the clubs whom Rangers felt ought not to belong to the same league in their proposals for streamlining Scottish football. And in the same paper's Cup previews, a 'comfortable' win for the Ibrox men was confidently forecast. It did acknowledge that there could be problems for Aberdeen at Dundee and for Dundee United at Hearts but not for Rangers at Berwick. No, the *Record* would have been ridiculed all the way to the border if it had suggested anything of the sort.

But the *Record* and Rangers, not to mention the rest of the world, had reckoned without Jock 'Jungle Fighter' Wallace. 'I had only been there two months,' he says in his best sergeant-major tones, 'and when I went the place was a shambles. I had the dressing-room painted and restored pride to the club. They had experienced players who had played in the Scottish First Division and it was up to me to lift 'em. I devised a new training routine, got everybody fit and raised morale.

'Berwick gave me my chance in management,' he continued, 'and I was grateful for that. It was up to me. I had been to all the coaching courses in England and served my time so Berwick was my chance to put what I'd learned into practice.' By coaching and coaxing, bawling and bullying, Wallace, one of the few men who could stay on his line yet still lead 'from the front', grabbed that chance with both gloves. Whenever his team attacked, his stentorian bellows could be heard as if he was alongside – which, of course, he was – in spirit. But up against his motley platoon of miners, joiners, plumbers, painters and teachers, were eight internationals – seven Scottish and one Danish. Rangers were the holders and had won the Cup on no fewer than 19 occasions. But the jungle-fighter was unimpressed.

Both teams were unchanged which meant that McKinnon, who had passed a late fitness test, took his place at centre-half for Rangers alongside John Greig, a formidable pairing for any attack to overcome, let alone one that trained only twice a week and was paid £8 for its pains. But Berwick were encouraged by Wallace who told them: 'With the exception of Greig, Rangers cannae tackle. When we get the ball, don't worry – we'll have more time than you think. We can keep 'em busy.'

But it was Berwick who were at full stretch from the kick-off as Wee Wullie Henderson mesmerised the part-timers' defence. Twice he went past Riddell and Rangers forced three corners in the first five minutes. A penalty appeal was turned down. Wallace hurled himself between the posts to thwart long-range efforts from Alex Smith and then snatched a cross from the waiting head of Forrest. The 'keeper-manager kept Berwick in the game when lesser men may have settled for the inevitable. Rangers took their corner tally to ten in the first half hour but the scoreline was 0–0. Wallace, cheeks puffing, hands burning, invective spitting like machine-gun bullets, was happy. The Borderers were still in it and he had been right – Rangers were not a team of tacklers, McKinnon did not look fit and even Henderson was beginning to lose his sting. The crowd were intent as the underdogs appeared to have weathered the Rangers offensive.

After 32 minutes, Berwick engineered a breakaway down the left. Kenny Dowds sent a low cross into the area and with McKinnon and Johansen rooted to their spots, Christie turned the ball to Reid. The wee inside-right, who had been told by a surgeon that his career was 'almost certainly over' when he fractured his left knee-cap two years earlier, did not hesitate, blasting past Martin for the goal that reverberated around the world. Berwick fans did not just go wild, thousands were still celebrating when Christie spurned a great chance to make it two. Martin's save brought them back to earth but for almost an hour the dream hung by a thin blue thread.

Rangers, pride wounded as never before, launched themselves *en masse* at Wallace's goal. But they met stiffer opposition now as Berwick's self-belief grew and Wallace himself stopped everything the Ibrox men could throw at him. Under skipper Greig, Rangers did not panic and tried to football their way through the Second Division defence. But every move would end with the grateful gloves of Wallace clasping the ball to his jersey, barking orders and belting the ball back – deep into the Rangers' ranks.

'Our improved fitness really told in the second half,' he says. 'Just when we should have been run ragged, we held on and then poor Willie Johnston broke his leg.' It was in the 65th minute and Johnston and Wallace went for the same ball which Wallace grabbed as the winger stretched. Both men went down in a heap but Johnston was stretch-ered off with a fracture. It was the last thing Rangers needed. On came Davie Wilson, who had scored a hat-trick on his last Cup visit to Berwick in 1960, but Wilson would have traded more than his match ball for an equal-iser now. Time was running out and it was Rangers who looked amateurish, lacking confidence and beginning to despair. With Wallace scaling new heights as a 'keeper, the *Sunday Post* reported, 'the Ibrox players must have been close to tears as he [Wallace] thwarted their every effort.' He flung himself around the six-yard box like a dervish, grabbing the ball from Rangers' toes, Rangers' heads, Rangers' hearts and in doing so lifted his own men to a new plateau of defiance. Wilson looked set to dash the fairy tale late on but Wallace hurled himself at the sub's feet and then brought off a stupendous save to foil McLean whose header looked destined to restore sanity to the scoreline.

But sanity was not restored, Dowds, Reid and Christie were magnificent in keeping Rangers busy at the back and preventing the all-out assault they required. Christie even contrived to miss another golden chance five minutes from time. At the whistle, mayhem ensued as Berwick joy bubbled over while Ibrox fury knew no bounds. An angry mob of Blues' fans besieged Scot Symon, calling for his resignation as the locals struggled to comprehend what the 10,000–1 outsiders had done. The *Post* compared the pitch invasion to the Dunkirk beaches. Certainly, Berwick and, in particular their goalkeeper-manager, had displayed the Dunkirk spirit.

But it was Rangers who were the retreating army, their once-proud blue shirts now bedraggled in the sweat of humiliating defeat. Kai Johansen summed it up when he said: 'I never thought a football result could make me feel so hurt, so ashamed, so disappointed and so sick.' The silence in the Light Blues' dressing-room was broken by a disbelieving Symon who had a private word with each player before calling for the guillotine after the weekend. He told the press: 'Our prestige has received a shattering blow. This is the worst result in the club's history . . . and these players took part in the game. That cannot be forgotten. I cannot find a word to describe adequately how I feel.'

Reid, the goal-scoring hero and Motherwell gear-cutter, had to cut short the celebrations and was back at work on Sunday morning. 'The foreman was good enough to give me a bit of extra time away,' he explained, 'so I had to make up that today.' As for the win, 'it is all due to Jock Wallace – he's a wonderful man and we really wanted to win for him.'

The gaffer savoured his triumph although he was heard to rasp: 'Christie missed two sitters – it should have been two-nil . . .'

Berwick Rangers: Wallace; Haig, Riddell, Craig, Coutts, Kilgannon, Lumsden, Reid, Christie, Dowds, Ainslie.

Rangers: Martin; Johansen, Provan, Greig, McKinnon, D. Smith, Henderson, Forrest, McLean, A. Smith, Johnston (Wilson).

Neil Young

MANCHESTER CITY 6 TOTTENHAM HOTSPUR 2
League: Maine Road, 3 March 1962.

Neil Young was born in Manchester on 17 February 1944. 'He is so majestic,' the Manchester Evening News *once wrote, 'that it seems an affront to the aesthetic eye if a 'keeper saves one of his shots.' With a left leg par excellence, Young came to be loved by the Maine Road fans, notching 108 goals in 399 (plus three as sub) League and Cup games. He first impressed with Manchester Boys and signed for City as an amateur in May 1959. He became an apprentice the following year and a pro shortly after his 17th birthday. He was capped at Youth level and made his first team debut in November 1961.*

One of the home-grown members of the great City side of the late 1960s, Young won a Second Division Championship medal in 1966 and the First Division title two years later. He helped City to win the FA Cup in 1969 and both the League Cup and European Cup-winners' Cup in 1970. A tall, elegant left-winger, he was relatively unsung nationally compared to stars like Lee, Bell and Summerbee, but he was a City hero. He eventually left City for Preston in 1972 and later played for Rochdale. Plagued by illness since his retirement, at the time of writing, Young had still to be granted a testimonial by the club he served so magnificently for 11 years as a professional.

Wembley winners are the stuff of dreams for most players and 'Nellie' Young is no exception. Few actually live out their fantasy and for those, immortality usually ranks a

252

poor second behind a reliable source of good dining. But Young, whose doses of ill-fortune and ill-health have dogged him since he left the Blues, always was a bit different. 'Different class' to the City faithful, he still does his own thing – even when it comes to choosing the outstanding match of his career. Dismissing the obvious candidate, when he scored the Cup Final winner over Leicester, as 'not an outstanding game', he opts for a League match with Spurs when he helped to shovel snow off the ground and which, he admits, 'probably shouldn't have been played'. No, it was not the celebrated 'ballad on ice'. And it was before Big Mal, before Summerbee came from Swindon, before Lee arrived from Bolton and when Bell was just a stripling. 'I was a groundstaff lad, myself,' says Young, 'and had only played three or four times in the first team. It was in March and didn't mean a lot to us in terms of League position. But it was the Spurs' double-winning side with Greaves, Blanchflower, Mackay and White. And we still had Bert Trautmann in goal and a few kids like me in the team. It should have been a thrashing.' It was.

'Where else do the fans get such a mixture of gloom and gaiety?' asked the *Manchester Evening News* before the game. On this wintry day, the fans very nearly got nowt as heavy snow covered the Maine Road pitch. 'I helped clear it off with a few other lads from the groundstaff,' remembers Young, as the aristocrats from North London wondered whether their journey to the frozen north had been necessary. 'I don't think,' says Young, 'that Spurs really wanted to play.'

Although results suggested that Tottenham had shed the invincibility that had secured the double the previous season, on paper they were even more formidable with Greaves having been grafted on to the side. Young says: 'I was looking forward to seeing them play,' and proved it by being one of the youngsters who went out to give the lines an extra brushing an hour before kick-off.' 'Every time we attacked, we seemed to score,' he recalls, 'but it

253

was a forwards' pitch – once you were past 'em, defenders couldn't turn.' Much to the amusement of City fans since, Young, probably one of the most blatantly left-footed players ever to grace the game, actually played on the right. 'But on this pitch,' he chuckles, 'it didn't matter and I gave their left-back a bit of a roasting. I also remember big Maurice Norman trying to cover for him and committing himself too early. I would just cut inside them both.' Some 30,000 City fans might add: 'To get it on to his left foot.'

City stormed at the Spurs defence from the outset, leaving Trautmann a lonely figure in the home goal. At the other end, Hollowbread, a capable deputy for the injured Brown, was the busiest man on the field as an otherwise full-strength Spurs seemed to be running on two cylinders. Trautmann shivered through inactivity but Hollowbread had to deal with shots from all angles and dived at the feet of Young in one of many early raids. Sensing that this was not going to be Spurs' day and with their own inferiority complex removed, the eager City kids kept sweeping forward but it still took them half an hour to break the Londoners down. The outstanding Joe Hayes hit the first goal and, two minutes later, one of the afternoon's other stars, Peter Dobing, made it two.

Spurs' worst fears were bitterly apparent. 'It seemed to run for us,' acknowledges Young, 'and they just couldn't get going.' As for his goal, 'I think I got either the second or third' is the most precise description this modest man will give. So it's over to the *Evening News* again: 'Young, tall and thin as an East wind, walked around both Ron Henry and Maurice Norman to score City's third.' It came two minutes before the break when Young does recall words of encouragement from Trautmann whom, he says, 'was brilliant with us youngsters. He told us to keep at them and not let them off the hook. We took him at his word.'

City maintained their siege of the Spurs' goal and, following their 'keeper's instructions, put the game beyond doubt (well, almost for City) when Dobing, who had a blinder, made it four in the 47th minute. The avalanche continued when Baker put through his own net six minutes later and, in the 58th minute, Dobing completed his hat-trick. 'I felt pleased with my first-half hat-trick against West Ham but this was even better,' he said. His speed and sharp-shooting coupled with the subtlety of Hayes and the incisiveness of Young had turned it into a nightmare afternoon for the treble-chasing hot shots from White Hart Lane. 'It was a day when all the youngsters came off,' said City boss Les McDowall, 'just as I had been expecting. I was particularly pleased with the teenagers.' But nobody had been expecting Spurs, who fancied themselves as the finest team in Europe on their day, to be hit for six.

Greaves did manage to salvage a little London pride with two late goals but they came, as the *Evening News* noted, 'only after City were gorged with success'. Young is more magnanimous: 'Jimmy Greaves scored one of the greatest goals I have ever seen,' he said. 'He beat four or five of our players inside ten yards. I'll never forget it.' Indeed, he remembers it better than his own. 'We had the run of the ball,' said McDowall, graciously, 'but you've got to have it to beat a team like Spurs.' Bill Nicholson said: 'It was awful. I don't want to take anything away from City's performance – they played well enough to have scored 12 – but I've never seen our defence play so badly.' Hollowbread, who was blameless for most of the goals, declared: 'I did my best but there were lots of gaps in front of me.' Trautmann observed: 'Most of the time I felt right out of it. But by gosh, it was grand watching the lads play so well.' Bobby Kennedy confirmed that it was grand playing, too: 'I have never enjoyed a game so much,' said the full-back.

It was City's day and, as the *Evening News* added: 'They drove Blanchflower & Co to despair.' Young recalls: 'We kept going forward and when we hit it, it would either go in or hit the scoreboard.' The fans, too, had to keep an eye on the score or they may have lost count or simply not believed it. As for those who didn't go, they kept jamming the paper's switchboard, being unable to accept the final tally. Says the *Evening News*: 'The incredible – either in defeat or victory – has ever been commonplace at Maine Road but City, the Sultans of shock, surpassed all previous surprises . . . so much so that hundreds of fans didn't believe the score.' Nellie Young was another who admits to 'losing count . . . and I was playing!'

Manchester City: Trautmann; Kennedy, Sear, Benson, Leivers, Oakes, Young, Dobing, Barlow, Hayes, Wagstaffe.

Tottenham Hotspur: Hollowbread; Baker, Henry, Blanchflower, Norman, Mackay, Medwin, White, Smith, Greaves, Jones.